THE PARA-INVESTIGATORS

Coming Soon from TAMA (The Age of Mass Awakening) Books:

THE CLEAR-HEARERS
52 True Tales and Concepts of the Great Voice

THE EXTRA-DIMENSIONALS
52 True Tales and Concepts of Alien Visitors

THE CHRIST BASED TRANSCENDENTS
52 True Tales and Concepts of REAL Christ Followship

THE EPHEMERALS
52 True Tales and Concepts of Ghosts and Seers of the Dead

THE WESTERN ABSOLUTISTS
52 True Tales and Concepts of Liberty in the Age of Mass Awakening

*Para-Investigators root out the deepest truths,
in this world and the next...*

Para-Investigators resolve mysteries and crimes using paranormal abilities. They are often people who don't know anything about the paranormal until they experience their own revelation. Para-Investigators are police officers, paranormal researchers, psychics, ghost-hunters, even ordinary people who somehow become involved in the search for truth. What they all have is common is that they use supernatural abilities to protect and serve a society that does not yet accept their existence. Para-Investigators are "over-crossers" who enter realms beyond our physical world. These are their true stories in their own words. Yet, to truly understand them, we must delve into the concepts that make Para-Investigation possible. It is vital to grasp what true investigation means, what real evidentiary value is and how "over-crossers" enter realms beyond our material world. At times, they do so without conscious knowledge that they crossed over and often without even knowing that they have these supernatural abilities. Understanding Para-Investigation is a key to opening our minds to greater truths that are not yet tolerated in this present reality. Once that door opens, we will finally understand that, in order to be complete, some investigations must reveal truth not just in this world but also in the next.

THE PARA-INVESTIGATORS

JOHN DESOUZA

TAMA Publishing

The Age of Mass Awakening

Edited by GOLDIE SERRANO
Cover Design and Internal Layouts by SCARLETT RUGERS BOOK DESIGN AGENCY
Printed in the U.S.A.

The Age of Mass Awakening

Inquiries should be addressed to:
TAMA Publishing
PO BOX 68964
Oro Valley AZ 85737
Business Office/Ordering Titles: (520) 544-3863

An Imprint of:

Transcendent

Planet Media

To order this title request from
TamaBooksPublishing@gmail.com
Library of Congress Cataloging in Publication Data
CIP available upon request

This work is dedicated to refugees from the mainstream: the former scientists, journalists, engineers, Ph.D.'s; and all those who broke out of the box and will never go back.

CONTENTS

THE TRUTH ABOUT EVIDENCE

PARA-INVESTIGATIVE FILES

PARA-INVESTIGATORS IN ACTION

PARA-INVESTIGATORS AND NON-HUMANS

PARA-INVESTIGATIVE AWAKENINGS

THE AGE OF
MASS AWAKENING

We are in it already. The circle of Mass Awakening has opened because of the expansion of what people believe. Despite what mainstream society tries to tell us, belief determines everything in life and beyond. Faith and belief are the *only things* that can transform everything. Eventually, we will no longer recognize the universe we live in. This may take a decade or an entire age—time is irrelevant in Ultimate Awakening because it originates from and concludes *outside* normal time and space. It is happening right now. The "Mass" in Mass Awakening only means breaking the six percent barrier in the population of any town, city, nation or planet. All over the world, we are bursting through that six percent barrier. People are awakening as never before in the history of humankind. The barrier is splintered, cracked and showing gaps. Escapees are increasing daily. Transcension is at hand.

"The Age of Mass Awakening" TAMA series is unlike anything done before. I know because I have scoured paranormal books for decades and been unable to find anything like it, except in science fiction or fiction-based books. Paranormal non-fiction has been the province of scientists, engineers and thinly disguised skeptics from the hard sciences who go "slumming" in the playground of the metaphysical. They indulge paranormal believers with tolerant phrases like *"residual emotional value of debunked belief systems"* or *"closely held unknowable assertions."* After we finish their books, they tousle the hair on our heads as if paranormal believers are petulant children and then douse us with more condescension: *"no one can truly know if these paranormal truths are real until more data is gathered and analyzed for a final conclusion by the authorities on these matters."* Those final authorities are invariably the learned men in lab coats and these phrases are scientist-speak for *"now get out of here you crazy kids and don't come back until my next debunking book."*

The overwhelming majority of such books are rife with apologies and embarrassed accommodation for the fact that there is such pervasive fascination throughout the world with the supernatural. Yet books, movies and media on these topics will continue to grow in popularity because among a global populace hungry and *even desperate* for information and material on the paranormal—*beggars can't be choosers.* If we can't get books that treat the paranormal as legitimate topics for truthful serious inquiry—then people will take whatever they can get. It's time to stop begging.

We, the paranormal experiencers need to start reaching out to enlighten the paranormal believers as our intended audience—without apologies, moderation, temperance or appeals for materialists to tolerate or at least suffer co-existence with our truth. We need to start speaking to each other and leave behind the old system of seeking the golden ring of mainstream acceptance. If you are a true believer, you will never get that ring and if you do, it proves you never were genuine to begin with.

The Age of Mass Awakening series is no mere collection of "spooky stories" or compendium of scientific case studies. These are paranormal concepts defined, explained, and illustrated in real events as told by "paranormal experiencers." The experiencers' identities are protected because most people in this volume are still active in their careers and that extra measure of safety is required to foster their overt disguises as normal members of mainstream society. Additionally, that anonymity adds to the emotional content they infuse into the retelling of their vignettes.

In law-enforcement especially, people most often do not share paranormal truth except with those who will understand and guarantee confidentiality. During two decades, I have received accounts that departmental psychologists will never be told because once that particular toothpaste is out of the tube—*you ain't getting it back in*.

There are three parts to the TAMA mission. The first is to change *the language of the paranormal*—to transform the labels and language of Newtonian scientists and 1950's pilots that still haunt these areas. I'm still not sure what "Unidentified Flying Object (UFO)" really means and I think that's because it means almost nothing. It's a horribly neutral term popularized only to convey a sense of uncertainty and vagueness. I also don't know what a "Near-Death Experience" is any more than I know about "Near-Pregnancy." A person is either dead or they are not. The people I have interviewed over the years who had this fatal experience—were *Dead-Dead*. They were clinically, provably and verifiably DEAD. Then, they came back to life even as physicians were busily mishandling and mislabeling them before their bodies were cold. There was nothing "near" about these experiences. These are only two examples of the pervasive and massive linguistic misinformation/mislabeling in every area of the paranormal. This is no accident. The paranormal is purposefully loaded down with coded language meant to convey fogginess and drowsy confusion. It is time to lift that fog.

The second part of the TAMA mission is to increase the *open* participation in the paranormal by young people—not just the provision of safe havens for discussion but the creation of "creative development zones" for paranormal believers of all ages. Dynamic change in any major area of culture requires young people as a primary moving force. Mentorship relationships and informal teaching clubs (outside the wingspan of mainstream institutions) between mature experiencers and younger believers are crucial.

The final overarching mission of the TAMA franchise is to reveal the hidden truth that Paranormality is a hyper-spiritualized alternative to the mainstream "control" institutions of conventional religion and Western materialism. The TAMA series depicts how we can understand and what we can accomplish in this new era, The Age of Mass Awakening—*once we believe.*

John DeSouza

THE TRUTH
ABOUT EVIDENCE

Scientists are yesterday's men. How do you quantify spirit? How do you peer-review the limitless gulf of Quantum Potential inside each of us?

I

TRUE INVESTIGATORS

Para-Investigations include the collection of rational, material-based investigation and data but the paranormal vetting component is not an addendum pasted on after "*normal investigation*" is completed. That was the old world, sheepish way of sneaking in "Para-investigation" once the "real investigation" was at a dead-end.

Para-Investigation– *a systematic inquiry or investigation that utilizes rational scientific methods initially but primarily relies upon intuitive paranormal mechanisms from Superconscious Abilities to resolve crimes and mysteries.*

Para-Investigative procedure will never detract from or diminish rational material based investigation but will only add confirmation of reliability to our "Investigative Conclusions." Para-Investigations will always add to reliability of evidence and never diminish it. Para-Investigative procedure can never be an afterthought. It must be used throughout every step of an investigation in a consistent and responsible manner. Whereas Para-Investigative methods have previously been instilled into investigations surreptitiously, they will be now be used openly from the initiation of every investigation or inquiry—*through the front door.*

We need someone new. The world of criminal investigations and the paranormal are already rife with fact-finders: scientists, analysts, engineers and academics sporting every possible combination of credentials; all working busily to gather and show mountains of data behind unsolved crimes and supernatural mysteries. Fact-finders reveal, organize and can even connect information and useful intelligence. They can uncover thousands of bits of data relating to a single crime or mysterious event. Generating of intelligence, analysis, and information completes the fact finder's job. Yet, so much remains unsolvable without something more, some alternate paths of ingress for the consciousness of the investigator.

The work of True Investigators is not complete until they enter the Superconscious Gulf to reveal hidden nuances of misdeeds or secrets. True investigators do these things instinctively/reflexively without thought or ritual. Police officers and even civilian truth seekers accomplish these goals and then disguise that process with terminology such as "having a gut instinct" or "pursuing a hunch." The process can be as simple as receiving an inspiration that reveals a crucial clue or as involved as an out-of-body plunge into a psychic re-enactment of a heinous murder. These investigators use paranormal sensibilities to reach the truth.

They are Para-Investigators.

Para-Investigators access the Cosmic Mind/Superconscious Gulf to resolve crimes and mysteries. There they uncover the evil deeds of criminals and the hidden plans of malevolent entities that have haunted our world for eons. Para-investigators begin their work with conventional modalities but then enter into transcendence and paranormal reality. Para-Investigators are not just investigators who happen to stumble into supernatural situations—their *own abilities transport them into paranormal realms.*

The only commonality among the diverse people in these accounts—these Para-Investigators—is their ability to reach into the Superconscious Gulf to experience truths that fact finders cannot bear to confront. A new sensibility and vision is needed in the world of criminal investigations and paranormal mysteries. It is for this reason that the Para-Investigators step forward now.

Do not labor under illusions. Those un-awakened minds that lay comfortably inside mainstream institutions with their mental restrictions will not gently leave their sanctuaries or happily co-exist with others who do. These *determined guardians* of their own mental slavery will monitor and punish any who dare to accept or promote Para-Investigation as a legitimate way of seeking truth. They will resist, ridicule and attack those who seek to find truth through unapproved modalities.

The best way to combat this resistance is *testimony*—testimony from all those who have been saved, helped and defended by Para-Investigators. They are out there. There are civilians alive because of the actions of those Para-Investigators. Those who are alive today because an Investigator jumped out of the strictures of the old ways; should step forward to stand up for the Para-Investigators who unfolded the abyss to save them. Only in this way, by the courage of these witnesses, we who defy those *determined guardians* will save more in the future.

The most basic models of investigation begin with the first exercise of the investigator's cognitive skills when they first encounter a crime or mystery. This is commonly known as First Investigator's Query. An initial investigator must ask these six "first responder" questions:

Who?
What?
When?
Where?

How?
Why?

The rub is contained in the mysteries and crimes wherein these basic questions *cannot* be answered in the material world. This is where Para-Investigators begin *their* process. Para-Investigators shall be the first responders for what is beyond our world but results in real world consequences that all people can see.

2

INDIGO KIDS

(After the 9/11 attacks in the United States, there were many stories of the "Indigo kids" going around the law-enforcement community but this one, submitted from a federal task-force member working counter-terrorism matters, stood out.)

"It was several years after the attacks on the New York City World Trade Center. I attended a Law Enforcement conference titled something along the lines of *Effects of the 9/11 Terrorist Attack.* It was a massive conference; attended by national security agencies and police departments from all over the nation. It was an appropriately somber affair, replete with dour expressions and heated patriotic statements for the benefit of the mainstream news outlets. Reporters were getting comments from the brass about how they felt on this anniversary of the attacks.

Nothing sensitive or confidential was discussed but there were furtive, officious-looking characters in black suits lurking among the officialdom. No one seemed to know who they were. As we broke into smaller "counseling sessions," a rumor spread that the black suits were "handlers" coming in to collect intelligence from field investigators in attendance. They wanted feedback on rumors that the government might have had a hand in the 9/11 attacks—or at least knew they were going to happen.

My group was welcomed into a conference room by one of the "black suits." Apparently, they were the previously announced "counselors" for this last hour of the conference. Our black suit was a middle-aged woman, hair pulled back into a tight salt and pepper bun—*pulled back hard.* Her horn-rimmed glasses kept trying to slide down the bridge of her nose. The silverish chains on each side of the glasses did nothing to soften the image she presented. The identity badge attached to her high-shouldered, Joan Crawford suit jacket had some agency on it no one had ever heard of. There were comments that she had the look of a "librarian-spook"—as if the CIA ran out of officers that day and had to deputize the library clerk.

After everyone settled in with introductions, she asked a rote series of questions about our psychological responses after the incident, the effects on our families, the reactions of friends and neighbors. Then, she asked about community activities that we were aware of or that we might have information on. There was a collective groan as she got deeper into the intelligence collection. Some of the veteran officers chuckled. One officer coughed into his hand. He coughed the word "spook" into his hand. Others took up the word-cough. Laughter and spasmodic *word coughing* filled the chamber.

Librarian-Spook didn't understand the word they were coughing. She pushed her glasses back up her nose and soldiered on.

"O.k., that's enough. Now who here can share the craziest thing they heard or experienced after the attack?" She was pleased when a couple of hands shot up. She picked the most eager guy, one in the front row.

"That's easy. It was *the Indigo kids*." There were murmurs of assent from several sections of the audience. Someone elbowed Eager Guy. He shut up but there was a shout from the back.

"Those kids were freaky!"

I came in late so I was in the front row. Her stern gaze locked onto mine.

"What, what is that—Indigo kids? Is that some terrorist group?" I fidgeted, not wanting to be the teacher's pet but she kept staring right at me with the *"I've got all day mister"* look.

I broke.

"Ma'am, *Indigo Kids* is just the way we refer to children who exhibit paranormal abilities like clairvoyance or precognition. In this case, it's just shorthand for all the kids across the nation who had dreams and visions about the 9/11 attacks—days or weeks before it happened. Usually, teachers, daycare workers and baby-sitters reported the incidents in to local, state and federal agencies about kids that had indicated the attacks were going to happen."

Her glasses skid down her nose and her nasal twang was exposed.

"Are you serious? But how did those kids know? Were they trying to warn the adults?"

I took her questions last first.

"No. They just did what kids do. They told their teachers or caretakers about dreams that planes were flying into skyscrapers. They did arts and crafts projects showing sculptures of rubble with two planes burning in the rubble. They told about visions of a terrible war starting the next day against America. Sometimes they told warnings and other times they were just expressing casual communication as best they could." She didn't seem to believe.

"And you personally spoke to one of these...*Indigo Kids*?"

"Yes Ma'am. Mine was a ten year old who hadn't gotten enough sleep the night before so he took a nap on the school bus and woke up crying about planes smashing into tall buildings and killing thousands of Americans. When I questioned him about it, he giggled and said it was just a silly dream. Like most of the Indigo interviews, his family had no criminal record or previous suspicious activity and no connections to terrorism. The boy and his family never even made the connection with the 9/11 attacks until I interviewed them."

Others piped up with stories of little boys painting gruesome scenes of people jumping from burning skyscrapers and little girls warning adults not to go near any very tall buildings the following week because *"bad things happen and low planes can go into high buildings."* Librarian-Spook was aghast. Every major police department and intelligence agency in that conference room had experienced first-hand the same "Indigo Kid—9/11" phenomena. She had many more questions. Blessedly, the alarm rang and the hour ended.

Outside as I was in the parking lot—I felt a hand on my shoulder. It was Eager Guy, who had started the Indigo Kid discussion.

"Hey, I just wanted to say thanks man for picking up the ball after I got shut down. I really don't think it should be a big deal to talk about these things." He rubbed his ribs in the spot where his sergeant had elbowed him.

"No problem. She wasn't going to let us go until we gave her something so I figured we might as well let it all out." Eager Guy laughed.

"She wasn't the only one. It gave me goose bumps to hear people talk again about those interviews. I'll never forget my Indigo kid. He was just nine years and he didn't really want to talk about his "phone dream" but I gently got it out of him. Weeks before the attack, he had a *very real* dream that he was standing in a white room with a black phone on a small table. He said it was an "olden day's phone like what Edison had." It rang and rang and he wondered why there were no adults to answer it. It seemed to get louder and louder so he picked it up and said "Hello." There was a man who was coughing and whimpering on the other end. The man didn't say hello or anything. He just started begging the boy to send someone to rescue him. He said he was trapped on the seventy-second floor along with a bunch of people from his company, there was thick smoke everywhere, and they couldn't go down any further because of fire. He kept repeating the floor and his name and the names of people with him and that he was too young to die. The boy kept telling the man that he didn't have anybody to send but it didn't seem like the man was listening. The man kept on going on about the fire and the heat getting worse. The boy said he never heard anyone as scared as the man on the phone was. The boy cried and apologized and hung up the phone—the dream ended."

His eyes became misty as he continued.

"I thanked the boy for being so brave. The poor kid began to well up with tears as I thanked the teacher and left. As I got outside, I started shaking and I couldn't stop. What are the odds that I would share something like that with a nine year old?"

Now, I put my hand on his shoulder.

"You showed compassion for the kid's trauma. That's all you could do."

Eager Guy looked at me sideways.

"His trauma? No, that's not what I meant.

Just before it happened—*I had the same dream—I got the same phone call."*

3

THE EPHEMERAL
POSTULATE

The crux of why science can never be trusted to determine the validity of paranormal truth in the physical world is best expressed by **The Ephemeral Postulate:** *paranormal truth can only be understood in proportion to the realization that genuine paranormal phenomena is never fully perceivable by our five senses in our physical universe, except partially or temporarily.* The fullness and truth of paranormal experience is perceived primarily through spiritual perception rather than five sense reality. We may hear sounds and see sights that flabbergast us during a paranormal experience but it is our spiritual perceptions and metaphysical awareness that gives us the full impact of each supernatural incident.

This postulate is the partial answer as to why much of paranormal phenomena have persisted in cultures around the world for hundreds, sometimes thousands of years and yet no civilization has supposedly captured concrete, scientific proof of these phenomena. It also explains why these phenomena will likely *never* be fully explained and accounted for by our physical scientific methods.

Extra-terrestrial flying craft are described in the book of Ezequiel in the Bible and they are depicted in ancient etchings of the ancient Egyptian Pyramids and on many other Megaliths left all over the Earth, yet scientists have never captured a "scientifically satisfying" sample of one. Nothing outside the material paradigm can ever satisfy them—by definition. Genuine supernatural phenomena tend to phase partially in and out of our physical existence due to vibrational distinctions. These phenomena might be contactable in our physical world by certain of our senses, but not by others. We may temporarily see the event with our eyes and even hear the event or *all five senses* may participate in the perception for a fleeting moment and then the phenomena blinks back out of physical existence. There have even been paranormal events can even overwhelm the five senses of the typical individual and even transcend into their consciousness—but it will be only for a moment.

In addition, some people exist, through their unique vibratory resonance, closer to the vibrational reality of a supernatural phenomenon than others, so that some can perceive the paranormal event but others right next to them are utterly "blind" to it. We all have slightly different vibrational settings but the greatest vibrational/perceptive difference is between *believers and non-believers.*

Those who believe will always be more open to perceptions of things that are beyond our narrow bandwidth of physical reality. Supernatural, Non-Terrestrial craft can be visible to the naked eye of people on the ground yet, at times, the F-18 Air Force pilots who come screaming to their reported positions never read them on their instruments *and* cannot even see them with their eyes. Such is the nature of the unstable reality platforms established during the vibrational flux of paranormal events. Genuine paranormal events tend not to be static in our reality.

Even the most apparently raw physical phenomena such as Bigfoot, the LochNess Monster and other crypto-creatures can never be captured and studied by men in lab coats in the present age because they may never be fully physical in this world. Like ephemeral spirits, Bigfoot may be seen by our eyes and heard by our ears and even be solid enough to leave hairs and tissue samples on the trees it tramples through— but it seems those samples just melt away into nothingness. Witnesses often smell the terrible stench of Bigfoot (sometimes referred to by Native American tribes as Skunk-Creature) and catch a glimpse of him but these same people do not hear the monstrous beast breaking branches or twigs. Other times, the reverse is true. People can sometimes clearly hear the monster breaking trees down as it pursues them, but never see him. The uniqueness of each individual's vibratory resonance ensures a lack of uniform results when it comes to the spiritual perception abilities of human beings.

Paranormal crypto-creatures cannot be captured and held here because they only manifest temporarily *or only partially manifest.*

Science as the study of reproducible results is wholly inappropriate as a way to examine paranormal events—irreproducible things. In paranormal matters, the higher value evidence is that which derives its energy from spiritual, transcendent and faith-based belief systems—in other words, from human consciousness.

Evidence *isn't* just about what you can see, touch, hear, taste, smell and reproduce under laboratory conditions. We've been tricked into thinking that only solid material and scientifically qualified data can serve as "real evidence" because the overseers of materiality want it that way. It gives them yet one more avenue by which to limit what people may think, feel and understand. Once they misled Western civilization into the belief that evidence must be solid or scientific in order to be reliable, then the evidence people could believe in or even consider was slashed by at least 99.9 percent. That's an important goal of the Elite Powers In Control (EPIC). This severe reduction in what the mainstream of humanity can trust as evidence means that most of "reality" has effectively been blocked from their daily consideration. This becomes crucial during quests for truth and it makes all people far easier to control. Control what people can consider as possible and you limit their hearts and minds.

Yet the truth is that often the most ephemeral is what serves as the most reliable and trustworthy evidence. Personal anecdotes, intuitive evidence, hypotheticals, even myths and legends have incalculable evidentiary value so long as they are true to human nature. If they are derived from the genuine impulses of a human spirit, then their source is the perceiver's consciousness. Your own quiet, still voice will tell you something is true to human nature. The great philosopher Joseph Campbell said *"myths are clues to the spiritual potentialities of human life."*

Myths and legends that reflect the inner essence of our collective humanity have lasted in written and oral traditions for thousands of years (during this latest period of recorded history). Similarly, anecdotes, hypotheticals, personal experience shown as testimonial or intuitive truth; all have connections to a supreme field of consciousness that ensures reliability and significance that no laboratory can ever measure or comprehend. As our globe enters a new paradigm of blossoming consciousness, it is vital that we wean ourselves from the organized madness of awarding "scientific" evidence a higher status than non-scientific evidence. Often, non-scientific evidence taps into a dispositive reliability that materialist-scientific thinkers cannot begin to approach. A reversal is coming. It will be a global switch in the area of evidentiary clarity and resolution.

Intuitive sensitivity is more important than fact-analysis. Individual personal experience is far more significant than statistical or analytical evidence which does not connect to any person's individual soul. Things like statistical and analytical vetting of data evidence treats human beings like machines generating activities that can be simply tracked and examined for standardized, automatic conclusions. Statistics about a certain area of crime do not tell us anything meaningful about the individual we may have as a suspect. Additionally, mechanical analysis of every bit of data from a person's various areas of background—financial, business, social, and investigative only reveal to us pieces of a person's physical life. We need to know about the elements of the *inner being* that caused a crime or mystery to occur.

An anecdote depicting that subject's behavior or an intuitive revelation received by an investigator confronted with material from the subject—reveals something much deeper of the subject's character than anything we get from a lab. Such personal anecdotes or intuitive flashes will cut right to the heart of an investigation or mystery: guilt or innocence, truth or deception. Simultaneously, in the same investigation; dozens of analysts and Ph.ds will be pouring out sweat over roomfuls of data and analysis indefinitely; only to arrive at *guesses* disguised as solid analytical conclusions.

Regardless of the nature of evidence contemplated, basic investigative muscle memory tends to follow similar patterns among investigators.

1. CRIME OR MYSTERIOUS OCCURRENCE REPORTED:

- a crime or mysterious occurrence is reported—this can be in person, telephonic or online but there should be a ground level indicia of stability (no incoherent rambling) in the person reporting. In the incident or crime being reported and the person reporting; there should exist a threshold of basic reliability—like the reporter's willingness to give their own full personal identifying information (no anonymity—the most common indicator of hidden agendas, grudges and ulterior motives against those being reported on).

2. PRELIMINARY INVESTIGATION:

- gathering evidence, collecting evidence, identifying witnesses
- determine classification of The Incident, identify elements of a crime or of a mysterious occurrence (i.e.: where does it fit?)
- conduct short interviews only to answer the First Query above
- preserve the scene for follow up investigation later

3. FOLLOW-UP INVESTIGATION:

- read over all reports from Preliminary Investigation, make sense of the situation, and look for leads; examine the scene of the crime or occurrence
- collect any evidence still available, coordinate any special units needed for evidence processing
- determine if a modus operandi (typical pattern of behavior that is a trademark of a certain type of criminal or paranormal occurrence) is present for a particular type of criminal or paranormal occurrence
- determine if a suspect exists or if the occurrence is genuinely paranormal

4. SUSPECT OR OCCURRENCE DETERMINATION:

- determine the results of trawling through evidence for leads
- increase investigator knowledge about this Crime/Occurrence
- attempt to establish a single suspect as the prime suspect, establish a strong link between that suspect and the crime or occurrence
- very thorough interviews, interrogations, secure confessions from the suspects or perpetrators and match suspect information against the data gathered

5. CASE CONSTRUCTION:

- legalize all information, evidence collected into a coherent, legally usable case
- investigator must think about reports and how the evidence supports theories of the case

- decide the narrative of the supported case
- conversion of all materials, knowledge and information into a standard that is legally admissible in a court of law

These same standards must be applied in paranormal phenomena as if we are constructing a case that will succeed in a court process. This is important because there are always cash and material rewards that follow any claim of paranormal phenomena that rise to a high level of credibility—with convincing evidence to display. There will always be people and institutions willing to pay whenever these phenomena come close to being proven to a courtroom standard of proof.

These five steps and The First Investigative query are the most basic building blocks of any investigation. They are in the reflexive muscle memory of most investigators and now we need to show the synthesis of the innate paranormal abilities of experienced investigators into all the basic steps of rudimentary investigation.

Many members of the fossilized scientific community have worked tirelessly to complicate this most basic model of investigation. Scientists and analysts can do many permutations on the basic investigative query model and all their complex elaborations only serve to impress other members of the same scientific class. However, the most serious damage to the investigative world by the obsolete scientific model is in the area of investigative vetting of evidence of paranormal phenomena.

Innumerable scientists and intellectuals have studied and reported on paranormal topics during recent years. The most educated and least intuitive among us gravitate towards subjects where they can pretend to command the topic without fear of contradiction. Sadly, few trained investigators have entered the study of the paranormal. It often goes against the nature of a professional investigator, steeped in the minutia of material physicality, to consider things that can't be perceived through the five senses. These are people trained to look at physicality even down to the sub-atomic level. They rarely lift up their heads from examining hairs, fibers, fingerprints and data records; in order to think or meditate upon ephemeral things. It is for this reason that paranormal topics have been left to the cynicism of materialist scientists and intellectuals. That time is gone.

Investigators and Truth-Seekers must reeducate themselves so they may be equipped to delve into a world that has been up to now the exclusive province of those most unfit to pronounce judgment over it.

4

THE GRAY BABY

(The following anecdote is recounted by a veteran state trooper—a man who had been tried and tested through numerous experiences with hardened criminals—various felony arrests, vehicle pileups on major highways with gory fatalities and even one shootout with fugitives. Yet nothing prepared this particular trooper for one gloomy overcast day in the late afternoon in Desert-Town.)

Trooper Lopez, sitting in his vehicle watching out for speedsters and drunks, caught just a flash of a dilapidated Chevy going at least 100 miles per hour as it zoomed past his hidey hole. He was happy for some movement as he had been feeling a bit stiff and out of sorts. The trooper was even happier when the vehicle immediately pulled right over right away deep into the spacious, sandy shoulder. He was not in the mood for a major high-speed chase today. As he stepped up towards the vehicle, his usual swagger dissipated. He felt as if he'd stepped thru a cold vapor—that made the hairs on his neck stand up. The normal sounds of birds and desert animals went silent. A wave of nausea swept through him. He bowed his head into the open driver's window.

Nothing.

No one was in the driver's seat—just an empty front seat on the driver and passenger side. He removed his sunglasses and threw them in his pocket.

Something crouched down in the back seat. He removed his sunglasses and threw them in his pocket.

The driver must have jumped into the back.

It was difficult to see. The windows were darkly tinted. It was already an unusually gray day for this desert town but there seemed to be an unnatural gloom inside that vehicle. Lopez could faintly make out that the driver was crouched down in the backseat and appeared to be holding something tenderly with both arms.

A terrible stench hit the trooper. Like a solid thing, the odor assaulted not just his nose but his eyes and he could even feel it prickling the skin of his face. It was the creeping scent of rank putridity. He had smelled something like this at autopsies but not at this level. His right hand jumped onto the handle of his holstered sidearm.

"Driver, stay where you are. Let me see your hands!"

A gaunt-faced creature jut forward toward the trooper and uncurled a long, bony finger against crusty lips.

"sshhhh, you'll wake the baby…"

He caught a glimpse of her eyes…or rather where her eyes should've been—instead there were large, almond-shaped pools of pure black. The trooper thought it must be a trick of the light or lack of it. He fought against the rising bile in his throat.

"MISS! DON'T MOVE! Driver listen to me, slowly show me what you have in your hands. Slowly!"

Her arms were preternaturally long because she thrust forward, out of the window, a tiny figure swaddled in a flower print blanket. The trooper recoiled. She had thrust it out so far that it hovered just inches from the trooper's face. He could only see a tiny body and a large puffy face. The "thing" was gray and stiff. It had been a baby once. The lips were dried and the eyes were swollen shut. The acrid smell of death buckled the trooper's knees.

"Oh my God."

He backed up to his vehicle, yelling as he went.

*"DRIVER, DON'T MOVE, DON'T MOVE.
STAY IN THE CAR."*

She could easily have driven off or run off or just slowly ambled toward the next truck stop and she would have gotten as far as she cared to because the trooper had no intention of intercepting her or The Gray Baby. As he frantically radioed for assistance, the trooper asked for local police, the FBI and anyone who would listen. He wanted as many bodies as possible between himself and the pair that remained quietly in the backseat of that vehicle.

Anyone who has been in law-enforcement for any period of time knows that part of the job is always *acting* as if you are in control of everything, whether you are or not. But once in a great while, something happens that can make even the most hardened officer lose that veneer of control and not care one bit. Whatever it might have been: fortune, happenstance, random luck or a plan contrived before that trooper was ever born; the trooper felt something life changing had just happened to him. The woman stayed in the backseat, happily mewling over The Gray Baby as if nothing was going on while assistance came from several directions. She continued making playful sounds to the thing in her arms as ambulances, fire trucks and police from several departments responded to the scene. Authorities brought her out of the vehicle. She was docile as a lamb. She only responded with screaming violence once medical personnel ripped The Gray Baby from her. Without wanting to, Lopez glanced at her in that moment and she looked back right into his eyes, as she screamed.

"Not our baby. Don't take our baby!"

The mother was subdued and faced a long list of charges. Trooper Lopez looked away and sat in the dirt. Turned out, she had fled the scene of a major meth lab take down, two states away. The mother was a known meth user who escaped after a shootout. She had seen baby's supposed father killed by police. That happened two days before the road stop. It was later found out that the baby had died from neglect *long before* she fled the scene. The mother took nothing with her but the clothing on her back, The Gray Baby and a generous stash of amphetamines. She had been driving ever since until this trooper broke her spell.

His comrades were very happy to inform Trooper Lopez that the baby had been dead before the female hit the road—that there was nothing he could have done to save *the baby*. They assumed Lopez was distraught because he felt guilt over the death of a baby but that wasn't the problem. Trooper Lopez truthfully didn't care about the baby—or the mother. Whatever they had been before, that was over long before he met them on that road. He felt sure "the baby" had become something else— something sinister.

Trooper Lopez felt certain that a dark force had targeted him that day—that it had sought him out specifically because *it knew his secret*—that he was (unknown to his friends and co-workers) *psychically sensitive*. The human baby was long dead and gone but he felt certain that The Gray Baby somehow lived. He knew that there was a dark force alive in that tiny cadaver that sought to find him and burrowed its way into his subconscious mind. That night and more nights than he cares to remember, he has had lucid dreams, more real and vivid than this physical life in which the scene played out again and again except that each time when the "dead" Gray Baby was thrust up into his face (it was closer with each succeeding dream) the end would be different. It suddenly opened its eyes—large almond pure-black eyes—like the woman—intelligent/malevolent eyes craving something from him…reaching out to him. Sometimes the Gray Baby's eyes would paralyze him, other times; he would take off running—whatever the result; he would awaken.

Trooper Lopez now believes evil seeks to go where it can do the most damage. Worst of all, Lopez *knows* that when the mother looked at him and screamed about *"our baby"* she didn't mean the human baby she shared the dead meth-head father. She meant that the Gray Baby now belonged to her and *to him*—Trooper Lopez—*he was the new co-owner of the Gray Baby and he would spend the rest of his life trying to exorcise from his life the horror of that ownership.*

5

THE BOX WITH
FIVE HOLES

During many years of studying paranormal events and supernaturally gifted individuals; I have come to several absolute conclusions.

The first is that the version of reality that we all learn from mainstream society, is utterly false. People routinely accept as truth that they are nothing more than flesh covered containers in a purely physical reality—that they will live the span of their lives in this box and can only understand the universe through the limitations of that box. Eventually, the box will crumble, fall apart and so will their reality, which was limited to the box. The best analogy to depict this illusion is *the box with five holes*.

Most human beings spend their individual lives inside this box. The worst part about that reality is that they only stay inside the box in obedience to society. This oblong box (*yes, like a coffin*) serves a dual purpose. It keeps the eternal soul and cosmic spirit of the individual safely contained so that they never, at least not in this life, find out about the indescribable supernatural abilities connecting what is inside the box with everything outside the box.

The holes do not emit anything. Rather, they are the poor apertures by which the resident of the box attempts to *take in* what goes on in the infinite universe outside the box. They represent a person's senses by which they take in very meager amounts of data about the physical world around them. The holes allow the perception of: sight, sound, touch, taste and fragrance. Absorption through these holes are the methods we are limited to in receiving the universe around us—*just five holes* by which to perceive our immediate physical surroundings filled with billions perhaps trillions, of stimuli. The rivers of information that compete for entry among these five holes would be still overwhelming to the boxes *even if the boxes had dozens of holes* by which to receive data.

As it is, the billions of data-streams are constantly shifting into new forms and data streams every moment of our lives—further adding to the difficulty of sifting, filtering and absorbing this information. Beside our immediate environment (where we are physically sitting at this point in space and time) there are also: the rest of the planet Earth, our solar system and all of time, space and existence; also producing stimuli and data streams that reach us through various media. How do the boxes deal with the overwhelming volume of data that doesn't come close to getting through the meager five holes available to let in data? The boxes ignore it—almost all of it.

They pretend it all doesn't exist, doesn't matter and they assert to themselves that only the infinitesimal bits that get through the five holes hold any real value for the boxes. "If we can't touch it, taste it, smell, feel, see or hear it; then it isn't real." This is the familiar refrain of all those contained by the oblong box. These boxes try their hardest to exclude entire universes of spiritual, metaphysical and *paranormal* stimuli, information and data-streams. Among these typical boxes, not a single strand of data from spiritual and paranormal realities is accepted through any of the meager five holes or the minds that manage them. When his apostles asked Jesus if they should delay God's work to go pay their respects at a funeral, He responded

"Let the dead bury the dead."

The contents of these oblong boxes are like the spiritually dead. They believe in nothing except what they can see, touch, taste or hear. They love nothing except themselves and those they see as an extension of themselves and they live for nothing except the fleeting momentary pleasures of the material world. They believe in nothing except what is first approved by their official cultural filters and then fed to them through mainstream institutions. Such boxes/people are like blades of grass that sprout in the morning but become nothing more than dry dead husks in the hot afternoon sun. Time and Space form the conveyor belt that is constantly moving the boxes forward in that hot sun, gathering what tiny bits of information they can through these small holes, as they move on the conveyor belt for a short duration until the boxes finally fall apart. Their short existence served no real purpose beyond the existence itself.

Those already spiritually dead are living in a lie, wrapped in deception, contained inside a prison. They live in the prison of the box because they have been duped into believing this is the only way they can live life. People believe they have no choice in this temporary material reality but nothing could be further from the truth. Those in the boxes can begin the process of rising out and above the boxes as soon as they make the simplest decision that they will not be held inside them anymore. Making that brave decision is the hardest thing to do. This is why so few actually make that decision. If the decision is made, then getting out of the box is the easy part. The truth, *down to the bone*, is that living outside this box is indescribably liberating and wonderfully thrilling. Instead of living the life of a dead person—we can be *fully alive* beyond the box.

Para-Investigators have little choice but to live outside the box because their quests for hidden truths, their investigations, already take them to far-flung metaphysical planes on a constant basis. They are the seekers of truth who have already broken out of this box. Para-Investigators have used their abilities to begin perceiving the outside world through clairvoyance, meditation, focused concentration, extra-sensory perception, clear-hearing and other extraordinary abilities of Awakened Minds. They have received gifts from the great swirling abyss that contacts the Mind of Creator-Source. Tragically, after unjustified attacks, many have withdrawn back to their boxes. Others have even had their careers destroyed by former colleagues who feared and hated them because of their abilities. It's time for the old fear and dread to give way to a new paradigm.

6

THE LIGHT VOICE

("The Light Voice" is an experience that has occurred to many different officers in desperate situations. Yet these "light voice" experiences always include the same basic elements—an officer caught in a hopeless, violent situation and supernatural intervention. The latest such experience was related to me by Dirk, a young man in his late twenties. He had recently started at one of the United States Federal government "three letter, law-enforcement agencies.")

Dirk was working a violent crime responsive squad in a major urban center on the East Coast of the United States. This young man was a former accountant probably more suited to investigating financial crimes than organized crime but he was very happy to work something new and different.

He was driving his government vehicle to lunch one day when he recognized the voice of one his squad-mates on the radio calling out:

"Shots fired! Need assistance from any units in the area!"

He took the address. His car ate up red lights as his vehicle screeched around corners and through intersections.

This is it…

Dirk knew this was his first real chance to prove himself and he would seize it with both hands.
who knows what this could lead to, transfer to any squad I want, transfer to any place I like…maybe even promotion?

His grasp was so tight on the steering wheel he could feel the plastic-carbon alloy splintering. As Dirk arrived at the radioed address, he saw uniformed police officers in front of a six-story structure arguing with each other and shouting at civilians at the front of the building. Dirk swung wide to avoid them. He drove down the side of the building and into the alleyway behind it. He would stash the government vehicle in a corner and approach stealthily from the side of the building. Dirk was a dark-skinned, Italian-American. He had it in his mind that he was in as much danger of being shot by white police officers as he was from criminals. He would routinely toss his badge around his neck on a prominent chain to lessen that possibility. Dirk fumbled for the chain in his glove compartment where he kept it. Dirk found a quiet spot in the alleyway and pulled close to the brick wall.

Dirk's car windows were down. Dirk heard a celebration nearby. Champagne corks popped and people yelled out:
> *"To Shar…good Black."*
> *"To Par….good Pack."*
> *"Shout it out!"*

Wait—there's no celebration here.

Blood had been roaring in his ears. He fumbled with the driver's side door as his hearing cleared. Men in the alleyway shouted at him.

"TOO FAR, MOVE BACK!
DIRK, TOO FAR, MOVE BACK!
DON'T GET OUT!"

Explosions all along his windshield.

Invisible hammer blows pushed back the door he was trying to open. The drivers' side mirror shattered. He hunkered back down into the bottom of his vehicle. He was face up on the floor boards as the upper half of his vehicle became a maelstrom of flying glass, metal and plastic. In his minds-eye, Dirk "saw" several revelations at once.

- Two shooters were in front of his vehicle firing automatic weapons with great accuracy.
- Police in front of the building had been arguing because *they didn't have heavy weapons to assist in the alleyway.*
- Dirk had driven his car right into a massive, deadly cross fire as rounds were striking his vehicle from the back as well.

Dirk laid face up on the boards next to the gas and brake pedals. He tried to focus. He triple-checked his gun was loaded but the car kept disintegrating above him. He could "see" the two men advancing on his vehicle as they continued firing. Dirk's friends were returning fire from cover. The attacking pair now used Dirk's vehicle for cover and continued their advance. They were pros. As one would reload, he would take a knee and call out, so the other would provide cover fire during the temporary pause. Upon complete reloading, they would call out again and would advance again together. For the six men crouched in the alley, returning fire now became a desperate effort to save Dirk's life who they thinly hoped was still alive in the car. Had any of them had something more powerful than mere handguns; there would have been no issue. Someone yelled into a radio for heavy gun support from police. Another yelled for assisting units *not* to come into the alley *unless* they had rifles.

Dirk's car was so shattered that the attackers, in seconds, would walk up, lean in through open areas; and fire at his shivering fetal position. He could hear them calling out to each other—approaching in tandem on each side of the car. Even if Dirk managed to shoot one, the other would get him from the opposite side. As death approached, Dirk did the one thing he never thought would do—*he gave up.*

Dirk made peace with his death/God/the Universe and consigned his soul to His Maker.

Then, *everything dropped out.*

Dirk stated this phrase is as accurate as he could say it in human language. The march of time and space stopped. The men attacking his vehicle froze. His friends returning fire from behind dirty garbage cans in the alleyway stopped—screaming police officers, traffic, birds and bullets in midflight—everything everywhere—stopped. A brilliant light with starry sparkles all through it filled the interior of Dirk's car. The light was intense, almost white but somehow, did not hurt Dirk's eyes. He looked right into the light and through it but there was nothing inside it except warmth and love. It filled Dirk with a sense of well-being and a voice came through the light.

FEAR NOT. YOU'LL BE FINE.

The light and the voice disappeared. That was it. No instructions. No specifics. But Dirk was filled with a solid peace and a feeling of resumed momentum as time and space clicked back into being. It was like a being a cork that had been bobbing in a standing pool of water but now that pool turned into a rushing river, driving the cork forward.

He knew what to do.

His hand with the gun darted out over the top/front of his dashboard. From where his front windshield used to be, he stretched his arm straight up so only his wrist with the gun jutted out. Without looking, Dirk began firing forward in a wide arc semicircle. He kept the rest of his body down as he pulled the trigger in rapid succession. His clip emptied. He reloaded.

He brought the gun out again but—everything ceased. But this time it wasn't time and space that halted—just the men shooting at him. Their fire desisted. The attack was over. Dirk peeked.

They were gone.

He looked back through where his back window used to be. His friends were in standing upright positions. They smiled back at him and gave him thumbs up. He looked forward again.

They're really gone.

Four of Dirk's friends took off in pursuit of the malefactors but two remained behind to make sure he was alive and uninjured. His friends assisted him out of his vehicle as they scoured the ruined insides of Dirk's government vehicle.

"Where is it?" Several of them asked as Dirk secured his sidearm.
"Where's what?"
"The machine-gun! That's what scared them off. Why did you stop firing? You might have gotten both of them." Dirk continued shaking glass shards off his clothing.

"There was no machine gun. It was just my sidearm."

It was later determined that Dirk had fired sixteen bullets from his semi-automatic pistol in just about three seconds. To everyone in the alley (and perhaps the two attackers) it sounded like a short burst from a machine gun. It's amazing how fast a person can pull a trigger when there's certainty and no aiming involved.

Dirk had driven the shooters off. The attackers had fled the alley back to their vehicle on the street in regular parking. They escaped. Each man had been wounded superficially several times but resisted going to the hospital until two weeks later when one of them got a vicious infection in his leg. They said at the hospital that they had come back from a hunting trip where an accidental discharge had occurred. An alert nurse didn't buy their story. An officer came to check them out and this led to their apprehension without incident. Again, they hailed Dirk as a hero as it was determined that his "spray and pray" stunt had actually hit each of the men, one time each, and given them serious wounds that made them flee and later be arrested.

Dirk didn't like the hero stuff. Sometimes this puzzled and even angered his friends, but he could never tell them the *full* story. Once he had finished recounting the complete story to me, his voice became low and throaty. Dirk confessed his enormous shame since that fateful day. He said he was no hero. To the contrary, he had been worse than a coward—*he had given up.* The only reason he hadn't run away was that he couldn't. If the Light-Voice had not come, he would never have survived. Dirk said he still doesn't know if the light-voice was God, his guardian angel or whatever but he does know he would have died that day if the Light-Voice hadn't appeared to him.

I advised him that I can't know for certain what the Light-Voice was but here's what I did know: the Voice and Light were a part of him and therefore whatever was done for Dirk that day, was not some alien outside force—it was a part of his persona, a part of Dirk. Even if he was no hero, he was certainly no coward. It took great courage to listen to the Light-Voice. This is because the Light-Voice can only show us the doorway—*we must still step through the door* as Dirk did that day.

7

DYNAMIC TRANSCENSION

The materialist medical establishment, materialist scientific community, rationalist investigative institutions; and all areas of human knowledge; face the installation of new paradigms. The universal perspective of reality itself is undergoing a rapid transformation. Some proponents even call it a revolution in which everything we used to think we knew has changed. The Age of Mass Awakening brings the convergence of:

1. Ancient spirituality and transcendence into the Cosmic Mind

2. with Quantum Science at the subatomic level

This convergence is counterintuitive and even unacceptable for much of humanity. Most wish to continue living in the box with five holes. It is restrictive but at least it's familiar to them—*and comfortable.*

Even as we enter an Age of Dynamic Transcension, far too many still live under and will even fiercely protect the fossilized materialist theory of the universe, which believes that *all reality* is just made of matter and energy. They defend unto their end— the supposition that anything which can't be quantified, examined and reproduced in a laboratory; must simply be the product of over-stimulated neurons misfiring in the brain. Those educated as scientists, physicians, and psychologists; under the old paradigm, continue to believe that humans are just material atoms, molecules and organs. They see us just as neurons, synapses and bundles of conditioned responses.

Their paradigm is expiring.

To avoid the natural consequences of recognizing the truth of the human soul/ spirit, scientists have tended to avoid discussion of consciousness as much as possible. Whenever physicians confront spontaneous healing through the power of faith and spirit, they will find alternate materialist explanations for the "miracle" or they use derisive terms they invented for these occasions like "placebo effect." When confronted with True Death Experiences that show the preeminence of the spirit over the body; they will point to massive billions of brain neuron cells firing simultaneously and creating "hallucinations." There are numerous specious arguments like these that materialist science uses to denigrate the new paradigm of mind/body/spirit unity; but these form a poor shield that has been crumbling for some time now.

The time is upon us for the next step in the evolution of police investigations and investigations of all types. We must now formalize the hidden intuitive processes that investigators regularly use but keep hidden as a secret shame under the current materialist system that restrict these investigations. Additionally, Para-Investigations will increase standardization and respectability of police investigations by synthesizing them into recognizable paranormal phenomena. What was known as mere mystic adventurism shall now become a legitimate new field of investigation and study.

8

PARANORMALITY AS HYPER-SPIRITUALITY

The world is starving for content that deals with the entire universe of paranormal topics as *truthful, serious reality*. Yet, such treatment is virtually nowhere to be found *even* as we enter The Age of Mass Awakening. Instead, in many areas of media and culture, we have examination of the paranormal going forward in the two most wildly inappropriate venues possible—scientific examinations and materialist skepticism. Consuming this type of mis-examination always has the same effect on our psyche. Although we appear to be venturing into higher areas of the metaphysical, it is analogous to consuming the empty calories of junk food. It feels good for a moment as if we are getting some real nourishment but ultimately we are left feeling weaker and more malnourished than before we consumed that garbage.

Human beings are hardwired by the Great Designer to crave spiritual nourishment—not the religious, group oriented brand of pseudo-spirituality but genuine direct-connection-with-Creator Source spirituality. We hunger for reinforcement of the innate truth that we are eternal spiritual beings just undergoing a temporary physical experience on this tiny shelf of existence known as the physical universe. We know this is true but we live in a dense fog of materiality and physical illusion that makes us forget who we really are. In some proportion of the population, this need appears to be partly fulfilled by participation in organized religion. Religion could only succeed in satisfying this need insofar as it promotes genuine spirituality rather than man-made morality. By its intrinsic nature, most mainstream religion offers *spiritual sedation* disguised as spiritual upliftment. Only true individual spiritual experience (found in very few places at this writing) satisfies the human yearning for real enlightenment. Organized religion, in the meantime provides comfort, security, reassurance and also control. Like mainstream science, mainstream organized religion is just another powerful force designed to *get us back into that box*.

A hidden truth of the unseen world is that *spiritual topics and paranormal topics* are both a continuum of the same radiant spectrum that satisfies the human soul.

Any division or segregation between them is artificial, created, and enforced by those who control the major institutions of our planet, the Elite Powers In Control (EPIC). Their media minions are fed propaganda and directed toward the purpose of keeping people divided into as many small, warring groups as possible. If paranormal believers and spiritual seekers ever realized that they are on the same quest, it could lead to unification of their quest. This, in turn, would help synergize humanity toward *The Age of Mass Awakening*.

Human beings instinctively know that they are more than just the box with the five holes but that knowledge has been conditioned out of them. Even if they did remember, the conditioning is so insidious that it neutralizes any desire or motivation they might have to do anything about it. Therefore, they quietly seek out spiritual and paranormal truths because the mere act of seeking seems to satisfy that urgent craving inside them. They desire a way to declare that they are more than just that box with five holes. Our common need to make this declaration is addressed: during meditations, during spirit-based rituals, at the séance, at the channeling or when we watch that UFO video. That commonality should lead spiritual seekers and the paranormal believers to stand together and declare that the box can no longer hold us. Understanding this simple truth will help render the box incapable of holding us: that Paranormality and belief in supernatural realities are a far more genuine form of Intensive Spirituality than any mainstream religion or set of rituals disguised as upliftment. That is partly because paranormal belief must always be sought out and struggled for—*against* the forces of mainstream culture. Mainstream religious beliefs are in obedience to mainstream culture and therefore simple to maintain and foster. For these reasons, belief in paranormal topics must emanate from the core of our beings while mainstream beliefs come from our easy obedience to society. Belief in the paranormal is not a substitute for spirituality—it is actually a form of *Hyper-Spirituality*.

As we enter The Age of Mass Awakening, an intense need for material dealing with all paranormal topics becomes more and more acute in our societies. This is carefully managed by those Elite Powers in Control (EPIC) who are desperate to keep us in the box with five holes. They have painstakingly built up entire professions whose jurisdiction it is to jam, stomp and shove people back into those boxes with extreme prejudice.

Think you saw something or heard something that doesn't fit into the current reality paradigm?

You better think again. Reveal your experiences in the wrong venue and they'll send you to a psychologist, psychiatrist or any of the cadre of "mental health professionals" who stand ready to tear you down, make you unsure and then medicate away any doubts you might have about their omniscience. If you won't stay in your box through gentle persuasion, ridicule or threats; then institutional powers *will forcefully stomp you back into your box.*

In the midst of all this truth seeking, we have foxes deciding whether hens should live. Any survey of television, cable channels, satellite channel programming, radio programming, thousands of internet programs available—depicts a steady stream of "paranormal" programming coming and going on a constant basis yet it is controlled to avoid the result that EPIC wishes to avoid (the awakening of large numbers of people to the true nature of reality). About 94 percent of all programming on paranormal topics is *through a scientific lens.* The standard filter used to determine whether there is truth to paranormal topics is the *same exact standard* that has, for eons, kept the human spirit trapped in a that cursed box.

Scientific instruments are, therefore, used to measure to trawl the black depths of the ancient LochNess Lake for presence of the ancient monster. Heat sensor photography and electro-magnetic resonance equipment are used to capture the presence of ghosts and spirits. DNA kits are used to collect samples of hair and tissue at the relevant sites in the great Northwest forests to prove whether Bigfoot exists. Worst of all, materialist scientists are interviewed to give **the final word** on whether paranormal phenomena actually happened or not. Even promoters of paranormal truth, writers on paranormal topics—sheepishly tout their scientific credentials (with M.D., PhD. or whatever academic degrees cause people to bow down) to create the inference that *if science finds this acceptable or even tolerable then it MIGHT be true.*

All this serves to empower the thinking that has kept so many inside that box, so that even if they begin the process of escape by inquiring into the truth of the paranormal; they can easily be recaptured and pushed back into that box. This is very much like having a committee of hungry foxes deciding whether individual chickens should have a right to live. This committee can promise objective, impartial, judicious verdicts all day long but chances are—*chickens lose.*

….if you don't see Nessie on the sonar then she's not there….it was all just an elaborate myth….

….if the ghosts don't register on the magnetic resonance equipment then they are not there and …this is all just primitive superstition…

….if the hair samples come back to a known animal, then Bigfoot doesn't exist and we can put all this nonsense behind us once and for all…

…..I've proven a hundred of these UFO videos were frauds this year! Do I have to prove every single one of them is false? How gullible are you people?

9

A MAELSTROM OF FRAUD

(Para-Investigators are formed even as children—children who will not be put off by adult indifference to pursuit of the unknown and who won't stop seeking answers to mysteries that matter. I have observed that many paranormal experiencers had their first encounters with the supernatural during the formative period of five to twelve years of age. This is my own such experience.)

It is quite possible that *all* children begin life as "Indigo Children" but the majority lose this innate status somewhere along the pedestrian journey of middle life. Tragically, from about the age of ten going forward, school system regimentation begins to stultify the imagination and spiritual powers of our children. That's exactly what the factory model, industrial age design school systems of today were designed to do. They limit and regiment the unlimited minds of children in spirit grinding institutions created for mega-corporate realities rather than for the flourishing of human ingenuity. They work to create cogs in the global corporate structure rather than leaders, artists and visionaries. This awful reductionism also suppresses our children's innate supernatural gifts as they acculturate into an academic system of enforced mind-limitations. Very often, these children lose these supernatural perceptual abilities and forget the experiences they enjoyed as a result. Sometimes, they even convince themselves in young adulthood that these were just childish dreams—*almost.* Then, something happens in adulthood to bring the re-emergence of the realities that first touched their lives during childhood. The universe finds ways to draw us toward the things that truly matter.

When I was about ten years old, I became very interested in Alien Visitors to planet Earth, partly because of my own experience observing a non-terrestrial craft. One late night, I was playing in a group of children on the streets of New York City. The play moved to another street and I stood alone under a moonless night sky as the 1:00am hour arrived. Only parked cars and tall buildings framed the night landscape. Although there was complete silence, I looked up for some reason. I saw something enormous hovering over the tops of some residential buildings. It was a silverish, metallic disk with a diameter of several hundred feet. The craft flashed strobing, multi-colored lights in its base and soundlessly descended towards me. Then, *we both changed our minds.* I ran away as fast as I could and the craft reversed course going back upward. It ascended again out of sight into a black cloud. I later embarked on a quest to find out what I had seen.

I began reading literature on the topic, both fantasy and non-fiction. I also discussed the event with my mother. She was reticent to discuss the matter except to say that I should continue to study before I came to any definite conclusions as to what I had seen. I lobbied my mother for permission to discuss this topic with my father. She steadfastly refused. My father was a hard-working man. He was *old-time tough*, a correctional officer who dealt harshly with violent felons on a regular basis—not a man who tolerated nonsense, especially not from his ten year old son. As scared as I was at the thought of upsetting my father, I just couldn't let this mystery go. He tended to be emotionally closed off with his family much of the time but I was determined to find the right moment. One morning, while my mother was out, I finally took the plunge. I told him about my experience seeing a paranormal hovering craft and about what I had subsequently studied about Non-Terrestrial Visitors to our planet. He surprised me with his response.

"*What did you see? What did you learn?*"

I had struck gold. I confessed to him that I had seen one floating above the buildings of New York City one late evening when I wasn't supposed to be awake, or carousing with friends, or on the streets outside. I described exactly what the craft looked like, how it moved and how it made me feel—like it was watching me *as much as I was watching it* and how it just disappeared without a trace. Finally, before he pronounced judgment, I regaled him with everything I had read and studied on the topic over the last few months. I told him about similar experiences others had undergone up to and including personal contact with Alien Visitors. I stressed that these Contactees were often responsible adults—with jobs! I related about the various theories some cutting-edge scientists had proposed about the origins of Alien Visitors and about why they are here and what they really want.

He responded, as he often did to my queries, *with a story.*

For a short period during his earlier life, my dad had been a long-haul trucker. One moonless night, he was driving one of the loneliest most desolate stretches of highway in these United States, Interstate route 15 between Las Vegas and Utah. It was a pitch-black night when my father was hauling a load and listening to the radio. Suddenly, the radio went dead and all the lights in the cab turned off. Going forward from over the cab of the truck an enormous glowing "vehicle" appeared. It seemed filled with living light as it zoomed low overhead and banked right. It was a spinning, transparent gyroscope with light-based clockworks visible through a transparent outer skin. It blotted out the night sky with a span of at least one hundred yards. It seemed to him like a living, floating squid-machine. After pausing for a moment over my father's truck, the craft, at impossible speed, shot far ahead into the distance. The

craft disappeared down over a ridge and was seen no more. My father coasted the
dead truck to a stop on the gravel shoulder as he watched the luminous traces of the
squid disappear into the Earth. Seconds after the object had passed, the truck turned
right back on again.

The object was three times the size of an airliner jet plane and yet made no sound
as it almost skimmed the top of his attached load. It floated over him with lights and
dials spinning. He thought something was wrong with the squid-machine because as
it passed down into a valley it appeared to be *leaking light like blood from a wound*. He
then did something he never thought he would do. He veered from his set course into
a dirt road leading to the valley where he had seen the vehicle disappear.

"So, what did you find when you drove in after the saucer you saw?"
My father's voice became low as he issued a grave warning.
"Are you sure you want to know what I found?"
"*Yes, yes*. What did you find?"

"*I found nothing*. Not a thing, because there *was never anything there*, in the air
or on the ground or anywhere. I had imagined the whole thing. There are no flying
saucers. They don't exist." He saw my disappointment so he affected a softer tone.

"*Look son....I had been working a triple shift without any sleep for a long time and the
brain is a very powerful thing. If a person does not allow themselves to sleep and dream;
the brain will force the issue by creating waking dreams and illusions to let you know that
not letting the brain sleep is wrong and will have serious consequences. I learned my lesson.
I quit the trucking business and from then on stuck to jobs that let me get decent sleep.
You aren't used to staying up very late. I think it was the first time you ever stayed up past
midnight. We'll discuss why you were out in the streets with your friends past midnight
another time. The flying saucer wasn't really there and you didn't really see anything except
what you wanted to see.*"

I mumbled about not wanting to see anything and shuffled away. We never spoke
of it again. I was crest-fallen and my mother could see how I felt. Later, she asked me
to tell her about the flying saucer I had seen. I wasn't in the mood and just uttered
the basic facts.
She seemed relieved and leaned back.
"Thank God. Our family was really blessed."
I leaned forward.
"Why?" My mother made sure my father was not within earshot and continued.
"Because you ran away."
"Why? What could have happened?"
My mother thought for a moment.
"I don't think anyone really knows what exactly those things are, if they are aliens
or humans from the future or spirits using the alien disguise to get access to humans;
but we know what can happen when people act *welcoming* toward things like what you
saw. People who do that *can disappear*. Sometimes they can come back a long time

later with no memory and things inside their bodies without any scars to show those things are inside of them. If you ever see something like that again, you do the same thing again—you run." I was amazed.

"How do you know all these things?"

My mother whispered in my ear.

"*Your father told me.*"

§

Para-Investigators are desperately needed in "modern ufology." That is because "ufology" is caught up in a maelstrom of fantasy and fraud. UFO's are the only paranormal phenomena that manifest two continuing, global epi-phenomena: the first is the fantasy aspect: a massive continuing production of fakes and staged events created by: semi-professional tricksters, future cinema students, video hobbyists, bored teenagers with "CGI" skills and people just seeking attention. I have seen thousands of exemplars of video and photographic recorded evidence of alleged Non-Terrestrial craft and I can testify that at least ninety percent of them are simple tricks put together by tech-savvy people with too much time on their hands and a desire to test their talents in public venues. Then, these fantasies are spread out virally to innocent individuals who are guilty of nothing more than wanting to believe. Although these are awakening individuals, they still long for something **concrete** to believe in— something they can take in through their five senses. They look to the skies and make premature cognitive commitments that much of what they see may be non-terrestrial.

The second epi-phenomenon is malicious fraud. It is malicious because it is not done to show off skills or to entertain but to actually deceive and distract. This malevolent movement consists of a sprawling, global group of experts and agencies who misinform and mislead us. That's their job and they do it well.

We are now in an Information Age when the Awakened Community is able to reach out to the mainstream and share genuine Non-Terrestrial craft information as never before. Communication of revelatory UFO media on the Internet has become immediate and global. Yet, instead of enjoying a renaissance of blossoming awareness, modern ufology has degenerated into chaos and confusion. Whenever a genuine such incident occurs and disperses virally throughout the globe, it threatens the stability of the mental prison the EPIC (Elite Powers In Control) have worked so long to build. Such stark evidence delivered to the cyber device of every member of the unawakened mainstream could destabilize the national slave-farms that hold humanity hostage. The response is immediate. "Shops" with enormous resources, time and determination, commence standard disinformation operations—dynamic, enjoying unlimited black funding and untraceable. These "ops" often consist of immediate production, uploading and distribution of duplicate media that very closely follows the details of the first media representing the Alien Visitor occurrence. But these duplicates have added elements which make it clear that these other versions of the same event are clearly detectable fraud, CGI, man-made tomfoolery. Now, the genuine paranormal phenomena are buried beneath dozens of "intentionally fake" versions of the genuine occurrence. That way anyone who hears about a video of genuine paranormal phenomena now will be confronted with numerous fakes and fraudulent versions of the same event. Problem solved. Awakening halted.

Those of us who have seen this concerted action take place again and again over the last decade know it is incredibly well coordinated, well-funded and is motivated by a single intention—to keep the truth from spreading. Notice I didn't say "to keep the truth from being revealed." Truth is revealed constantly—it's only the spread that is halted. Genuine paranormal phenomena, Non-Terrestrial craft and Alien Visitors are uncovered continuously among the Awakened Community. EPIC doesn't care about that. They only want to prevent the spread of such (potentially awakening) truth to those in their gentle care—the mainstream majority herd of society ruled under their institutions.

Here is a typical fact-pattern: let's say tomorrow you happen to catch a giant black triangle ship landing in your backyard in Parsippany, New Jersey (it's a big backyard). Two beings of light emerge from the craft and speak to you for ten minutes about why they have come as Alien Visitors to Earth. Amazingly, they are not the least bit perturbed about the video camera you have filming the entire exchange. They give a message about a dimension shifting change that is about to come upon the Earth, about how we must all raise our spiritual vibration as quickly as possible. They urge withdrawal from all human systems that advocate violence, slavery and hatred (i.e.: respectively: politics, economics and mainstream organized religions). Then, they re-enter their craft and disappear—leaving no trace—not even a bent, irradiated blade of grass.

Subsequently, here is what will happen. Once you upload the video to the Net, it will cause a global furor and will garner significant attention from believers all over the world. You think, rightly, this is it. *This is the final spark to light the final great bonfire of Mass Awakening throughout the Earth.*

The problem is that within 24 hours after you emitted that thought, there will be dozens of duplicate videos that look eerily similar to your authentic video. These doppelgangers will have Hollywood-level production values requiring enormous investment of financial resources. Some of the after-loaded fakes will actually look even more authentic than your true video—complete with fake aliens and a civilian that sounds and/or looks *very similar to you in the original video*. The backgrounds will bear an impossible resemblance to Parsippany, New Jersey. These fakes look like big money production studios put them together with access to enormous resources. Yet, it still would have taken an incredible state of readiness to produce such expert fakes on such short notice. Now, only 24 hours after your original event, anyone who searches **"Backyard Aliens In Parsippany, New Jersey"** experiences a barrage of videos that all look very similar, have common elements (that match up to advertised search terms) and similar supposed "Alien Visitors." The only difference will be that all the after-loaded fakes will carry tiny tell-tale signs of Computer Graphics Interface (CGI) elements, photo-shopping or other breadcrumb trails of fakery intentionally left for the debunkers to attack and knock down. Then, the entire incident and all the versions of the incident will be pronounced "debunked fakery" *including your original paranormal video.*

All but the most determined will simply give up sifting, filtering or trying to differentiate between versions. *Which among all these versions could be the genuine one all my friends were talking about the day before?* They will simply revert to the default mainstream programming—*"yeah I looked at that and it turned out to be a fake/debunked/a well done fraud."*

Sometimes, EPIC's efforts are double-rewarded by not just averting this potential awakening incident but by even creating new conditioned responses in formerly open-minded members of mainstream society.

"Why am I spending all this effort anyway on paranormal phenomena? All these things are probably fakes. I need to live in the real world."

How do I know for a certainty that the Parsippany, New Jersey, incident would happen this way? Because it has already happened—numerous times in the modern age since video and the net have existed. During the last few decades, there has been an enormous increase in access to high quality video devices and in the ability to show videos around the world in an instant. More authentic sightings and contacts come to us on video than ever before. Yet, the fact-pattern above emerges right on schedule whenever a genuine supernatural incident is displayed to the world. The mainstream paradigm preserves itself every time. The members of the mainstream are trained that they can only rely on "hard evidence" but when hard evidence of genuine paranormal phenomena is presented to them, then extraordinary measures must be used to keep them from ever getting to the truth.

Although only about six percent of UFO incidents are genuinely unexplained and paranormal, this still adds up to hundreds every year and that number is rapidly increasing; as are what we call "mass sightings." These are instances when anywhere from a dozen to sometimes *thousands* of people all see the same paranormal, Non-Terrestrial craft. Also on the rise are: alien abductions of humans, alien experimentation on humans, alien device implantation and cattle and livestock mutilations. Telepathic communications with Extra-Dimensional beings continue through channeling, visions and even dreams. Contact cases with Alien Visitors are also increasing to a level no one ever expected. The maelstrom rises in genuine supernatural incidents in this area just as it does in the fantasy/fraud aspect.

We can't afford to wait for fact-finders and "hard evidence" to resolve these issues because it won't happen that way. Only True Investigators can lead us to truth of Extra-Dimensional Craft and Extra-Dimensional Visitors. This is the 6% solution to the problem of sifting through the constant global tsunami of "UFO" sightings. There are already dedicated Para-Investigators using new perspectives and expertise to slice through the 94 percent that have bogged down or discouraged so many in the past. Their work has led to several cognitive breakthroughs that will lead us into The Age of Mass Awakening.

The "Extra-Dimensional Visitors and Craft" phenomena have covered the Earth for almost seventy years in the modern media age. The Alien Visitor theme has saturated our culture through the global media complex. Hollywood-produced cinema has projected and shaped this topic even as its output on these topics has increased geometrically. Humanity's involvement with Extra-Dimensional realities continues to expand toward a climax undreamt of during common hours. We are quickly coming up on the endgame in the Extra-Dimensional milieu. If all we have to rely upon in the hour of climactic crisis are a cadre of myopic, materialist, scientists and ambitious government bureaucrats; humanity will truly be lost.

10

THE EXTRA-DIMENSIONALS

Breaking away from the mainstream labels and control language is the first major step in understanding paranormal Alien Visitors. False neutral labels, like "UFO" are put in place to limit discussion and imagination, not to encourage it. Ludicrous descriptors "little gray/green men" are invitations to ridicule anyone who opens a paranormal topic for discussion. Breaking from this "control language" will be crucial for Para-Investigators.

The Extra-Dimensionals—non-terrestrial, intelligent life forms who are visiting our dimension of time and space as transitory beings *from outside* our plane of physical time and space—e.g.: from outside our material existence and who return to outside this physical existence.

PLASMAS—is the replacement for the old mainstream trigger word: "UFO." PLASMAS is an acronym for:

Paranormal—having supernatural qualities such that no explanation or qualification can be provided for this particular event or thing in the physical/material iteration of time and space.

Living—a living creature, sentient, intelligent but also programmable like a computer

Aura-Reading—able to read the auras and emotions of living creatures, especially humans

Soul-Printing—able to record, collect and store a blueprint of a soul/spirit for later reference

Mobile—able to move through physical or non-physical media and even able to dematerialize

Aerial—most likely to be in the air because it wishes to be seen by as many humans as possible

Scanners—these are unoccupied scanners constantly roving to carry out their programming—to collect soul-prints of as many "interested" humans as possible.

PLASMAS are the "vehicles" that often accompany the appearances of Extra-Dimensional Visitors. Much of the Awakened Community has come to the common conclusion that, like the Extra-Dimensionals themselves, these craft also tend to phase in and out of our physical dimension of time and space. (*For a more detailed explanation of PLASMAS see the book: The Extra-Dimensionals by John DeSouza.*)

Paranormality—is it extraterrestrial, earthly-governmental or extra-dimensional in nature? There are hundreds, perhaps thousands of reports over the last twenty years that fall into the final category of credible, reliable, unexplained paranormal phenomena—true PLASMAS. This minority of incidents include video records made by: astronauts, air force pilots and other government officials, sometimes on duty and sometimes off duty. They created reliable and credible records of PLASMAS that had no plausible earthly explanation before or after the event. To date, several hundred such witnesses have been identified throughout the world and spanning every branch of the armed services, the Intelligence Agencies, and numerous other current and former officials from all the nations.

In the past, the corporate mainstream media has sufficiently stigmatized the witnessing of such incidents to the point that if an incident comes dangerously close to qualifying for genuine PLASMAS status; the old media in television broadcast and print media typically join ranks to discredit the witnesses. This has given government officials license to ignore the witnesses. It has been a simple matter for governments to keep a lid on the four to five percent of PLASMAS phenomena that are genuinely supernatural.

The continuing, unspoken alliance between the old mainstream media and old government institutions worked successfully to keep the global populace's attention fixed on UFO's so that few would notice the tiny portion of *PLASMAS's* that would crop up from time to time. This happy alliance has been shattered in the last twenty years by the global democratization of information through the Internet and non-mainstream alternative programming in all areas of media. PLASMAS's now receive attention outside the control wingspan of the old media and their partners in globally controlled national governments. All they can do now is continue to flood genuine PLASMAS incidents with a withering barrage of disinformation operations designed to discredit and distract any who are seeking the truth.

Genuine PLASMAS exhibit the following hallmarks:

1. The sudden appearance of a sky born object that appears to defy gravity, move intelligently, without noise or emission of any sort so that it qualifies as possible anti-gravity technology or unknown breakaway technology of some sort.

2. Travel speeds or maneuvering that human technology cannot duplicate or explain. The appearance and disappearance of these craft at rates of speed that are inexplicable, shape-shifting or apparition and dissolution from our physical plane of existence; are prime indicators of PLASMAS.

3. Reliable credible witnesses who do not gain by the reportage but rather take great risks in their professional lives to maintain the truth of their stories. These should be assertions made by people with responsible positions and offices who put those positions in danger to continue asserting the truth of the PLASMAS incident. In law, this is called the "inherent reliability of admissions made against interest." *Why would they invent these claims since it only hurts them professionally and in their social circles?*

4. No credible natural or terrestrial explanation for the witnessed phenomena (e.g.: is the proposed government/material explanation just a ludicrous attempt to distract people?

Typical Event—concise paraphrasing of the Phoenix Lights incident:

AIRFORCE OFFICIAL: *Concerning the mass sighting of that supposed Gigantic Triangle craft over the city, I've been cleared to show you publicly that we released military flares in a pattern on the night and time that people thought they saw a Giant Triangle Craft over the city. The light patterns people thought was a single craft floating over the city were just our flares floating down.*

AWAKENED AUDIENCE MEMBER: Sir, a close reading of your video of the flare exercise shows that the release of the military flares exercise occurred on the same weeknight and listed time of the mass sighting—*but a week after the event over the city.*

AIRFORCE OFFICIAL: *That's all we have. No further comment.*

5. A reliable record of the phenomena that occurred complete with chain of custody record and high indicia of reliability in that media to guarantee no alteration or tampering.

When these five elements are present and Para-Investigators are present on the scene, it becomes impossible for EPIC to prevent truth from spreading, even to the docile masses in the mainstream they guard so jealously.

II

THE PERSISTENT
CONSCIOUSNESS
COROLLARY

By scientific standards, nearly every paranormal topic has been utterly disproven, debunked, exposed as untrue, explained as misunderstood physical phenomena, discredited and demystified, shattered and pounded into the ground with the surface soil thoroughly salted so that no outside-the-box concepts *should ever grow there again.*

This has occurred over the past century not just dozens but hundreds of times with each topic from Spiritual Channeling to Ghost-hunting to the LochNess Monster and all crypto-creatures. The truth of the LochNess Monster has been attacked with numerous sonar-searches, deep-water photography, trawling of the bottom of the LochNess; all of which found nothing. Yet LochNess Monster and all these topics are more popular than ever. Why? Because *we* instinctively know something scientific materialists will never grasp: that physical science can never disprove Superconscious Truth—truth that comes from a realm that is beyond our ability to quantify, measure and reproduce—truth that is both spiritual and cosmic simultaneously.

This is why frustrated, fossilized, cynics/debunkers/critics/haters/flaggers/non-believers will **never** put an end to the paranormal topics that continue to fascinate, mystify and enthrall generations of those in the throes of the Awakening Process. Paranormal topics that are truly infused with authentic human consciousness have a quality that guarantees they cannot be debunked or "disproven" out of existence. They have a quality of *regenerating energetic stamina* that guarantees the frustration of debunkers. How can this be? It is because of the "Persistent Consciousness Corollary."

There is a growing comprehensive theory of existence that states that the basis of existence is not really time, space, matter and physical reality—but rather *it is consciousness.* Just as Creator-Source "spoke" the universe into existence by infusing

His consciousness into non-matter, we also co-create and re-shape existence through our conscious attention and energy. If the basis of all reality is actually consciousness, intention and belief—not time, space and matter, then this truth shifts the priorities of all things.

Persistent Consciousness Theory: *things come into existence and remain in existence because we give them our energy in the form of attention, belief and our energetic consciousness.*

The chicken and the egg have been switched. We do not give them our energy because they already exist—they exist because someone/something somewhere has given them energy in the form of consciousness and continue to do so.

The Persistent Consciousness Corollary—The necessary addition to this comprehensive theory is therefore that *if any spiritual or paranormal subject/idea/concept/belief has persisted in human consciousness for decades, centuries or eons, that persistent existence is the best evidence that it is real, that it truly exists and that its existence is incontrovertible.*

Otherwise, that subject would have just disappeared from human memory shortly after it was suggested. That is especially so in light of the automatic mainstream resistance that manifests in so many forms: debunkery, secular cynicism and culturally conditioned responses against metaphysical reality. The moment we understand this truth, the fruitless search for scientific minutiae becomes irrelevant. We know it exists because someone believes it exists. The LochNess monster is real because it has persisted in human consciousness for centuries and perhaps eons regardless of what technical scientific equipment does or doesn't reveal on that topic.

Here is a partial list of paranormal topics in which popular interest is currently at all-time, historic highs:

- Bigfoot/the Yeti/Wendigo/the Abominable Snowman
- Innumerable Cryptids from all over the world ("scientifically unknown animals"—unknown to conventional Western science but often accepted in scientific circles of 3rd world nations that tend to be closer to original/Shamanic/aboriginal ancient knowledge (e.g. Chupacabras In Mexico)
- UFO's as vehicles for non-terrestrial alien beings
- Existence of the Hollow Earth
- Ghosts/spirits/ethereal beings temporarily in our physical world
- The Channeling of Ancient spirits/ Ancient warriors and Alien Beings
- True Death Soul Experiences after Death aka: Near Death Experiences
- Out of Body Experiences
- Lucid Dreaming

- Psychic Abilities
- Unsolved Animal and Human Mutilations
- Crop Circles as Messages from Alien civilizations or from our own planet Earth
- Megalithic Ancient Structures that were not created by early humans (like the Big Three Giza Pyramids)
- Vampires, Reptilian Humans, Zombies—Undead humans
- Magic spells/Witches/Sorcery
- Anti-Gravity Technology/Free Energy/Tesla Devices
- Reincarnation/Past Lives Regression/Astral Projection
- Time Travel/Parallel Universes/Multi-verses
- Clear-Hearing/Clairaudience
- Shadow-People
- Humans Who Develop Extraordinary Supernatural Powers

Additionally, despite the angry, often shrill and desperate, efforts of cynics and debunkers; many spiritual phenomena also continue to attract the interest of truth-seekers around the globe. The fuel of fascination with the paranormal never runs out and often blends into spiritual topics along the same continuum of faith.

CONSISTENTLY POPULAR SPIRITUAL/SUPERNATURAL TOPICS :

- Weeping/Bleeding Miraculous Statues
- Virgin Mary Apparitions with Messages for Believers
- Spontaneous Healing and Curing of Diseases
- Power of the Holy Spirit—Ecstasy and Transcendence
- Miraculous Power of Prayer
- The Shroud of Turin as Jesus' Burial Linen
- Messages and help from various Angelic/Heavenly/Celestial Beings
- Exorcism of Evil Spirits
- Speaking in Tongues and Deciphering Ancient Unknown Languages
- Christ Based Transcendence (CBT)

Despite centuries of domination by the scientific establishment over institutional thinking, the rationalist debunkers have failed to extinguish persistent belief and even yearning for information on these topics. How can this be?

Once again, it is because humans are hard-wired by Creator-Source to know the truth—that we are greater than the box with five holes and our spirits crave to lift up above the box in search for higher reality—the reality that there is so much more beyond this poor box than what we can see, touch, taste, smell and feel. Both spiritual truth and paranormal truth allow us to transcend that box and perceive so much that cannot be taken in through those five holes.

12

DEATH BY BROKEN HEART

(A famous incident of intuitive policing occurred during the Olympic Park Bombing.)

In 2004, during the Olympic Games, there was an unusually astute young man who worked as a security guard for an hourly wage. It was honest work but like many security guards, this young man dreamed of being a police officer or an FBI Agent. He had taken the test for his local police department but had not passed. He was over thirty and living at home with his mother, in a job that required him to wear a nametag. Adding to that, the fact that he was overweight, under-educated and spoke with a slight southern drawl, and there seemed little hope that Richard Jewell would ever emerge as anything more heroic than a mall cop preventing theft.

Jewell was working as a security guard in Centennial Olympic Park, Atlanta, Georgia, at about 1 a.m. on July 27, when he noticed a suspicious unidentified package and began moving people away from it. The package turned out to contain a very powerful bomb, which eventually exploded killing one person and wounding more than one hundred others. Had Richard Jewell not acted as quickly as he did, those casualty numbers might have been nearly reversed—many dozens of fatalities with only a few surviving wounded. The detonation of the bomb captured the imagination of the public as the moment was caught during numerous, live-recorded broadcast interviews of Olympic athletes and local celebrities. The frightened natural reactions on camera greatly impacted the psyche of the American people as did the pithy name for the suspect terrorist—The Olympic Park Bomber.

Initially, Jewell was hailed as a hero for moving people away from danger with extreme alacrity and efficiency but then some law enforcement began to review some of the various videos that were turned in of the entire incident. Jewell had spotted the suspicious looking backpack—advised his supervisors by radio and then cordoned off the area around the backpack with police tape. He then urged people to clear the area but then he doggedly used all his physical abilities and even some shouting to make sure people left the area. In view of the dense crowds that had been streaming on both sides of the bomb, his actions probably saved *dozens of lives*.

Some videos of the incident had audio as well and Jewell could be heard speaking to people right after he discovered the unattended backpack. The average security guard upon finding the same hiking backpack that Jewell found, would simply have hauled the discarded backpack over to the lost and found for its owner to reclaim, even if that was against regulations. Other security guards would have spent precious minutes physically searching for their supervisors and consulting other officers on what to do. What was it that made Richard Jewell such a man of action that he acted with such decisiveness in this crucial moment of high emergency? The answer becomes clear in listening to those videos, repeatedly, of his voice inflection, pitch and tone as he repeatedly yelled for people to clear the perimeter around the package. Even as they were trying their best to ignore him, Jewell screamed and gesticulated for civilians to follow his orders and worked to *clear even the outer perimeter as well as the immediate area*. As investigators played those tapes repeatedly, they listened to the urgency in his voice rising to an intense pitch to get people to obey his commands to evacuate faster and faster—the truth became obvious:

He knew it was a bomb.

You don't have to be a profiler or experienced Para-Investigator to recognize the certainty and panic in his voice. He did know there was a bomb but how did he know? Federal Investigators made the only assumption that materialist, scientifically inclined, analytical thinkers could make. They made the assumption that he could only know it was a bomb because *he planted the bomb*.

They determined that he planted the bomb to give himself an opportunity to be a hero. He fit the profile of a frustrated, would-be cop, who would do just about anything to be a public hero especially in the eyes of law-enforcement whom he idolized so much. It became known that, as far as federal authorities were concerned, he was "a person of interest" in the bombing. For weeks, reporters and camera crews camped outside Jewell's Atlanta apartment, capturing every move that he made. "Journalists" repeated the same jaded stereotypes and convicted him in their newspapers and television broadcasts. For many weeks, they pronounced him to be "The Olympic Park Bomber." They reported voluminous false information about Jewell that fit into the neat pattern of "the would-be-cop manufacturing himself as a hero" narrative they had decided on. They were ruthless.

After 12 weeks of relentless scrutiny following the bombing, the FBI and U.S. Attorney Kent Alexander cleared Jewell in an unprecedented government acknowledgment of wrongful accusation. Jewell made a statement for reporters after his public exoneration.

"*I am not the Olympic Park bomber. I am a man who has lived 88 days afraid of being arrested for a crime I did not commit.*"

The federal government, Jewell said, trampled on his rights "in its rush to show the world it could get its man," while the news media "cared nothing about my feelings as a human being" in its rush to get a story on the bombing.

In April, 2005, Eric Robert Rudolph, a notorious domestic terrorist, pled guilty to the Olympic Park Bombing, among other bombings. Authorities captured Rudolph in Murphy, North Carolina, in May 2003, after one of the largest manhunts in U.S. history. Again, there was further exoneration for Richard Jewell. Jewell sued several media organizations that perpetuated the worst accusations against him. These organizations settled with him for enormous sums of money for the destruction they wrought in this hero's life. Unfortunately, the real damage to this Para-Investigator was already done. Jewell's heart had been broken. The police organizations that he had held in such high esteem and admired all his life had turned on him and crucified him for doing nothing more than using his supernatural intuition to save peoples' lives.

Instead of being rewarded like the life-saving hero that he was, the police agencies that he admired so much tried to burn him at the stake. Medical authorities say that Jewell, at the age of 44, died of diabetes and kidney failure. Yet to this day, I fully believe he died of a broken heart.

§

Still today society is continuing to burn the witches—those with supernatural abilities and who care so very much for their fellow human beings. Such care can be greater than their own sense of self-preservation. Society's record of dealing with Para-Investigators has been one of mostly punishment, harassment and persecution. A few of the more fortunate Para-Investigators were able to hide their abilities behind dissemblance and alternate explanations, rationality, and "cover phrases." They sometimes were able to deflect further queries into "how they knew what they knew" by simply pointing to things that offered material explanation for unknowable supernatural realities. Others who did not have an adequate material explanation for their supernormal intuition would suffer the full measure of a fearful law enforcement community. Like Mary Shelley's Frankenstein monster, such individuals are reviled and persecuted, even when they peer into the abyss in order to save many civilian lives. Yet misinterpretation and fear impel even the supposed compatriots of fellow law enforcers to treat those utilizing paranormal abilities with suspicion and contempt. Society will accept *the benefits* of "Para-Investigative abilities" but are unwilling to accept those who use paranormal methods to protect them.

The pioneers on any great new frontiers "take all the arrows." We are now past the frontiers of the bold new world of Para-Investigation and are proceeding into the Age of Mass Awakening. It is time to adjust all our institutions to accept and even encourage those who unfold the abyss to their benefit. They will be leaders who show the way into this bold new paradigm. Institutions must adjust themselves to compensate for the treatment of these pioneers in the past. Failure to do so will leave those institutions in dusty irrelevance.

13

REAL EVIDENCE

Evidence in its broadest sense includes *anything* used to determine or demonstrate the truth of an assertion or that can make that assertion more or less likely to be true. The assertion proposed can be whether someone is guilty of a crime or it can be whether the supposed subject of an elusive mystery really exists. In science, there is systematic collection of facts and data in an attempt to assert a proposed investigative conclusion often labeled as a hypothesis. In the world of the paranormal, this is a dishonest process from its inception. The final investigative conclusion of a scientist or any materialist-physical world investigator *must* fit within the parameters of the scientific world—otherwise how can those people refer to themselves as members of the scientific community once the investigation is over?

In the area of evidence, scientists and physicians trained in the outdated scientific mold; continue to promote the same false premises we have seen now for nearly three centuries. The most damaging of these suppositions is that "scientific evidence" is inherently more reliable than any other types of evidence.

SCIENTIFIC EVIDENCE INCLUDES:

Anything that can be objectively demonstrated, tested and experimented upon under laboratory-controlled conditions like: chemical residues, fingerprints, DNA samples, blood or bodily fluid samples, computer hard drives, computer data, any objects utilized in the performance of crimes or mysteries. Another form of scientific evidence that is highly utilized among scientists in the area of crimes and mysteries is statistical evidence. Statistics is a mathematical science pertaining to the collection, analysis, interpretation or explanation/presentation of data. It also purports to depict prediction and forecasting based on data.

Non-Scientific evidence is derived from human experience and is often rejected in Western jurisprudence as unreliable. It consists of or uses any combination of:

• Individual personal experience
• Intuition

- Testimony from credible witnesses
- Anecdotal evidence
- Hypothetical's that utilize our basic understanding of human nature
- Myth and legend

Para-Investigators know that the latter class of non-scientific material can serve as more reliable evidence than the scientific category.

Karl Marx said all the history of man is the story of a continuing struggle between the classes. In the world of investigations, especially law enforcement, there are several classes locked in a continuing struggle for preeminence in the world of investigations. They are always present at the scenes of high-level investigations or mysteries.

- Street Level Investigators (Police, Federal Agents, Government
- Investigators, Field Investigators of all types)
- Scientists and Analysts
- Psychologists and Profilers
- Psychics

Street level investigators: police, private investigators, detectives, corporate, governmental investigators; tend to profit greatly from their intuition in finding the solutions to crimes and mysteries. Yet they must be careful to cover the use of their natural and supernatural abilities. They must always have ready materialist, purely rational, "scientific" explanations for anything they do out of a sense of "knowing," abilities from a place that is not within the five ordinary senses. Our legal system demands legalistic phrases to cover the reality of their paranormal abilities.

I developed probable cause based on my previous knowledge of similar circumstances in the past during many years of investigative service...

I feel there was reasonable suspicion in light of my experience with similar patterns of behavior as significant indicia of suspicious activity...

In view of my knowledge and experience in this area of crime, I immediately recognized the telltale signs of criminal activity on the part of the observed parties, etcetera..."

Of course, their ordinary history and experience does play into "what they know" in their queries but it's the *diverse paranormal abilities* they possess which serve as the Superconscious Conduits that channel the cosmic power of the universe into ordinary investigative activities. Ambiguous, unquantifiable phrases help those investigators: "suspicious behavior, suspicious activity, probable cause, reasonable cause" to maintain the illusion of ordinariness that is so vital for legal prosecutability. This is why these phrases must be so flexible and ephemeral in what they can mean. The time is upon us when we must liberate these individuals from the requirement that they be secretive about investigative supernatural abilities.   By formalizing the use of these abilities, we will resolve crimes and mysteries to a degree never dreamed of before and most importantly; *we will save more lives.*

14

RED SHIRT

(This story is familiar among East-Coast law enforcement. The officer involved in this anecdote suffered many queries and even some suspicion from colleagues who were present on the scene and could not explain how the officer knew what he knew.)

A plainclothes police officer heard a report of drug dealing on his police band radio. He exited his vehicle and approached a group of individuals standing on a street corner in an urban area. He determined, from their appearance and demeanor, that they were drug-dealers and drug buyers. As he approached the group, several individuals broke and ran in several directions. The officer didn't even get a look at them before they ran. The officer broke off pursuit and returned to his police radio. All he recalled was colors of clothing. He broadcast to other officers in the immediate vicinity.

"Get the one in the red shirt. He's got a gun."

Based on that transmission, several officers in the general area intercepted that suspect. They drew their weapons on the man in the red shirt. They carefully brought him under their control and placed him under arrest. They searched him. He did have an illegal handgun that turned out to be a match to a gun used in several other violent crimes committed recently. One officer later asked the reporting officer how he knew that the man in the red shirt had a gun when they all ran before he even got to observe them?

The officer answered only in strictest confidence.

"I don't know how I knew. I just did."

There were several officers around the perimeter who knew there was no physical opportunity for the officer to see the gun. More cynical officers murmured about the criminal possibly being a previous associate of the officer (possibly his former snitch) who was no longer useful to the officer. Many in law-enforcement tend to be locked into a miserable claustrophobic paradigm where the only people who display these non-physical abilities are "scamming" in some way. Yet Para-Investigators, men and women of action, must ignore such meanness of character in order to preserve the safety and security of those who still don't understand them.

Under our present legal system, intuitive certainty is an impermissible element in articulating probable or reasonable cause that a crime is being committed or has been committed. What if Para-Investigators could save many lives by following "a hunch?" Should they choose between stopping the perpetrators or letting them go free because "hunches" are not permissible in court?

Blessedly, True Investigators always choose to save lives but the severe limits on this system must change for the sake of honesty, integrity and for the sanity of Para-Investigators.

15

THE SIX PERCENT RESOLUTION

During decades of paranormal research, it has been revealed to me that in almost every paranormal topic there is a reliable repetition of certain numerical patterns. Whether we are talking about paranormal Extra-Terrestrial Craft, Crypto-Creatures or any other supernatural topics on which people report every year; such reports reveal a similar repeating breakdown.

The Six Percent Resolution: *In paranormal areas, approximately 94 percent of reported incidents are those in which there are natural, physical or even fraudulent explanations ultimately provided or proven. This resolution still leaves an average of six percent of reported paranormal phenomena that are genuinely paranormal or supernatural in origin.*

There are thousands of credible reports of UFO phenomena every year, in the United States and again throughout the major nations. Once we discount about ninety-four percent of Unidentified Flying Object accounts as: weather balloons, elaborate kites, Chinese lanterns, space junk, teenagers practicing mischief, future film-makers practicing special effects and the over-active imaginations of people observing new aircraft and satellites for the first time; that still leaves us with dozens of accounts *with reliable evidence and testimony* that have no explanation in our physical world except for the supernatural explanation. Every year, several major countries have exploding amounts of Extra-Terrestrial Craft reportage such as Mexico, Israel, Russia, China, India, Brazil, Chile and many more which continue to seek out methods for dealing with this ever-expanding phenomena.

The Six Percent Resolution utilizes a very conservative estimate, allowing for a great deal of artifice, prevarication and misinterpretation in the world of paranormal reality. (Although no generous allowance for deception and mistakes would ever satisfy cynics and debunkers.) Yet, the remaining six percent is an undeniable confrontation to the conventional view of our physical reality.

That means that every year in the United States there are dozens (throughout the world—hundreds) of genuinely paranormal "UFO" events occur which have no physical/material explanation except that they are truly otherworldly. This is true when considering just a single area of paranormal phenomena such as Extra-Terrestrial craft reports.

Add to that six percent: the credible six percent remainders each year in areas such as: Chupacabras, the LochNess Monster, Mothman, Ghosts/spirits, Alien Beings, Crop Circles, Reptilian Humans, Zombies/Undead humans and numerous other Crypto-creatures that roam the unknown recesses of alternate realities and occasionally pop into ours. Further, add to this, the many reported supernatural *personal experiences* such as Remote Viewing, Clairvoyance, Extra-Sensory Perception, Lucid-Dreaming, Out Of Body Experiences, Alien Abduction experiences, etcetera; the enormous volume of active paranormal topics and the overall accumulation of the *many 6 percentages* begin to add up to huge overall numbers.

It would look like: 6% + 6%+ 6% + 6%+6% + 6%+6% + 6%+6% + 6%+6% + 6%+6% + 6%+6% + 6%+ 6% + 6%+ 6% + 6%+ 6% + 6%+ 6% + 6%+6% + 6% + 6%+ 6% + 6%+ 6% + 6%+ 6% + 6%+ 6% + 6%+6%6% + 6%+ 6% + 6%+ 6% + 6%+ 6% + 6%+ 6% + 6%+6% + 6% + 6%+ 6% + 6%+ 6% + 6%+ 6% + 6%+ 6% + 6%+6% +6% + 6%+ 6% + 6%+ 6% + 6%+ 6% + 6%+ 6% + 6%+6% +6% + 6%+ 6% + 6%+ 6% + 6%+ 6% + 6%+ 6% + 6%+6% + 6% + 6%+ 6% + 6%+ 6% + 6%+ 6% + 6%+ 6% + 6%+ 6% + 6%+ 6% = An astounding number of genuine paranormal occurrences happening all over the world.

This is more than a confrontation—it is a *clear repudiation* of the materialist-scientific world view as it exists today in our mainstream culture.

However, we must admit that there are exceptions to the Six Percent Resolution. There are certain paranormal topics in which the explanations for genuine occurrences can only be **100 percent** paranormal or supernatural. These paranormal topics have no physical or natural explanations at all. Yet predictably, conventional science and medicine also ignores these. One of these areas is "cattle mutilations" which have no real terrestrial explanation due to the above-human technology that is used in accomplishing them. Cattle and other livestock (and even humans at times) are left as bloodless carcasses with organs and parts removed by technology that leaves behind: no scar tissue, no entry or exit wounds, no blood traces on the ground or in any part of the immediate environment, tripod markings but no footsteps or tracks. Wild scavengers will not come near these carcasses and no security measures on Earth can stop these mutilations. This has been the subject of many books by fearless Para-Investigators but the institutional scientific community has steadfastly refused to lend any aid to desperate ranchers victimized by this ongoing phenomena.

Another "One Hundred Percent Supernatural" area is soul experiences after death aka: "Near Death Experience's (NDEs)." There is no scientific or medical rational explanation for clinically dead people, people whose hearts have stopped beating and were documented either by doctors or instruments to have no life signs at all, continuing in Mind-Consciousness when they are provably without brain activity of any sort. These experiences are not "Near" anything. They are actual *True Death Experiences*. These are TDEs—not NDEs. Truthful nomenclature frightens those frozen in the materialist scientific model but it's still the truth. No amount of scientific obfuscation or medical tap-dancing can account for a clinically dead person with *no* brain activity; returning to life and then telling doctors several events and conversations that occurred during the period that they were dead. Numerous TDEs have medically documented complete *absence of life*. The subjects were hooked into machines that showed no brain or biological signs of life at the time. Yet these people later come back and tell us what people said about them and what actions that took place while they were gone. These are *one hundred percent* supernatural.

Genuine True Death Experiences reveal to us that our brains *do not* produce our consciousness...*they only receive consciousness* from somewhere else. This is the result of non-local transmission of that human consciousness. Consciousness can only persist after death if the experiencer's brain never was the original source to begin with. Our consciousness is being produced/generated/created somewhere else outside our bodies and is then beamed in to our brains and bodies.

To primitives, a functioning radio may seem like a box that produces the voices of tiny people from inside the box. It might seem that the radio device is the source of the voices and music. We, as moderns, know that the radio does not produce *anything*—it only *receives* the signal produced from a very distant but powerful radio tower and that beams it out to millions of radios even from a long distance away. The radios are not the producers. They are receivers. Our brains are likewise for human consciousness.

Current conventional science attempts to appear aloof from such unacceptable concepts but the truth is that they are just incapable of dealing with these facts. A few daring thinkers have "gone rogue" and have left behind the atrophied role of scientist to become Para-Investigators. There are numerous books and literature available to give a better understanding of just how egregious the medical establishment has been in ignoring the incredible wealth of new understanding that TDE's offer. This is another reminder that deepest truth is only available to those willing to follow the quest for truth, *no matter where the quest might lead.*

16

HIGH PRIESTS OF NOTHINGNESS

There is a world religion that has as its most holy sacraments: cynicism, nonbelief and an absolute rejection of all nonmaterial realities. Since the highest value here is willful ignorance of nonmaterial realities; there is no amount of fraud, artifice and outright deception that is too extreme in furtherance of the sacrament of nothingness. As they pursue the sacrament of nothingness, they put all their faith (ironically) in *excluding all matters of faith.* This is what conventional science has become.

Old world Newtonian science is a methodology of reproducible results that prove the truth of a phenomenon by quantifying and measuring that phenomenon in a form that can be recreated under laboratory conditions. Therefore, using scientific method we know that lemon seeds will germinate under certain conditions of natural light, moisture in the soil and temperature, because we can reproduce those conditions precisely again and again and we will (allowing for controls and variables) always get the same results. Growing a lemon tree is perfect for scientific query, measurement and methods. Under the old scientific methodology, advances and forward strides have been made by man which have propelled him into an age of technological marvels that were unimaginable only one hundred years ago.

Yet, institutional science, much like conventional mainstream religion has now come to be terribly misused. Science is now a religion for rationalists who employ it as a filtering lens and worldview by which to determine what is real and what is not. Just as religion is misused to control what people may believe, science is being misused to restrict people from believing in anything at all, at least anything that really matters.

Religion is often the filter by which people view the world and determine what concepts are valid and which are unacceptable. Science presently attempts to do the same but is monumentally unfit for this purpose because, rather than widening our perception, it narrows the field of vision of the inquirer. Science would be the worst religion because rather than putting us in communication with greater truths, it only reduces things down to the point where they can fit through those *tiny five holes*. Conventional science is essentially *the religion where nothing happens*.

Science is inappropriate as a worldview and even more, it is ludicrous to use it to evaluate the validity of paranormal phenomena.

Paranormal events, by their nature, *tend to be unique*—they tend to be occurrences that happen the way they do only once. There is a slim exception for ghostly traumatic events repeated at regular intervals with emotional resonance. Conditions in the universe, at times, may meet certain thresholds and create an emotive-cosmic recording. These are actual events that generated earthly emotional trauma, like a grisly murder, wherein the ghostly spirits commit loops of reenactment until they somehow escape from the macabre spectacle. Apart from that rare exception, spirits, ghosts and shadow-people will appear a certain way only once. Genuine paranormal UFOs do not appear on the anniversary of their last appearance. Despite what mediums charging money may say, spirits cannot be summoned to appear in the same way repeatedly. This is one more reason why the method of reproducible results is inappropriate for determining the reality of paranormal phenomena.

Few minds are ready to grapple with this truth. However, if you have acquired this work, chances are you are sufficiently awake to grasp several premises that can be extrapolated into virtually unlimited spiritual understandings necessary to expand consciousness—so here goes…

PREMISE # 1

There is a portion (even if it is a tiny minority of incidents) in each area of "paranormal" activity that is genuinely supernatural.

PREMISE #2

The people who are qualified to make the determination of what portion of these incidents are genuinely paranormal, are those who **do not** use the severely limited materialist-physical worldview and the scientific method to determine what is real.

PREMISE #3

Therefore, only those investigators and seekers of truth who are *already* paranormal/ spiritual believers can judge and determine what is real in paranormal topics. That is because *only these believers* have the ability to absorb, comprehend and explain the truth of such expanded realities in their paradigm. Thinkers frozen in the old scientific-materialist mold are, by definition, disqualified from any possibility of serious examination of these putative truths.

How can a scientist, on a break from the lab, standing outside smoking a cigarette on his break, explain that a Bigfoot creature emerged from the forest and attempted to communicate with him for several seconds before it vanished back into the woods? Once he gets over his disbelief and terror, how will he explain that he now knows Bigfoot exists? How will he communicate that to others? A phrase would occur to him: *don't even think about it.*

Once he's calmed down and gotten back to his "rational mind" he will conjure acceptable explanations for what happened to him—explanations that won't cost him his grant, that won't cause him to be ridiculed by co-workers, that won't cause him to be ostracized by superiors and won't cause him to be ejected from the peer-review process for his publications. He will likely find for himself some explanations that fit neatly into the paradigm of the institutions that imprison his mind, his imagination and his life. He will quickly shake his head free of novel thoughts and obediently crawl back inside his box.

Paranormal truths are beyond the ability of the materialist-physical paradigm to comprehend or explain. Therefore, the tendency will always be to find the paranormal to be a fantasy. *This will especially be so when the supernatural incident is genuine.* A materialist-physical alternative explanation is the only way to preserve the only comfortable reality they know. Comfort can be a prison of its own.

Only those who are already believers in the paranormal—i.e.: those who already exist outside that poor miserable box can serve as honest brokers in the world of the paranormal fact-finding. Like eagles walking on the ground, they can alight onto a more pedestrian reality. They CAN decide that an alleged incident isn't supernatural at all—that it's a fake, a fraud, an honest mistake, a misinterpretation, a trick of the light/shadow/nerves—because they *can* function and move about in the purely physical, non-paranormal, concrete reality. Yet the reverse is *not true* when it comes to those who are purely physical, materialist paradigm believers. They simply cannot soar along the edges of the deep, dark maelstrom of the genuinely supernatural. They don't want to and they couldn't even if they did.

We have allowed people who have no ability to emerge or *even peek out of the box* to say that other realities outside the box—can be evaluated by them from inside that tightly sealed box. It doesn't work. No one can examine items that exist on a different plane of reality from the examiner. We have consistently used hard, scientific standards to dismiss events that will never qualify *as real* under criteria that are irrelevant to paranormal phenomena.

THE PARA-INVESTIGATIVE FILES

To move forward into the Age of Mass Awakening, we must leave behind the cynics, the debunkers and all the naysayers who demand you stay inside that box.

17

THROW IT DOWN

(One female officer, Courtney, related a unique story that happened to her "on the job." She only had a few months before she would have completed "probationary status" at her new position.)

During a multi-agency raid in a major city, in the mid-west of the United States, Courtney darted down the back of a building to cover the rear. She carried a heavy shotgun as the raid proceeded at the front of the building. Courtney heard the muffled clamor of arrests inside the building on the radio she had clipped to her belt. The shouts in the distance reverberated in static echoes on her radio.

"Get down on the ground!"
"Police, don't move!"

She turned down the volume on her radio so she could advance in stealth mode.

She stood in the alleyway looking up through the rusting metallic fire escapes and tried to pinpoint which second floor window she was supposed to focus on for potential escapees.

"I suppose it's the window somebody will be climbing out of."

As her thought finished she felt that someone was watching her but not from any window. She felt a shadow pass and she spun. Courtney came face to face with a young black man holding a pistol on her. He didn't climb out the window but snuck up from the back of the alley. As the man held the gun on her he glanced up sideways at the same window Courtney had been watching.

He was coming to climb in the window.

He suspected the front of the building was under surveillance so he did his business by climbing the low ladder and going in and out of that back window. That didn't matter now. All Courtney could see was the desperate look in his eyes and the giant front barrel of that gun. He had the drop on her. She remained frozen. Suddenly, Courtney heard something.

THROW IT DOWN

Courtney looked at the young man's lips. They hadn't moved.

THROW IT DOWN

The voice came from inside her head.
She tossed the shotgun to the ground. It fell with a dull clatter.

The noise seemed to snap the young man out of his hesitation. He looked at the shotgun on the ground and threw his own gun into the side-pocket of his baggy pants. He turned and ran. He went faster than Courtney had ever seen anyone run. He was out of sight in seconds. She couldn't believe it was over so quickly.

She recovered her shotgun as her radio kept squawking. She never told anyone about this experience or her encounter with the young black man or The Voice. At first, she was terrified that her agency might fire her because she allowed the man to escape. She was still on probation. Fortunately, no information ever came up about him so she never felt any real obligation to speak up about what happened—he was not one of the wanted subjects or even known to the investigators in charge. Yet, even now, years later, Courtney asserts she can never admit publicly what happened in her work context because it fits too neatly into all the stereotypes her male counterparts "are already anxious to believe about her." Courtney would assume a husky male voice.

"Awww, poor little Blondie, couldn't hack it. Couldn't handle being a cop. Threw down her gun. Surrendered at the first sign of trouble. Don't want her backing me up but at least we already know what she'll do when the stuff hits the fan! Haw, haw."

She came back into her own voice. "It wasn't like that at all. It wasn't a cowardly response. I didn't feel scared when it happened. *I felt…peace.* I obeyed what The Voice told me to do without thinking. It all happened so fast I didn't realize what almost happened to me until after the guy was gone."

I could see a great weight lifted from her. Her eyes welled up with tears as I responded.

"Courtney, you did the right thing in doing what The Voice told you. I've had experience before with The Great Voice that comes forward to help people during desperate moments. Whatever the source of the Voice is, I know this: The voice comes from something that knows much more about what happens and what can potentially happen than we do. Also, the source of that voice loves you. Had you not done what the voice told you, the

consequences would have been much worse than we imagine. You not only saved yourself but also probably saved many others around you. Otherwise, the Voice would not have come forward at that moment."

Now her tears flowed. Courtney approached me as if she sought an embrace but she thought better of it. She turned away. Courtney thanked me and asked me to remember my assurances about confidentiality. That was the last time I ever spoke to her.

§

Like Courtney, all the law-enforcement officers depicted in this work have shared that cursed/blessed moment when all their cognitive filters and perceptions change. This is the *Para-Investigative Shift*. In a broader sense, all the investigative classes are undergoing a radical shift. Scientists and analysts tend to be wholly on the rational materialist side of the investigative equation. They believe that through scientific method, any investigation or mystery can be solved. This is because they believe in the myth that science is objective, but of course, this is demonstrably false even according to scientific definitions. "Science" is alternately defined as:

1. The methodical observation, identification, description, experimental investigation, and theoretical explanation of phenomenon.

2. Activities restricted to a class of natural phenomenon.

3. An activity that appears to require study and method.

"Science" typically denotes unbiased assessments of observable events, and exclusion of a subjective mind but even basic definitions show that science tends to be very different from what it claims to be. Science always, even in the most pristine laboratory setting of control groups and perfectly reproducible results; at least at the conclusion stage, lets in the subjective opinions and biases of the human scientists involved. Even the decision to exclude any possibility of bias through double and triple blind systems, due to the vital importance of the results of an experiment, betrays a bias.

Psychologists and profilers are part of the same investigative class. Many profilers tend to be psychologists and this class of investigators tends to examine the mind of the putative perpetrator of a crime or of a mystery under the same frozen materialist model. They view human beings as mere bundles of nervous system connections and conditioned responses. They will often ignore the human brain's true significance as a receiver/transmitter for the soul/spirit/consciousness. This is ironic since some of the original pioneers finally recognizing the human mind primarily as a conductor for consciousness were themselves scientist-psychologists such as Karl Jung and Sigmund Freud. Their work from over a hundred years ago opened doors to understanding that are now being further developed in advanced quantum physics, the branch of physics that concerns itself with the study (observation) of the subatomic realm. Advanced quantum physics is now showing us that Jung was right when he referred to our own minds as being transmitters and doorways to the great Cosmic Mind that longs to provide us with all knowledge and understanding from all the Multi-Verses. Yet, since this great and innovative work, psychology has sheepishly retrogressed back into the ancient materialist model.

Psychics are still a badly kept secret throughout the investigative world. Sometimes their help may be accepted but only in the quiet desperation of ice-cold, unsolvable homicides and kidnapping cases. Most investigators, in public, cautiously dismiss the work of psychics as unacceptable even if it only for "lead value only" to be kept outside the structure of "case construction" of legally admissible evidence for a court situation. But in private, each proven psychic's work is considered on an individual level, case by case.

Psychics will have about the same average percentile of competence as any other profession. When I was at university, my favorite professor was a famous writer named John Gardener. He was a man who was prone to make bombastic statements in public and in the media. We loved him for that quality. One of his public statements was: *"the average level of incompetence for just about any profession is roughly eighty percent. About 80% of any profession is incompetent and has very little idea what a skilled professional in that particular profession should actually be doing—whether you're talking about lawyers, doctors or writers."*

His basic concept is correct. Psychics are not exempt from certain levels of incompetence any more than other professions such as physicians, attorneys or police. However, psychics working with law-enforcement *will self-filter* to a much higher degree of competence and truth because they are taking great risks to step forward against great cultural resistance and reflexive animosity. Suspicion and resentment from law-enforcement are often their rewards for helping desperate victim's families. Psychics tend to mostly step forward when they are highly confident in their own abilities to help those people. As a class, they have displayed a high percentage of success in cold investigations, often under cover of anonymity and for very little reward other than alleviating the terrible pain of victim-families.

The classes must unite. All categories of official investigators: street level investigators, scientists and analysts, psychologists/profilers and psychics; must experience a *Para-Investigative Shift* in their attitudes and realities in order to enter a new paradigm together. They will live the creed of the interconnectedness of all things. There is a process to become a Para-Investigator and the first step is to contemplate the subject of the investigation while shutting down the rational mind.

Shutting down the rational mind, which we use for everyday tasks, is the way to prepare to connect in non-sensory ways with information in the Quantum Field of Potentiality.   Here we temporarily neutralize the rational, analytical thinking mechanism that we use in everyday life.   This opens up the non-rational state of consciousness that is intuitive in nature and often unexplainable in the material world.

18

PARA-INVESTIGATIVE ASSESSMENT AND EMPATHY

Para-Investigative Assessment is feeling what the situation really is—not from this physical world, but from the unseen abyss wherein resides the Cosmic Mind that connects us all, every member of the human race and all the races who animate this reality through their consciousness. This assessment is intuitive listening and feeling what the abyss contains in reference to the investigation. It is akin to a spiritual review or inventory of the case—divorced from rational, material based sensibilities.

Detectives and police always called this sort of thing simply "their gut or their intuition" because that's as far as they are allowed go or to say in the rational world. With Para-Investigative assessment, these investigators can detect when a subject is lying and why the person is lying—no machine or list of deceptive body language signals can give anyone this kind of knowledge. The hardest part is for most investigators, once they have this certainty of deception, is to resist the temptation to jump to conclusions about why any particular deception is happening. Deception can be happening for reasons entirely removed from actual guilt for the main crime or mystery.

Para-Investigative Assessment which leads to connection is using a great truth in narrow ways. Quantum science has shown us through the behavior of subatomic particles that all matter was connected at one time and can behave as if it is still connected. From the time of the original Big Bang that started creation until now, there is a very high probability that at one time, all things were directly connected as matter to everything else in a single container about the size of a pea. Then, what we know as the Big Bang separated and spread throughout the universe we now know in its present ever-expanding pattern of solar systems, galaxies and the cosmos. When one subatomic particle is joined directly to another, it can later be separated from that first particle and even carried across enormous distances so that there exists a huge void of space between the formerly joined particles. After separation, stimulation to one of those particles will cause an instant response by the second particle. This is like an identical twin grabbing his arm and yelping in pain because his/her twin in another state had its arm pinched.

We, as Para-Investigators may be completely connected even to the most heinous liar, criminal, con artist or even murderer. There is usually a moment during every interrogation, when the investigator reminds the subject of something—anything the subject of the investigation dearly loves or has in common with some portion of humanity. That investigator will suddenly come upon the correct combination of factors to remind the subject of his/her connection to other human beings. In that moment, at that perfect pivot point, the tumblers flip, rock solid resistance and deception melt away and the subject realizes...*my God what have I done?*

Para-Investigative Empathy goes even beyond ordinary understanding and providing the person's reasons for lying. This ability is not just grasping the person's reasons for lying but *spiritually becoming that person* and justifying every action, every thought, and every deception down to the smallest action or omission. The investigator temporarily assumes the persona of the subject and becomes the subject's greatest advocate. This is connectivity at the deepest possible level. The investigator steps out of their shoes, not to become "good cop" or "helpful friend" to the subject; but to *become the subject.*

19

THE INVESTIGATIVE CONCLUSION

True investigators (whether they are Para-Investigators or civilian truth-seekers) do not merely collect, assemble, organize and present facts and evidence in an objective manner so that the receiver can then peruse these and come to their own conclusion. That is what mainstream journalists, old world scientists, scholars and other fact-finders do. *True investigators* collect facts and evidence but then go deeper to connect clues and explore hidden truths that play a part in any crime or elusive mystery. Then, they apply their own knowledge and experience and distill everything they've uncovered into a final product called *an Investigative Conclusion.*

The Investigative Conclusion is the culmination of the True Investigator's knowledge, experience *and intuition* as applied to the clues and evidence revealed to that investigator during the span of this investigation. The Investigative Conclusion is the answer to the question of "What really happened? Who committed this egregious act and why did they do it? Alternatively, "does this paranormal entity really exist or is it just a product of the observer's overactive imagination?"

This final product is what they present to the receiver. The receiver can then accept or reject that conclusion but it will remain with them as the undeniable culmination of all the investigator's skill, knowledge, experience and abilities. A worker in a widget factory has to provide a certain numbers of widgets at the end of the day or else he is just a person hanging around the widget factory. The True Investigator, at the end of the day, must also provide the Investigative Conclusion or else he/she has done nothing that a fact-finder couldn't do. The receiver will then accept that final investigative conclusion or it will be clear that the receiver was never interested in the truth at all—rather they were only desirous of the outcome they hoped to receive. Para-Investigators are *not* dispassionate, objective, balanced finders of fact. They are vigorous and determined advocates for revealed truth. That revealed truth finds its culmination in the final Investigative Conclusion.

In the investigative world, there are numerous incidents of extraordinary paranormal perception. Law-enforcement knows these stories are true because they have the ring of authenticity and they live with these specially gifted investigators every day. These stories—these *true* stories reveal far more than lore and tales of the supernatural. They reveal that some who are in law-enforcement themselves have supernatural abilities. While they tend to explain away these sporadic supernatural events by referring to a developing sixth sense or uncanny intuition, it is much more. My research and work collecting paranormal vignettes over the last two decades have led me to a paradigm shifting Investigative Conclusion: people *do not* have paranormal experiences because they come across supernatural entities: "That house had ghosts." "I was in the forest and I came across Bigfoot." "Alien Visitors came in through the walls of my house and I couldn't move." They have paranormal experiences because *they themselves are temporarily translated from physical into supernatural articulation.*

20

BLUE JACKET

(This story has been told in various versions throughout the mid-West. The officer that related it to me was long since retired but he was the younger officer in the story.)

Two police officers responded to a call reporting a possible dead body at a suburban residence. Someone had looked in the front window of a residence of "a sweet little old man in the neighborhood" who no one had seen in his routine movements for several days. As the officers arrived at the residence in question and peered in the window, they saw a body slumped down in the kitchen with a cat nuzzling it. The police had been told the old man lived alone so after ringing the doorbell and knocking with no result; they started trying the windows and began trying to "jimmy" the door. Suddenly, a little gray-haired fellow swung wide open the door. He wore a brand new blue jacket with "New York Jets" insignia like he was getting ready to go out for a stroll. The officers felt like burglars caught in the middle of a break in. They stammered about the call they received but the little old man just pointed toward the back of the house.

"He's back there on the kitchen floor."

They advanced deeper into the house. The front door was closed and the older man was close on their heels as they came upon the body. The dead body on the floor was apparently the brother of the man who had let them in the house—the same age and description. With their latex gloves on, they shooed the cat away and turned the body over to get a look at the freshly deceased face. This dead body was not just the brother of the man who opened the door. He was *an identical twin* with the same glasses, hair and the same...blue New York Jets jacket as if... *he was about to go out for a stroll.*

The two men looked at each other. They turned to the dead man's twin. He was gone. They searched the house, calling out for the greeter. They had not heard the door. The windows were all shut tight. The cat stared at the officers unblinking as if to say *"you won't find him."* They went outside. The younger officer insisted on walking around the neighborhood and calling out for the greeter. Their voices came back as echoes. They began to notice odd things—no sounds in the neighborhood, no people, not even insects or birds. It was daytime but a misty gray dullness pervaded everything. Strangest of all, there were no sounds from the radios on their hips— normally a constant squawking distraction. They tried to focus on the task at hand— finding the old man who let them in the door but it was getting harder to focus for some reason.

How could both radios be dead at the same time?

The former officer recounting the story to me began feeling the same emotions of that day as if he were back playing the role again. His eyes betrayed his fright as he replayed the scene in his head. He was in the street on one side of the cul-de-sac as his partner looked around on the opposite side around a couple of other houses. His partner had pulled his flashlight to shine in some windows to see if he could rouse some souls out into the street if only out of curiosity. From a hundred feet away he heard his partner curse as he shook the flashlight.

"Dammit, it's dead, just like the radios." He answered in a calmer tone.
"Just like everything else around here." Suddenly, they regarded each other as if some terrible truth had been uttered. The young officer shouted out for the little old man but really he was shouting out for anyone—*anyone at all.*
Both officers began to feel sluggish and heavy. Their brisk step became a slow shuffle. Neighborhood was deserted and there were no sounds. The older officer became alarmed.

"Kid, we gotta get out of this here the way we came in."
"I knew he was right. Somehow, *I don't know how,* I knew he meant we had to get back to that front door of the little old man's house or else we could stay trapped in this place." The young officer shivered at the thought of what "this place" really meant.
They labored to orient themselves in the right direction. All the empty uninviting homes looked alike but they had to get to the right one.
"We began to feel drowsy as if some sort of cloud was settling on us or like *we were coming out of a cloud.*
For some reason we felt an urgency to make it back to the front of that door before our final bit of energy ran out. We both knew what we had to do but we were breathing hard. It was like climbing uphill through molasses but our time was running out." Both men finally made it to that front door and then not knowing what to do, the younger man reached for the doorknob but the older officer stopped him.
"I don't think going inside again is the answer. Let's do a prayer for the little old man's soul—that he should find peace." The younger man agreed and they both removed their hats and bowed their heads. Something lifted from them. Suddenly the younger officer felt the bright sun on the back of his neck. Fear turned to elation but he kept his eyes closed so as not to break that wonderful spell. Chirping and insect sounds came back and even a horn beeping in the distance could be heard. Then, a Voice came.

YOU ARE ALRIGHT...

Both men came back into their senses.

"Are you guys alright? I'm so sorry to disturb your...meditations but I just wanted to know if you needed anything from me." It was a neighbor from across the street. He had his hands up, clearly not comfortable with sneaking up behind two armed law-enforcement officers and tapping them on the shoulders. I wouldn't have disturbed your prayers or whatever you were doing but I thought maybe something was wrong—it was strange how you guys just stopped. The older officer eyed the neighbor suspiciously.

"Where were you before? We were walking and calling out in front of your house and there was no one in there." The neighbor looked puzzled. He pointed back at his wife standing in front of their home across the street.

"We've been home all this time watching you guys since you arrived. You both parked your police car and came up to the door, bowed your heads and you been in the same position for a long time." Both officers looked at each other and then at the man's wife standing in front of her house unwilling to come any closer. She stood with her meaty arms crossed in front of her fidgeting from side to side. A half-hearted wave was the most involvement she was willing to commit to this situation. The neighbor continued.

"I'm the one that called it in to you guys. I was coming out to talk to you but when I saw you guys meditating or praying or whatever, I figured you knew him and I didn't want to disturb you...but it's been a while and I just wanted to know when you're going in."

The younger officer was bursting.

"*We were inside.* We saw everything in there—the cat in the kitchen, the old man's body in the blue jacket." The neighbor smiled.

"You couldn't have been. We were watching you the whole time. You didn't move from the front of that door since you arrived."

The neighbor turned toward his wife who gesticulated for him to let the officers do their jobs. He ignored her as he turned back to the officers.

"When you guys stood there with your heads bowed I figured you were trying to figure out my note that I used to seal the front door for police a couple of days ago. I didn't want anybody but you guys breaking that in case there had been foul play." He wished them good luck and finally joined his anxious wife. They scurried back inside their home. The officers looked down below the doorknob on the front door. There was a piece of white bond paper sealed across the seam of the front door with two pieces of transparent strapping tape. No one could open the front door without ripping the paper and the tape that sealed the entrance. The neighbor had scrawled a message for them in black marker.

OFFICERS CHECK
THIS HOME

Another officer arrived. He was upset about why these two decided not to answer their radios today. They sat in their vehicle, happy to let the third arrival break the seal and enter the home. They sat in stunned silence in their vehicle as the third officer verified everything they had previously found—the cat, the body, the jacket. Yet, there was no brother, no relatives at all, only a note on the kitchen table that the deceased wanted all his belongings, including his cat, to be given to a local church and that he wanted to be *buried in his favorite New York Jets jacket.*

21

QUANTUM
PARANORMALITY
THEOREM

The Quantum Paranormality Theorem—Individuals who encounter genuine supernatural situations are not merely stumbling across metaphysical phenomena. Perceivers of the paranormal phenomena are themselves passing through a quantum flux field (or being forced by supernatural forces to pass through this field) so that they are translated temporarily into a parallel field of existence.

Experiencers will resonate with this way of stating it: despite all appearances to the contrary, *paranormal entities are* not *coming to us—it is* **we who are going to them.**

Supernatural entities do not, in most cases, enter our physical world but we enter into the plane inhabited by the supernatural entities for a brief period of extraordinary perception. We are not peering into another dimension—*"I saw a shadow person."* Experiencers are actually passing through a veil for a short period and then we snap back. Most often, we have no clue that we were ever gone. We automatically believe that we remain in our physical context unless something radical forces us to realize that we are not—as we float high above the bed we suddenly look down and see our own inanimate body laid there. Then we realize that we are translated.

In the story of "the blue jacket," it is likely that the two officers never actually had any physical door opened for them. They likely passed through a veil of transmogrification at that front door. They *believed* that they had a door opened by a spirit that had *no ability* to open a physical door. The two officers were translated onto the same plane that the spirit inhabited but could still view a version of the physical universe even in that state. They passed through the physical door to the inside of the house but eventually they translated right back into the physical world.

The spirit of the little old man didn't want his physical body to rot in his kitchen. He wanted more than anything to have his physical shell buried in that jacket. So his spirit was allowed to bend the laws of the universe; to borrow and translate the spirits of those two officers temporarily toward his purpose. It was no coincidence that those officers were picked to go to that door and participate in this potentially awakening incident. These men already had a strong propensity toward the supernatural as some people in law-enforcement do. That's why they were the ones drawn to come to this scene. Everything happens the way it does for a reason.

Contrary to what people might think, individuals don't become interested in the paranormal because they have supernatural experiences. Rather, they have paranormal experiences because *they are already paranormal themselves*, e.g.: they already have paranormal abilities and propensities. This is what the Para-Investigative files represent. Although they might appear to be stories of investigators who stumble across supernatural phenomena—*they are not*. These are stories of official investigators and even civilian truth-seekers passing through the Quantum Flux into a field *to somewhere else*. Sometimes they translate into that other place for just a moment but that's enough to change their material outlook forever.

22

THE SMOOTHIE

(Among East Coast law-enforcement this true story is a commonly recounted by veteran law-enforcers use to teach young recruits to listen to their intuition.)

A state trooper was on duty. He was driving down a well-traveled highway when traffic in both directions on this route slowed down due to congestion. Suddenly, he saw a young man in a slow-moving dark sedan, traveling on the other side of the highway. He locked his gaze into that of the young man's bright clear face. They entered a timeless moment as each driver stared directly into the other's eyes and the young man's expression changed. The trooper "sensed" the young man exclaim two words:

"Oh Sh*t!"

The trooper thought that maybe he read the young man's lips but the problem was that he clearly "heard" the phrase inside his own head. The hairs on the back of the trooper's neck stood up. An alarm went off in the pit of his stomach as the words reverberated through his brain. The trooper sped up to find the cross over to the other side of the highway. He found the crossover, swung around and sped up to locate the dark sedan. He found the sedan and pulled it over to the side of the highway. The young man had the appearance of a successful executive, wearing a suit, white shirt and tie. He also sported an expensive European briefcase displayed on the passenger side. The driver had all the appearance of what law-enforcement refer to as a "Smooth Operator"....one of those confident young men who move easily between the business world and the criminal world depending on what was convenient on any given day. Smoothie smiled. He appeared calm and cooperative.

Could this be the wrong car?

The trooper dismissed the thought as quickly as it came. The trooper was an experienced hunter of automobiles and men. A single glance and his photographic memory would retain the exact color and features of any vehicle or person. He also recognized the perfectly symmetrical features of the Smooth Operator's head and face. The driver was a clean-cut, attractive young black man, who despite his professional attire and appearance still had more than a hint of "street" in his demeanor.

The trooper had to say why he pulled Smoothie over. "You seemed to be swerving and changing lanes in an unsafe manner."

The trooper was surprised when the young man did not protest or object and instead displayed a rock-steady smile as he provided identifications that were all in order, including insurance cards. The driver asked what other documents the trooper might require. There were no warrants on the young man and all his inspections, insurance and license were up to date. The inside of the vehicle was immaculate and offered no clues in plain sight as to the driver's activities. The trooper had developed no probable cause at all to go any further but his uneasiness intensified.

The trooper resorted to the standard first investigator's query of who, what, where, how and why. The young man explained he was returning from a business trip from New York City and he has family living there also. He was only passing through the trooper's state in getting back to his home in Pennsylvania. He enjoyed driving through the suburban parts of the trooper's state because the scenery was quite beautiful. When the young man was peppered with the detailed questions that often make suspicious characters stumble; he responded without hesitation every time.

What family lives there?
My older brother and his family...
What kind of business?
It's import/export for household products.
What town in Pennsylvania?
Hershey.
That's a very long drive isn't it?
Yeah, but I love to drive.
About how long is that?
Two-hundred thirty-six miles from Hershey to New York City.

The trooper was defeated.

He could find no probable cause to search the vehicle. Smoothie had given him not a scintilla of suspicious behavior, not an odd moment, furtive glance, no fumbling that could be interpreted as suspicious in the least. After all this alarm and effort on the trooper's part to get to the truth of this matter; he had been blocked. The worst part of having to let this man go was that the trooper's knowledge and experience told him that the absolute lack of anything remotely suspicious, the rehearsed perfection of all the answers and behavior; *absolutely confirmed* that something very suspicious *was* going on.

Any average citizen or person who is not involved in some sort of planned operative behavior, would show some bit of nervousness or a stutter or stumble here or there as a normal part of ordinary behavior. None of that "ordinariness" was present here, which told the trooper a pre-planned mission of some sort was in full operation. He fought back the urge to question Smoothie about his "oh, sh*t" comment. Regardless of all his intuitive knowing, that ephemeral based certainty was not an available asset. He could tell no one about the words he "heard." The trooper knew he would have to let the young man go and by the looks of his grinning face, *Smoothie knew it too.*

The trooper grudgingly gave him back most of his documents and he prepared to leave, Smoothie knew his victory was complete. The young man carefully placed his insurance and registration papers back into the slots where he had them neatly kept. The trooper held the driver's license waiting for him to take it. Like a super-villain savoring victory, Smoothie began to monologue.

"Man, you guys do an incredible job. Anything us citizens to make your jobs easier, you just let me know." Smoothie undid the parking brake and reached for his final document—his driver's license.

The trooper pulled back the license.
"*Well, now that you mention that*...it would make my job a lot easier if I did a quick search of your car."
Smoothie's face shifted.
The trooper continued like he was just gabbing with a close friend.

"It'll just take a minute and it would make my bosses a lot happier when I can say that I did a complete job when I stop a vehicle. It's just like a *checking the box type thing.*"

Smoothie still didn't speak and just kept his hands on the steering wheel as he stared straight ahead. The trooper put the license back in his breast pocket as he watched Smoothie doing mental calculations...the kind people do when they are toying with the idea of gunning the car and taking off. The trooper now moved back from the car and assumed a more menacing pose, hand on the holster.

"...so just pop the trunk for me and walk out here to my vehicle while I do a quick search."

Finally, Smoothie paused a long moment as his eyes became glassy.
"If it's all the same to you I think I'll just be on my way now."
The trooper acted wounded.

"But it's not all the same to me. *You volunteered. You said about helping in any way possible.* I didn't make you say that. You said that on your own. Why would you change your mind about that unless... *you're hiding something?*"

Smoothie smiled and regained his composure.

"Aw no man, I'm just in a hurry. That's all. But no...you can search as much as you want but I have to warn you that this car...I just got it back from my friend Maurice who was using it for about a month."

With that, Smoothie unlocked all the doors and popped the hood of the trunk. He then obediently stood at the trooper's vehicle as the trooper made a discovery of an enormous quantity of cocaine from a hidden compartment in the trunk. The value of the seized drugs added up to the greatest single cocaine seizure in the state's history by a single officer acting alone. This extraordinary accomplishment raised eyebrows and questions.

How could the trooper possibly have known?

Others in law enforcement will most often cut off their own queries by just ascribing the whole event to "dumb luck and good procedure." Only the trooper himself knew it was much more. Only he knew that his historical drug seizure would never have happened had it not been for his unshakable faith in what he heard and what he knew to be true, and *now you know it too.*

23

TOO PERFECT

(Here is another true story commonly recounted by veteran law-enforcers use to teach young recruits to listen to their intuition.)

As we entered the new millennium, there was a young man crossing into the United States from Victoria, British Columbia, aboard a ferry boat that was loaded with vehicles that were all doing the same thing—crossing into the United States of America for the upcoming New Year's celebration. Out of many cars that came off a ferry from British Columbia that day, something caught the attention of a female Customs Inspector that made her select this young man's vehicle for thorough inspection. It turned out his documents depicted that he was a citizen of a country that is a friend of the United States: Canada. There was nothing suspicious in his manner, demeanor or actions.

Yet this American female Customs Inspector got a severe and uneasy feeling about the young man with plenty of identifying documents. He seemed to have a standard and correct answer for every question asked and even had easy replies for spontaneous queries the Inspector generated to elicit some variation in the young man's steady demeanor. Everything seemed in order with the young man but the Inspector still could not shake the feeling that something was awry. The Inspector asked for help from another Inspector who noticed the young man's answers seemed rehearsed. He also seemed to delay in letting the Inspector's into the vehicle for the standard search. It was as if he was just finishing mental calculations before he allowed the search to go forward. The female inspector was on alert for any possibility of serious drugs.

After a long and thorough search, they found copious amounts of white powder in the wheel well of the vehicle.

"Jackpot—cocaine in huge amounts."

As the female inspector celebrated in her mind, the first of several twists occurred. The suspected traveler broke free from inspectors. He bolted from the station and carjacked a driver at a nearby red light to try to escape. The armed Inspectors reacquired him as he attempted to drive away with the vehicle. The traveler was dragged from the car and placed under arrest. He was facing numerous felony charges and that was even before the preliminary tests came back on the cocaine. Then after they secured the prisoner, the bad news began. Numerous tests on the white powder and field tests with kits and drug sniffing dogs turned out negative for cocaine and *for drugs of any type*. The white powder was inert material without any purpose. Perhaps drug-dealers had ripped off the young man by selling him a few pounds of chalk-dust as cocaine or told him it was granulized methamphetamine. It wouldn't be the first time they had seen such things along the border.

Then, the Inspectors realized that their search should not have stopped with the white powder. They resumed the task of ripping apart the vehicle to possibly find out clues on the function of the whitish powder. They discovered in more secret compartments: little black boxes complete with circuit boards, timers, and watches— items that looked very much like bomb-making components. Notifications and the young man's identifiers went out to the FBI, ATF and the Royal Canadian Mounted Police. His fingerprints turned out to be a match to a known international terrorist. This known terrorist went to America in order to blow up major landmarks during the celebration for the New Millennium. The traveler and his associates (later arrested inside the United States) would have accomplished their mission unmolested had it not been for the faith this lone Customs Inspector had in her own supernatural intuition.

24

NO HUNCHES ALLOWED

(The following account is the painfully public prelude and aftermath to the 9/11 attacks in the United States.)

The 9/11 Commission report was put together in order to determine if any government gaps were responsible for a lack of preparation for the terrorist acts on 9/11/2001.

A U.S. Federal Government Agent who investigated terrorists on a regular basis throughout the United States was noticing a disturbing pattern during the opening months of the year 2001. Among Middle-Eastern subjects that were routinely under surveillance by National Security agencies, there were an inordinate number of them, beyond the statistical probabilities, that were signing up for and taking flight lessons. At aviation colleges, private airports and government sponsored aviation facilities; an expanding number of Middle-Eastern students were taking flying lessons. The typical profile of these aviation students made them very unlikely be the type of people who would want to be pilots. In some cases, the aviation students were terribly inadequate at the English language, sometimes barely able to make themselves understood to bewildered flying instructors. Others were qualified in academic areas that diverged wildly from anything to do with flying—linguistics, chemical engineering, mathematics, geology mineral derivation. Yet even these, when questioned by instructors, would insist that they were taking flight lessons in relation to their majors at university.

The Government Agent in question was a person who throughout a long career in National Security had already exhibited numerous instances of prescience above and beyond any ordinary expectations. He had known, on several occasions, what terrorists were going to do even before the terrorists themselves had laid out their plans to their compatriots. However, this particular instance of clairvoyance would shock the world.

There were further reports from flight instructors who added anecdotes about Middle-Eastern students who were uniformly uninterested in learning how to land planes. Others were indifferent to the mechanics of how to take off in a plane or land the plane, while insisting on learning the fundamentals of steering and handling planes already in the air. Flight instructors tended to, in many cases, be former Air force personnel—a more patriotic group than the average. They sometimes reported this strange behavior to local or Federal law-enforcement without really having a well-defined suspicion as to the agenda behind the strange behavior they were reporting. The new millennium had left the United States of America and entire globe with a feeling of having "dodged a bullet." Ringing in the year 2000, did not produce any of the promised and even expected "Y2k catastrophes," the meltdown of computer system networks, the malfunction and even crashing of all planes, trains and automobiles with computer chips in the guidance systems. Best of all, there had been no terrorist attack on the nation.

A dangerous terrorist fully equipped to create havoc in some of our major cities was neutralized at the border America shared with Canada. As the United States sailed through 2001, there was a general feeling that many major catastrophes had been avoided.

Yet this Agent reported publicly that he had been seeing "preparatory behavior" by many of these subjects and had been hearing "increased chatter" among major terrorist groups. Alarm bells went off for this particular Agent. He unfolded the abyss and what he uncovered necessitated that he, against great bureaucratic resistance, create the following warning letter on July 10, 2001, which is excerpted here from the publicly released portion.

> *"The inordinate number of these individuals attending these type of schools and fatwa's…*(**deleted by the U.S. Government**)*…gives reason to believe that a coordinated effort is underway to establish a cadre of individuals who will one day be working in the civil aviation community around the world. These individuals will be in a position in the future to conduct terror activity against civil aviation targets."*

(Document Credit: Government Document/Public Domain)

The balance of the communication went on to cite immediate measures to avoid catastrophe and gave voluminous anecdotal evidence that supported the Agent's conclusions that a grand terrorist attack was imminent. The memo then stated several defensive and counter-active measures to deter, defeat and disrupt any impending attack.

The "911 Commission" in their public report noted "that the memo did not contain any recommendations that would have prevented the terrorist attack." They also cited the statement that "the Agent was pursuing a hunch and that government officials *do not act on hunches.*"

Unfortunately, truer words were never spoken.

25

THE SORCERER-KING

(From the history of ancient England we have a recounting of a story that is commonly used at Law Schools, Police Academies and Technical institutions in relation to the usage of and the shortcomings of polygraph machines.)

To call someone is a liar is a harsh and inelegant thing.

Most people are not actual liars—they equivocate, they straddle, they omit and they give off indications of discomfort and deception. They prevaricate. Prevarication is an ancient word from old English: pre·var·i·cate; to act in collusion, literally, to straddle. It means to straddle the line between the truth and falsehood. This implies telling some truth, as far as can be afforded and indulging in falsehood, as much as is required.

Most people straddle the line between truth and deceit, others simply believe whatever is convenient to their worldview or outlook—truth is a constantly shifting reality for them. Some cultures do not see truth as an obligation unless they have a special relationship to the questioner that morally imposes an obligation for truth telling. This is a *special* obligation beyond normal relationships. Westerners with their restricted linear thinking often cannot conceive of these non-Anglo-Saxon perceptions. In the world outside of Anglo-Saxon culture, things rarely come down to truth or lies, black or white. That's why "prevarication" is a far more appropriate term for investigations than the invective term—"liar."

In medieval England, a king suspected that his queen had been having an affair. He decided to hold a mock combat contest among his knights. However, the king changed the rules of engagement so that this combat instead of being until any combatant yields for any reason would continue "until honor ran out." Combat had to continue until the first grievous injury occurred or until one knight could no longer continue. This greatly changed the nature of the combat. Due to requirements of honor that knights felt so acutely, the increased level of seriousness involved in this type of combat could result in permanent injury or even death. The knights would insist on continuing no matter how bad their injuries became—until broken bones, concussions or some horrible injury required them to accept the shame of asking for quarter in front of their king and queen. Because there were no sharp edges to these weapons, there would be no clean injuries—only terrible blunt force trauma.

This king also changed the roster so that the knight suspected of bedding the Queen would come into the final pair of the mock combat. Moreover, he passed the rumor that a kiss from the Queen as she awards the medals would be among the prizes for the last champion winner. The King who considered himself well versed in the arts of truth detection (this was one of his sorcerous areas of expertise) had placed a powdery chalky substance in the palms of his hand. Then, he insisted on holding his Queens hand while the knights trotted out into the open-air arena, pair by pair, for mock combat with wooden practice weapons.

The Queen wishing to appear calm and collected advised the king that she was looking forward to this amusement. She remained exactly in that condition throughout the contest as dozens of knights clashed, suffered injuries and were removed from the competition. As the contest progressed, the king said that in view of the prize—a kiss from the Queen—it was necessary for her to hold his hand throughout the contest as a symbol that the kiss she would give would be simply a formality required by her office. As the afternoon went on without any catastrophic incident, the King kept checking the powder in his hand to find it perfectly dry.

However, when it came the turn of the alleged paramour of the Queen, she began to fidget slightly, her eyes began to dart in several directions, and she pointed her toes toward the opposite side from where the king sat. As the final pair's combat intensified (because it was this handsome knight who was more determined than any to win this prize) she appeared very uncomfortable. She seemed ready to pull her hand away at any moment. The King checked the powder in his hand. Soaking moisture had obliterated the powder. He asked unthinkable questions.

"Do you have any special feelings for the handsome knight who lost his helmet and may be in danger of losing his good looks?"

"Are you concerned that should he win the competition, the kiss he will get from your highness may reveal something more than a majestic obligation?"

And finally….

"Is your Majesty concerned that this event may reveal what is already whispered by gossiping old women…that your Majesty is having an affair with the gallant knight?"

The Queen failed in her attempt to withhold indicators of deception from the King. Her body language, facial tics, perspiration, the pulse the King was measuring from her hand, tone of voice—all went off the scale with indicators of deception as she issued the standard denials and proper moral outrage. What happened next is sometimes romanticized in legends but the more brutal version (which I believe is the truthful version) was that the King immediately cancelled the contest and had his Queen and that knight beheaded promptly by the next sunrise.

The pair vigorously protested their innocence—even saying that they were guilty of thinking of such sins but never even came close to committing them in the material world.   There was an outcry against the penalty throughout the kingdom and even from neighboring kingdoms.   Many people knew of the Queen's tireless work for the poor and needy.   They considered the Queen "a saint."   The King's response to all this resistance was a hardening of his position.   He proclaimed the pair guilty of: adultery and treason.   The King also made it clear how certain he was of their guilt by saying that if God would grant him the power; he would bring the pair back into this life several times over, only so he could behead them several times more as befitting the heinous nature of their crimes against the kingdom and nature.   The execution took place on schedule.

The King no doubt thanked his "wizards" for teaching him the absolute foolproof system for knowing when a person is lying and for saving his kingdom in the short run.   In the end however, internal elements already against the king increased their support after his universally condemned brutality.   Perhaps due to karmic justice or just due to already-brewing rebellion that only required a catalyst/rallying cry, the Sorcerer King's reign and his line were brought to a swift and bloody end shortly after his Queen's demise.

Yet, I believe that Queen was most likely innocent of what she was accused and the reason is that his methods of detecting lies were about as reliable as the modern technological methods we use today,

This medieval King's lie detection methods function essentially in the same way that our modern machine methods function.   These treat the human brain and body as a material machine with various autonomic responses and circuits that fire based on involuntary responses.   Like the Sorcerer King from many centuries ago, we are *still* measuring perspiration in the palm, heart rate speed up and slow down, voice pitch and various other machine-like responses; for the supposed purpose of knowing when a person is lying.   We are still engaging in the same mistakes the medieval king did, by acting under the pretenses that our bodies are purely material machines instead of what we now know that they really are: conductors for consciousness and spirit that technological means cannot gauge.

Consciousness is far too complex for machines to assess or measure.   We have brain surgeons who treat the brain like a mechanic fixing an automobile, but those same brain surgeons cannot locate that vital decision maker called "individual human consciousness."   It's not there.   The temporary bodies we enjoy in this limited physical existence are merely conductors for something we cannot yet touch, measure, or examine.

We make the decision to deceive at the deepest levels of consciousness generated by the untouchable decision maker we all have but that few can understand. The reasons that motivate those decisions to deceive are as complex or as twisted as each person's soul. In the medieval conflict cited above, I believe the Queen was not guilty of the charges made against her but I *do not believe she was innocent.* There is a difference. The Queen was probably guilty of "wanting to" have an affair with the knight in question. The moral teachings of the time were that thinking about sin should create as much guilt and therefore generate as many explicit autonomic deception responses as would be caused by *actually doing* the sinful deed.

Today, as advanced as we are in the information age, we continue to promote the myth that we can tell if people are lying through the technology of measuring physical autonomic responses. This is a fantasy based on the old myth that our bodies are merely mechanical physical machines like a toaster that when set to the highest setting will always burn toast. Those who believe that polygraphs or technical-based lie detection can tell us if a person is lying, also believe the human body, like that toaster, merely has mechanical settings that it cannot help but trigger if someone pushes the right lever.

We can no more tell with any measure of certainty if a person is lying than we can tell if someone is a good person or a bad person. That is why polygraph examinations are excluded as evidence in court—because they are evidence only of emotional stability or turbulent personality. The myth of polygraphs, voice stress analysis and mechanical lie detection of any sort are just more flotsam and jetsam left over from the old Newtonian-materialist era when we believed that we were just physical human bodies. In truth, we are eternal conscious energy temporarily inhabiting biological coverings we call human bodies. Polygraphers are little more than modern technocrat witchdoctors who continue the Sorcerer-King's work today.

Real truth detection can only be done by Investigators without machines because they are ultimately using spiritual perception as their final filter. In this area, old world skills are most useful but they require dedicated practice and they don't involve machines. Detecting body language—Look for body language that might indicate someone is lying, such as not looking you in the eye when speaking to you, being fidgety, or acting nervous or uncomfortable. There are literally hundreds of body gestures, facial tics and body micro signals; that a person can look for in assessing is someone is exhibiting deception, anger, fear or concern. The old saying is that "the words lie but the body tells the truth."

Most people assess deception only based on one or two signals. That's wrong. True Investigators must cross-reference three, ten or fifty such body language signals in order to acquire a fair assessment of the person's mental state. The problem with this and all old school investigative skills, is that the autonomic signals are nearly the same for lying and deception as they are for many other states of mind: love, hatred, discomfort with a topic, anger with the subject matter or questioner, dislike of the questioner for reasons may have nothing to do with the subject matter and a myriad of other mental conflicts. Often deception detection terminology sounds more impressive than it really is: gestural slips, unilateral contempt and micro-fear. When the snake coils, we know that it will strike but *what if* it becomes vital to know whether the strike is due to fear or anger?

Which group of people are the best at gliding smoothly while telling their tale? Is it truth-tellers or prevaricators? Listen for inconsistencies in what the person tells you, such as different stories on different days, different time frames and mistakes in remembering details. This important skill reveals deception but is not very useful in real life because no matter how true a story might be, it's a natural human inclination is slightly vary a story each time you tell it. We are not machines. Only machines or a tape recorder could perfectly in every detail duplicate a story each time they tell it—unless it's been rehearsed.

Therefore, investigators can always find as many inconsistencies depending only upon their determination in any particular case. At the same, practiced dissemblers tend to be more consistent in their repetitions of the same stories. They must be so in order to engage in their favorite activity—deception. Only masters of deception can glide along smoothly without ever stumbling.

26

TRICKS OF THE MIND

An old police trick is invaluable to teach new recruits shows how easy it is to create deception in the human mind. Police veterans will tell new police officers that if they accidentally or prematurely fire their weapon without direct witnesses, they should immediately shout aloud **"Stop or I'll shoot!"**

Then call an ambulance and act as if nothing had gone wrong. Neighbors will hear the shouting. They will experience cognitive realignment, which means their minds will try to make sense of sensory perception that, at first, makes no sense at all.

"Why would anyone shout STOP OR I'LL SHOOT after they have already shot the gun?
It makes no sense. But isn't that what I heard? No it can't be."

This process is subconscious and most often the neighbors' minds will rearrange reality to convince themselves that they heard the shouting first and the shots second. Then the police officer in the unfortunate situation can tell his version of events: *that the officer was feeling threatened coming into a dangerous situation against a dangerous criminal. The desperate criminal kept making furtive movements despite repeated warnings. There was no choice but to shoot.*

The only caveat is that if any of the neighbors are young children *this mind trick doesn't work.* The prison-like parameters of logical thinking have not yet regimented the minds of young children. They don't suffer these cognitive phenomena. Children tend to witness, assess and say exactly what happened without the adult need to make sense of things before our minds accept them as true.

The human interrogators first red flag is usually detecting extreme avoidance/resistance. Detecting high levels of resistance or avoidance—if the person steadfastly resists answering any questions and exhibits defensiveness could mean that he or she is trying to hide something. This happens all the time during investigations but it may indicate nothing more than discomfort. Because we are complicated souls, this discomfort can be for any variety of reasons that might have nothing to do with deception or criminality. Any myriad of reasons can cause discomfort. It depends on culture, upbringing and customs. Cues learned from cultural conditioning, habits and inculcated social reactions caused most of our natural responses and behavior.

It never fails to impress me how many people go out of their way to give a person a firm solid handshake, only to (at the last second) avoid eye contact with the person they are greeting. Avoidance of visual contact during physical contact is a very telling sign of acute discomfort or contempt. It is the reason for the discomfort that *we do not know*.

Another important sensitivity for the interrogator is detecting the counterattack. A useful old world skill is detecting false accusations from a subject against the questioner. The subject accuses the questioner of lying or being deceitful. This often reflects the other person's own underlying behavior, which he or she is projecting onto the questioner. Again, it means the false accuser is guilty of something—but of what we don't know. That question is for Para-Investigators. Para-Investigators are most difficult to deceive. They utilize all the old school skills of front-line investigators but they add intuitive abilities that increase the potential for rooting out deception. Dissemblers cannot deceive them because Para-Investigators have already overcome the world's greatest lie—*that this material world is all there is.*

27

SORCERER KING— CONCLUDED

In returning to the story of the Sorcerer-King, it is possible to turn even these ancient historical actors into Para-Investigators.

The medieval King should have assigned someone the Queen would find non-threatening in this age of segregation between the sexes, a person who could speak to her on sensitive topics without raising suspicions but whom the King could completely trust—his oldest most mature concubine, who we will call Gertrude. The mature woman would have put the basic investigator's query to the Queen: the "who, what, why, where and how" relating to the suspected affair between the Queen and the dashing knight. The Queen would have parried with the usual denials, avoidances and even deception that the older woman would expect. The Concubine would have then employed what was, in an earlier era, known as "a woman's intuition." From our perspective today, the older woman would be employing the skills of Para-Investigative Assessment and Empathy.

"I know of the feelings between you two but I also know you would never betray the King by adulterous union with another man. Yet I could never resist the lips of that gallant knight if he offered them to me. Deny those arms crushing me? I think not. You are Queen, a majestic and regal Lady yes, but you are still a woman to whom the King does NOT accord rightful affection as befits her role."

At this point, the Queen might begin to well up with tears at the memory of stolen moments as the older woman, having completed Para-Investigative Assessment/ Connection, would then enter into Para-Investigative Empathy: *"I dare say I would have put off my regal self and leapt into his arms hoping never to leave that embrace ever again. I would forsake my cold king and forsake this barren kingdom. I would have to follow my heart!"*

At this, the Queen would break open a clear honest moment.

"Gertrude, after the midnight hunt a month ago…we embraced and kissed by the river under the full moon. Nothing more and we agreed that nothing else could ever happen between us."

Gertrude, the concubine could then have taken the report back to the proper authorities and acquire a generous punishment of banishment from the kingdom or exile into a foreign land for the Queen. She could have saved the younger woman from ignominious execution under a false accusation of mortal sin. The fate of this kingdom would have changed. The King who ruined himself with his people, who wrongly accused and executed the most saintly woman in his kingdom, could have saved himself and his dynasty through the use of Para-Investigative skills.

Para-Investigators will never make the mistake of using or participating in the use of polygraph machines. Polygraphs cannot tell us if someone is lying or telling the truth. Many practiced liars beat the polygraph and many truthful people fail them. Additionally, polygraph results are not allowed in any of civilized court systems for exactly these reasons. The polygraph's only legitimate use is as a weapon against "guilty" subjects in order to elicit a confession of wrongdoing. Unfortunately, due to bureaucratic cowardice and lethargy masquerading as leadership; polygraphs have wormed their way into many aspects of life. They continue to be used for employment, background investigations, and many other routine matters where they cause far more harm than any benefit they provide.

True Investigators and Para-Investigators can tell the veracity of a witness just by listening carefully to them relate testimony sometimes in a single instance. Once you add the hundreds of possible signals of ill ease or truthfulness present in body language, it is almost impossible for a Para-Investigator to avoid knowledge of truth or deception in any subject.

PARA-INVESTIGATORS
IN ACTION

The Para-Investigators have warned us, saved us and led us to truths so shattering that the world has burned them at the stake again and again

28

FEVERED DREAMS OF GOD'S MANDATE

The convergence of modern Information Age skills and ancient hatreds allow a radical manifesto to circle the globe within seconds and inspire many like-hearted individuals with the same burning desire for destruction. Radical ideas are lit like the fuse of a bomb. The potential for destructive power is magnified from where it was before 1980 to a magnitude that is almost incalculable. The main determinant of this magnitude is the power of the ideas. The unification of modern technology with the fire of faith can have devastating results.

This relates to terrorists because they are always religious figures. Terrorists are distinct from murderers as a class in the aspect of faith. Murderers kill one, two, or even three people out of hatred, envy, avarice, anger, betrayal or pride. Their motivation can be any along the spectrum of destructive human emotions. These simple emotions provide a damaged soul enough motivation to kill but often are not enough to keep their deeds secret once the fever of that emotion is past. These are the *fevered dreams of temporary madness.* Once that fever is past, they often find it a relief to confess and reveal their terrible deeds.

Terrorists are individuals attempting to effect societal change through violent means and methods that can terminate extraordinary numbers of human lives. The human psyche demands a far greater justification for real terrorism than it does for simple murder. Mere greed, anger or hatred is not enough to fuel the terrorist's mind towards his deeds. The much larger level of destruction to human life requires *religious faith* to justify this path. True terrorists have a profound religious faith at their core. Whether it is an established religion, recently invented religion or just a personally created religion; *sufficient investigation always exposes it.*

Terrorists believe God gives them their mandate and the universe awaits their success. Without this outlook, their psyches simply could not justify the massive cognitive commitment required to evaporate so much human life. This backing of faith is what makes them far more dangerous than mere murderers. How do you stop someone who believes in his cause so much that he's willing to die for it? Terrorists are willing to give their lives and everyone else's lives for the same cause whether they are innocent women, children or even babies—God's mandate can demand nothing less.

Faith...the substance of things unseen and the knowledge of things hoped for must also back those who investigate such formidable individuals. Faith is the greatest power in the universe. That's why so much cultural dark force is devoted to keeping people from true faith. Para-Investigators will have faith in their own ability to pierce the Superconscious Gulf of Cosmic Overmind and unfold the hidden knowledge that swirls there. It is the same place that terrorists go for inspiration and those who oppose them should reach out for the same privilege—the privilege of access through faith.

29

YOU ARE WAHI

(This story comes from overseas in the ongoing battle between Western intelligence agencies and the supposed enemies of the West.)

There was a Middle-Eastern man suspected of being the leader of an operational terrorist cell in a major Western nation. The intelligence agency of a major Western power tracked his every move. A Government Agent who was the best in the world at what he did, carefully monitored everything he did. His specialty was to deter, disrupt and defeat terrorist groups already in motion. Yet, no matter how many resources the Government Agent used or how closely they watched the Middle-Eastern man, no one could detect how he was getting out instructions to his organizational cells throughout the country. His sworn followers and associates were simultaneously acting from the same trigger point in time, as if they had all received detailed instructions in a coordinated manner. Yet no phones, computers or cyber networks of any kind transmitted instructions, codes or communications that anyone could see. The Middle-Eastern man, Nemesis (Not True Codename), was confident there was no way on Earth his methods would ever be detected and *he was right.*

Government Agent went to his national courts and advised that "he had information through reliable informants" that led him to believe that Nemesis was meeting in public areas with his lieutenants who were passing out his instructions *on audio-recorded cassettes*, distributed to his cell members, played on antiquated cassette players and then destroyed. Twenty-four hour surveillance had been unable to capture the passing of any media of any type but the informant information was enough. Courts granted arrest and search warrants. However, they failed to find the cassettes with the instructions and every member of the cell, when interrogated, said they never existed.

Despite this evidence never being found, the cell had been disrupted and almost all of the cell-members were deported back to their countries of origin. The arrest and interrogation of Nemesis lasted several months. Nemesis pleaded ignorance and bewilderment to Government Agent during all those months. He never admitted to any terrorist plans or terrorism related activities of any sort. Nemesis never gave any information about his network and six months later he was also deported back to his nation of origin. His own nation of origin imprisoned Nemesis but eventually Nemesis acquired his freedom after signing agreements with his government not to engage in any further such acts. After his release, he assumed his place as a respected leader of his own group of radical followers.

Years later, Government Agent happened to travel to that same foreign nation for training. During one trip to the capital city, the vehicle he rode in was returning to the embassy when it stopped just short of the embassy due to some sort of disturbance on the street. There was a protest going on against the regime in the area of the embassy and there was no way past it. The Western government convoy was stuck in place—unable to move forward or back. Agent obtained leave to depart the convoy and find his way on foot back to his embassy housing. He began walking but it would be a circuitous route to avoid the crowds. Government Agent was actually interested in the protest and stopped to watch a small knot of fundamentalist Muslims protesting bitterly against corrupting Western influences in their country.

"Such a small group caused all this commotion?"

The observers and the national police who guarded their protest were larger numbers than the protesting group itself. Government Agent, a Caucasian blonde man in dressy casual attire must have looked out of place. A Pakistani man approached him and smiled. He motioned him to his taxi and said he would take him back to the embassy. He said he would cut through an excellent route past these crowds so that Government Agent wouldn't have to walk twenty minutes out of his way. The Agent went with him and settled in the backseat. The vehicle sped off but was heading not toward embassy housing but in the opposite direction toward the outskirts of the city. Government Agent shouted questions at the driver as he tried all the locks and realized the vehicle was set up as a police car—locked from the outside and with an impenetrable plexi-glass barrier separating him from the driver. The driver just smiled at him and motioned for him to sit back and relax.

The Agent had made a mistake. The driver no longer responded to his questions. The protest riot in the street had been a distraction. He'd read stories about incidents like this and he knew how they ended. He faced torture and death at the hands of one of the groups he had prosecuted in the past. His mind raced to think which of his former opponents could be involved in this. Agent's thoughts drifted to his loved ones and their final words to each other as he steeled himself for what was to come. The vehicle finally stopped and the driver made his announcement: "We're here. You will go with these nice people. "

Instead of burly Kalashnikov-bearing Arabs grabbing him—more diminutive, gray-garbed Pakistanis took him inside. There were no handcuffs or bags over his head. Their friendly demeanor shocked him. He followed in a daze.

Agent arrived, not to a barren safe house for torture/interrogation, but to a very elegant two story Villa on the outskirts of the capital. A slight Indian man dressed in an immaculate white uniform appeared inside the home. He bowed and motioned for him to follow. It was a beautifully decorated home. The servants ushered him in to a Great Room where the sweet smell of Hookah tobacco smoke mixed with hashish wafted through luxurious pillows strewn about a silk curtained room. Inside he saw the outline of a familiar silhouette.

It was Nemesis.

He sat smoking the Hookah. He appeared to have gained about 30 pounds and living a good life in the several years that had passed.

"Welcome my friend. I'm so glad you accepted my invitation."

He was bright, happy, and very different from the orange-suited, chained up prisoner that the Agent remembered from so many years ago in the West. Agent came back to his senses.

"I was kidnapped by your people." Nemesis acted alarmed.

"No, no, my friend, I only wanted moments of your time and my driver will take you right back to your embassy. I swear. After so many years have passed, I still need to find out a single truth from you...and you will be on your way. I swear it." He clasped his hands as if in a Christian prayer.

"I am begging of you a small indulgence for a Servant of God. Many of the same associates I had in the West when you knew me are with me still and I need to know directly from you—which one of my men betrayed me. *How did you find out about the recorded cassettes?"*

Government Agent calmed down. The door was left open. He could hear two Arabs out there chatting with the Pakistani servants in English, the only language they all had in common. Nemesis was telling the truth. This was no kidnapping—*this was a forced reunion.*

"No one told me anything." Nemesis again acted bewildered.

"Then how did you know the way my messages were getting out to my people?"

He could tell Nemesis was deadly earnest about his need to know the truth.

Nemesis had tracked the Government Agent, bribed *who knows how many* of his government officials to keep informed, created the fake riot that occurred on the streets just as Government Agent returned to the embassy; all just to get this quick answer that had plagued him for years.

"I just felt it."

Nemesis studied Agent's face.

"What do you mean by that?" Nemesis offered the hookah pipe, which Agent waved away.

"I knew…I felt that you were somehow getting the instructions out but we had no way to show how exactly you were doing it so I went into the silence to help me figure it out. I saw images of you paying cash for clean audio cassettes. Then I saw you labeling those discs in Arabic—"Listen and Destroy.""

Nemesis laughed and clapped his hands. A terrible weight had lifted from him. For years, he had dreaded finding out which of his trusted lieutenants was the betrayer—he dreaded ordering the death of a male blood relative. Government Agent released him from that burden. Nemesis knew Agent was telling the truth. He pointed at the Agent.

"Now I understand all. You are Wahi. I am also Wahi. It is common in my circles, for men of action and spirit to be Wahi… we acquire revelation through a way that is different from the common mind. We call it the "mindless mind." The mindless mind lets us see into unseen worlds—through sitting dreams, walking visions and great voices that speak to us. The honored dead will come to us with glorious news of future dead. Worlds are revealed to us made up of glowing matter called nur, existing in sheaths within sheaths, nurun ala nur. Man is connected with all these worlds whether he knows it or not. He has only to look and he will see with his mindless mind as I have and as you do."

With that, he took an elegant looking curved dagger down from the wall and approached Government Agent. Agent swallowed. His host slipped the highly polished, jeweled dagger into a leather scabbard, reversed it and offered it handle-first to the Government Agent.

"You have made a new man of me today. This dagger is priceless but it is still not enough to make you understand what you have done for me this day. This day, with your words and your truth, you have saved lives, sacred trust and love."

The Pakistani taxi driver spirited him back to the embassy as promised with many apologies for the deception and inconvenience. Government Agent determined never to tell anyone of what had happened. He knew bureaucrats would find fault in him somehow and besides—*he didn't want to give up the dagger.* As Government Agent arrived at the Embassy with his prize wrapped in his jacket, he couldn't seem to shake the feeling that he had just left, for the final time, the presence of a man who understood him better than anyone else in the world ever would.

30

THE BOUNCE BACK EFFECT

(Here is the story of one of the most notorious terrorists in history from the perspective of a Para-Investigator.)

According to all open sources, one of the most successful individual terrorists in history of the Western world was known as "the Unabomber." This assessment is plain using the measurements of:

1. the enormous amount of resources and manpower used to pursue his identity and his crimes,

2. the expanse of time (two decades) he was successful in his killing activities and

3. the terrible level of violence he successfully committed against Westerners.

This terrorist continued his highly publicized murderous activities during a span of over twenty years while evading the most intensive, continuous domestic manhunt in U.S. history. The resources both human and technological that were brought to bear against the Unabomber were staggering. Every law-enforcement organization, most major civilian organizations and even the civilian population were at some point involved in a widely publicized search for the elusive bomber, yet he seemed to effortlessly glide in and out of his killing activities like a phantom; a deadly phantom that could solidify and kill.

Like all true terrorists, his was a religious fervor that drove his damaged psyche to kill. Nearly all profilers predicted the Unabomber would be a person of extraordinarily high I.Q., a very highly advanced strategic thinker. The Unabomber ultimately turned out to be a brilliant PhD. mathematician and former professor from University of California, Berkeley University. The Unabomber's religion turned out to be a lethal brand of Luddism.

The Luddites were a social movement in England which began in 1811 and who protested in violent illegal ways against the changes produced by the Industrial Revolution. This religion sees technology as a diabolical plot to destroy people's souls, spirits and to take away everything that makes them human. The movement clashed in battles with the British Army. The Luddites were crushed militarily and at a mass trial at York in 1812, they were disposed of in mass executions. The only thing the Luddites have left behind in the Western world is the actual term "Luddite" which is still describes anyone violently opposed to technological progress and change.

In 1971, Theodore Kaczynski, was preparing to become the person known as the Unabomber. He moved to a remote cabin in Lincoln, Montana and began his preparations and training for his upcoming role on the world stage. Finally, from 1978 to 1995, Kaczynski sent 16 bombs to targets including universities and airlines, killing three people and injuring 23. If we count his preparation time, self-training and trial runs from about 1975, he had a terrorist career that spanned over twenty years and struck constant fear throughout the civilian population of the United States.

The manifesto that laid out his belief systems reads like an amateur professor boring his class into submission. The Luddite anti-technology beliefs are the only things that clearly come through the staid diatribe.

> *1. The Industrial Revolution and its consequences have been a disaster for the human race. They have greatly increased the life-expectancy of those of us who live in "advanced" countries, but they have destabilized society, have made life unfulfilling, have subjected human beings to indignities, have led to widespread psychological suffering (in the Third World to physical suffering as well) and have inflicted severe damage on the natural world. The continued development of technology will worsen the situation. It will certainly subject human beings to greater indignities and inflict greater damage on the natural world, it will probably lead to greater social disruption and psychological suffering, and it may lead to increased physical suffering even in "advanced" countries.*

(Document Credit: Government Document/Public Domain)

My own introduction to the evil genius known as the Unabomber came in 1994 when I was summoned to the home of an advertising company executive who had received a small brown package postmarked from Lincoln, Nebraska. It was a small box with strange, handwritten markings on it. The package had been delivered to Thomas Mosser's million-dollar mansion in New Jersey. It was a bomb.

Although the victim, Mr. Mosser lived in luxurious surroundings, he had *not* inherited his position or wealth. According to his public biography, Mosser had been a highly admired naval officer who spent his career building up and innovating in the Navy's public relations department. Later in civilian life, he climbed the corporate ladder at various companies in the highly competitive world of advertising and public relations. Every company he moved to as Director or in any executive leadership position, showed a marked doubling or tripling of profits due to reorganizations and advertising innovations he effected.

Mosser eventually became the CEO of his own highly successful public relations and advertising firm. Mosser was in the kitchen of his New Jersey home, when he decided to open a recently arrived package with the strange markings. Mosser placed the package with the Lincoln, Nebraska, markings on his kitchen counter and began to open it. A metallic contact tapped in. A bright flash emitted from the package. Mosser realized he'd made a mistake. The package erupted upward sending dozens of nails out as bullets. He died on his kitchen floor.

An evil man would not have deserved a death this horrendous...but Mosser was no evil man. He was a hard-working, dedicated, decent man who improved the positive quality of life everywhere he went. It was reported in the news that when his friends and co-workers heard about the murder of Thomas Mosser, their first thoughts were that it might be another Thomas Mosser because his name was rather common and *this* Thomas Mosser had no enemies—only friends and supporters. He was a good man who actually cared about improving the lives of those who worked for him. The Unabomber had never met Thomas Mosser or knew anything about him except that he was an important CEO of a leading advertising and public relations company. Somehow, in the Unabomber's mind, advertising had a causal link to the technology-related sins of our modern society. So he targeted Thomas Mosser for his twisted brand of retribution. Mosser had made his achievements through his own hard work and dedication to his people and his companies. He had only helped people all his life but he died like a petty dictator.

As one of hundreds, perhaps thousands, of investigators assigned to track the Unabomber, I tried receive images of the Unabomber's identity from the Cosmic Mind. I saw a tall slouched over man shambling through forest woods in faded green army fatigues. I had scheduled quiet times to continue to try to see the rest of the man but my introspections were interrupted. Like all those around me, I became consumed in the full time, rational, scientific slog through swamps of potential Unabomber data, Unabomber victim analysis and more mountains of information for data mining. Bureaucrats, who believed that chaotic motion, furious activity and investigative progress were all the same thing, foisted these activities upon investigators.

"the victims can't truly be random. Keep searching for a connection between any single individual and all the victims."

So urged onward, we continued to examine every bit of minutia from the backgrounds of the victims for some commonality with someone, *anyone* who could be the Unabomber—with no success. Some of us even (surreptitiously) searched our dreams, meditations and even projected our thoughts toward each other to find an answer to the identity of the Unabomber, all to no avail. One of my fellow investigators had "seen in dreams" that the Unabomber was a woman. He was sure of it but was unable to convince others.

The constant demand for full attention to the rational side of this investigation left no energy, resources, or time for the more important work of examining the Superconscious Abyss that already had the answers we sought. Yet, a short time later, a man identifying himself as the brother of Theodore Kacinski, turned in his brother as the Unabomber. The investigators assigned to this case, assumed we had failed and that we had only been saved by a strange series of incidents that had nothing to do with the mental power we had projected outward. We were wrong.

Our mental projections during our meditations on the identity of the Unabomber had not come back with the identity of the famous terrorist; but it did manifest in a different way. Whenever people come together and create a massive psychic surge into the Ekashic field there may not be direct result revealed but the psychic exertions can create *"a bounce back effect."*

That's why very often when a damaged person wishes someone a particular evil in their life, that evil wish tends to bounce back and manifest that exact evil in the life of the person sending that negative energy. Those who wish poverty upon us will become poorer. Those who wish failure upon us, sink further into their own despair. Those who hate us, only succeed in becoming more hateful. That psychic energy tends to swirl up into the periphery of the Ekashic field and it "bounces back" into our reality as something else *yet similar* to the original energy. We agitated the great Superconscious Abyss for revelation of the Unabomber's identity and that exact revelation came, albeit not in the way we thought it would.

Sometimes even a negative jolt can create a tremendous positive charge into the life of the target. People can create blessings in the lives of those they mean to curse. We must be careful when we release psychic energy for a particular purpose. It returns to us in another, albeit similar, form. Although our conscious psychic efforts appeared to have failed to uncover the identity of the Unabomber, I now believe that this energy succeeded after all. That psychic energy may have been the final ingredient that influenced Kacinski's brother, against terrible internal conflict, to discover and even turn in his brother to authorities, for the greater good of the world.

§

Had fully dedicated Para-Investigators been put on the Unabomber case utilizing their own techniques, his terror could have been stopped long before it was. The best we can do against people like this is to arm investigators with the tools of the unseen as well as the machinery of the known world. All the rational science based investigation and law-enforcement resources in the world could not come close to finding the Unabomber for over two decades. If the Unabomber's brother had not finally turned Theodore Kaczynski in to authorities, it's likely that to this very day, the Unabomber would be sending out packages to the objects of his twisted hatreds.

31

PANTOMIME OF RATIONALITY

(This true case study of a murder investigation is commonly taught at police academies but is actually a study in Para-Investigation.)

Murderers kill from base motivations: greed, hatred, resentment, anger, pride and envy. They can kill as a result of decisions arrived at on a whim: during robberies, sexual assaults or any crimes during which they decide they can afford no witnesses. Murderers of this low-grade stock may still have some vestige of humanity left within them and ordinary human responses persist in their psyche. For this reason, it is often possible to get them to confess to their crimes. Often, their crimes were born of passion and once the passion is gone, there is guilt and despair—these are usually the normal condition of their minds that they mistakenly thought would be permanently eradicated by the ecstasy of the murder. That relief from their normal state of acute anxiety only lasts for minutes once the killing is past. Then the typical killer is back to his ordinary state of guilt and despair except is now more acute than ever before. The only option left to diminish this state of mind is more killing (usually not an option as the person is an opportunity killer and that opportunity is gone) or the other option is confession. As we see at the beginning of the Old Testament, killers can feel that it is God Himself that demands their confession.

Genesis 4:10

The Lord said, "WHAT HAVE YOU DONE? LISTEN! YOUR BROTHER'S BLOOD CRIES OUT TO ME FROM THE GROUND."

What if we could create a cadre of investigators as a massive deterrent force against ordinary killers before they strike? This deterrent force would prevent many homicides and in completed cases of homicide, they would reveal the hidden perpetrators of murders already done, thus avoiding later crimes from those unknown killers. Not only is this possible—it is possible to do right now. A cadre of Para-Investigators with the ability to pierce the veil of the great Cosmic Mind can find out the identity of any killer, victim and uncover any vile deed, no matter how hidden. Such teams can be assembled at this moment with the human resources available to us right now. If our society could prevent just a one murder under ordinary circumstances, it would mean *they could eventually all be stopped.*

A great writer named Phillip K. Dick, aka: Philip Kindred Dick (December 16, 1928 – March 2, 1982); had such a vision. Dick was a brilliant science fiction writer who said that he can only write about the world as it should be, not as it is, because the world as it is does not live up to his standards. His imagination and stories were transcendent in their foresight and originality. Many poets and novelists, like Dick, claimed that they "received" their material rather than consciously constructed it. Many of Dick's stories have been adapted into some of our most stunning and original films to date, including "Blade Runner," "Total Recall" and "Minority Report." Dick had an uncanny ability to draw upon the great Superconsciousness and receive creative ideas and visions of the future that were both shocking yet wholly believable. The adjective most often used to describe Dick is *visionary.* He was far ahead of his time in his thinking and in his imaginings. Yet the time has come, many years after Dick's death; that we as a society can no longer afford to forego being visionary. We must all imagine that which we previously thought inconceivable—*that we can create investigators who can deter crime.*

Now here is the great news—they already exist. As we have already seen in the Para-Investigative files, they are already preventing terrorism, felonies and murders. They are already stopping crimes and tragedies while still only in thought-form (like the Pre-Crime Investigators of Phillip Dick). They just can't reveal exactly what they are doing or how they do it—*yet.*

Over the years, I have received many accounts of psychically gifted investigators who have used their abilities to save lives. One such gifted investigator was faced with an unsolved disappeared teenage girl who he "felt" was murdered by her stepfather who had a history of conflict and battles with his step-daughter—but the suspect had no criminal record, an alibi during the murder of the step-daughter and no suspicious behavior. The investigator interrogated the man extensively utilizing Para-Investigative Assessment. Over the course of this examination, the Superconscious Abyss revealed to this investigator that this man had indeed killed the young stepdaughter. Unfortunately, the rational evidence did not assist in arriving at this investigative conclusion.

The physical facts revealed to the investigator were of almost no help in determining guilt or innocence except for the following revelations:

INVESTIGATOR NOTES:

- the suspect was physically attracted to his daughter-in-law, but also thought she was lazy, spoiled, and promiscuous.
- suspect had been at the home the day of the disappearance to mow the lawn (corroborated by other witnesses)
- suspect's wife had warned him not to disturb the daughter while mowing the lawn, as she was sleeping (corroborated)
- suspect claimed to only having entered the garage to retrieve a tool (corroborated)
- suspect had returned to the home the day after the girl's disappearance to clean carpets, as they were dirty from dog urine and hair (corroborated)
- suspect had no overtly suspicious responses, behavior or defensiveness.

There were reasonable explanations, backed up by witnesses and physical clues, for every action that brought the suspect anywhere near where the young girl slept. There was not a single iota of physical evidence to tie the suspect to her disappearance and suspect had no criminal prior history or record. The suspect immediately volunteered for the polygraph. Both the suspect and his wife had provided the above alibi for the suspect that placed the suspect outside the home at the time she was home. The polygraph was predictably non-conclusive and the suspect did not appear the least bit perturbed. There was no physical evidence of struggle in the home.

Para-Investigative Assessment was successful in revealing that this suspect was in constant psychological conflict with his stepdaughter. Now this investigator shifted into Para-Investigative Connection and Empathy. He connected to the suspect's feelings in this situation and then "put himself directly into the soul" of the suspect.

"You were just trying to enforce some discipline weren't you?
She tried to use her sexual power to tempt you too, didn't she?"

This would allow the subject to vent his feelings about the many boys the victim kept company with and therefore minimize his own role in assaulting and killing her.

"What else could you do? You were forced into it by the mother who saw what was happening and didn't do anything to help you control her.

You were practically forced to kill her."

The suspect volunteered some very revealing information about his rocky relationship with the deceased but then just stopped himself. He refused to answer any further now that the interview had fully shifted into interrogation. The suspect got up and said, *"I'm going to leave now… I need to go talk to her mother…I need to find her. Then, I'll come back and tell you what I know."*

The gifted investigator described massive unfoldment from the Superconscious Gulf: the Investigator stated he had "a gut feeling" that allowing the suspect to leave could lead to another murder. "Gut feeling" is traditionally in law-enforcement one of the few permissible terms that investigators can openly use when referring to Para-Investigative abilities.

His strategy shifted with the urgency of the suspect's responses:
"Why do you want to talk to her? What do you want to tell her?

He told me that he needed to tell her what happened. I told him not to tell me what happened, but practice telling the mother. I switched the interview to the third person. He confessed to the murder in the third person. I asked him to put it in writing."

This prevented the suspect from going to *"meet with his wife to explain to her the situation."*

A later search of the suspect's automobile revealed a shotgun and shells, purchased *the morning of the interrogation.* The missing female's body turned up several weeks later, near a river. In addition to the shotgun and shells, as well as the body, turning up later, the crime scene was again scrubbed with more intensive laboratory tools. These now revealed recent human bloodstains.

§

This bold investigator not only used his Para-Investigative abilities to unfold the abyss, but also was daring enough to put aside legalities and rational niceties in order to stop this perpetrator from committing more murders and mayhem. This Para-Investigator probably saved, not just the mother's life, but probably also saved the lives of several others who would have been lost in a renewed effort to bring this man to justice. The majority of investigators and analysts are brave beyond reason when it comes to facing criminals, terrorists and killers but are far more sheepish when it comes to defying their own procedural requirements. Most investigators would not be as bold as this man was—not without support from the society they have sworn to protect.

There have been times when the Abyss has clearly opened itself and transferred energy and data to an investigator so clearly that the transfer may be obvious even to civilian observers. However, when the accomplishment of the investigator is so great and the number of lives they save is very substantial; then society may turn a blind eye to the supernatural skills at play. So long as some effort is made to put forward some bare bones of rational explanation, this will be enough to satisfy the pantomime of rationality required by societal standards.

32

TENTACLE OF LIGHT

(The following publicly-known encounter details a well known terrorist incident and reveals a great deal about the mechanics of Para-Investigation)

The subject known as Timothy McVeigh was definitely a person with murder in his intentions but the full possible extent of his accomplishments as a one-man terrorist wave has always been a point of contention. What is *not* in contention are the skills of the Para-Investigator who caught him against long odds. The capture of the bomber of the Oklahoma Alfred P. Murrah Federal Building was adequately covered by rational terminology so as not to raise suspicion that the investigator was getting data from a forbidden place like the Superconscious Gulf.

Among the permissible terms which cause little stigma are:

"I had a feeling there was something bizarre about this guy."

"My gut just told me that this guy was involved in something real serious."

"My sense just told me that I should not walk up to that car like normal procedure."

These are the acceptable phrases when investigators are referring to their own paranormal abilities.

On Wednesday morning, April 19, 1995, at approximately 9:00 a.m., Central Time, a huge explosion destroyed a Federal Building in downtown Oklahoma City. In the minutes that followed, the world realized that the worst terrorist strike against a single civilian target in history had just occurred causing the deaths of hundreds of innocent civilians.

What followed became one of the greatest manhunts, in American history. Resources dedicated to this effort were massive but utterly useless because all the leads followed were based on an incorrect scenario. The original reports from witnesses described two "middle eastern males" in blue jumpsuits or jogging suits spotted running from the immediate area of the Murrah building. The mainstream media promoted this scenario and numerous international law enforcement agencies rapidly becoming involved, working feverishly to track suspects under this mistaken scenario. A middle-eastern male was apprehended in London at Heathrow Airport, allegedly with explosive materials in his luggage. He had left the U.S. earlier that day and came under immediate scrutiny due to his description, age, timing and profile. The self-reproducing hysteria created dozens of false leads, which reinforced the mistaken scenario. The "middle-eastern males in blue jumpsuits" scenario was pervasive and went global in the minutes and hours following the destruction of the Murrah Federal building.

Again, a brave state trooper was Para-Investigator for the day. As plausible rumors were flying and regenerating themselves about Middle-Easterners bombing the Federal building, this trooper executed a routine traffic stop of an individual for driving without a proper tag on his license plate about two hours after the deadly bombing. The trooper broke from normal procedure. He did not walk up on the driver's side of the vehicle. The trooper decided on this occasion to stay at his vehicle and used the intercom to blast out orders and instructions to the driver. He instructed him to take the keys out of the vehicle, throw them out and exit the vehicle.

This is the procedure for a violent felony car stop, not for a routine traffic violation. This type of procedure should only be appropriate when a law-enforcement person already is aware that a violent crime was committed by this person; and is *almost impossible* to justify for an improper car tag. Yet, not only did this trooper follow an extreme procedure to preserve his own safety; but once he had him out the car, the trooper could clearly see that the subject was not a Middle-Eastern male. To the contrary, he now saw that Timothy McVeigh appeared to be a sandy-haired, crew-cut wearing, all-American boy—more likely to be an off-duty U.S. Army Ranger rather than part of the "Middle-Eastern crew that bombed the federal building." Yet the Trooper, for some unseen reason, still stayed behind the door of his patrol car as if he expected a hail of bullets at any moment. The trooper's mental processes in that moment show that he was being fed information from a place wherein all knowledge resides.

The trooper covered McVeigh with his weapon as he barked orders out.

"I don't claim to be the best shot in the world, but from that distance I'm not going to miss."

Yet on a rational level, even when the gun in the waistband was revealed, the trooper still had no reason to believe that this subject was anything more than a U.S. army recruit driving through town. The Trooper later said, far from acting nervous or fidgety; the subject was emotionless, bloodless, calm and bland in his demeanor. This behavior and demeanor did not add up to probable cause to stop and detain.

The Trooper also related: *"You would think that someone that committed something that terrible you would see something in their emotions. He didn't have any emotions."*

That begs the question: then why did the Trooper treat the subject as a dangerous criminal ready to shoot the trooper?

1. McVeigh was not acting nervous

2. McVeigh only had an expired tag on his license plate

3. McVeigh did not fit any description of the rumored bombers of the Federal building.

4. He did not know that McVeigh was armed.

The answers to these questions cannot be found in the rational material world.

The Trooper had McVeigh get out of the Mercury Marquis and raise his hands far above his head.

"I really feel like that if I had walked up on that car that day that I would have been shot."

McVeigh later confessed he did consider having an "old-fashioned shootout there on the side of the road" when he was stopped. During the spin around the trooper noticed the bulge of a loaded handgun underneath McVeigh's jacket and arrested him for a suspected illegal firearm. Two days later, federal agents found McVeigh was still in the Noble County jail after identifying him as a suspect in the bombing. Ultimately, McVeigh was executed in 2001 for the vilest act of terrorism on American soil.

There is no limit to what can be accomplished by individuals who are utterly dedicated to their mission. They will sacrifice everything they are and anything they have in this temporary physical plane of existence for goals that speak to their eternal selves. The unlimited power that resides in what Emerson called the "Oversoul" or what Jung called the "Cosmic Mind" opens a portal and pumps torrents of spiritual power into individuals willing to open themselves to it. McVeigh had tapped into those enormous resources of power and energy to meet the horrible requirements needed to accomplish his massive act of terrorism but then, at a certain hour on April 19, his deed was done.

In order to accomplish the staggering level of success that he achieved in this historical act of terrorism, McVeigh was himself drawing upon the Superconscious Gulf for the extraordinary levels of energy, creativity, mental powers, and physical powers to accomplish his monumental task. For McVeigh to compose a single truck bomb containing at least 4,600 pounds of ANFO explosive mixture, to innovate the engineering needed to do the damage required to bring down that building is no less than miraculous. Also, for one or two individuals to mix so many barrels of ammonium nitrate by hand at some obscure park in a major population center without being detected is hard to conceive. Adding that it was all accomplished within a short time frame, the totality of the deed is almost beyond what can be done in the rational world. Only a monumental effort of the spirit and super-human determination could have accomplished what McVeigh did. Evil men and good men live by many of same rules of the universe.

Finally, McVeigh, infused and animated with power from the Superconscious Gulf for so long, at last, finished his mission. His wormhole to that enormous gulf was closed. The tentacle of cold energy had withdrawn from him. He was driving away feeling listless and uninspired probably for the first time in many months. All the inspiration, power, and creativity of the Superconscious Gulf had left him just a shell trying to figure out what he had lost and why he felt so deflated.

Here's where it gets weird.

When McVeigh's window to the Oversoul closed, the great Universal Consciousness saw the Trooper as it was withdrawing from McVeigh. It decided to render a few final moments of inspiration and insight to this astute trooper. Like a plasma funnel, the great energy transferred from the "Para-Terrorist" to the "Para-Investigator." Like a fever breaking, McVeigh went suddenly cold but the inspirational fever, that tentacle of cold light, found a new host. Because of that switch over, instead of a dead trooper on the road riddled with bullets and a desperate armed fugitive on the run, a very different result came about. That "plasma funnel" of energy and inspiration doesn't really care where it goes—it just wants a vessel for its terrible power. So must all Para-Investigators remain ready at all times to receive the unlimited power that resides in that tentacle of cold light. In this way, many will be preserved alive and well who otherwise might fall victim to tragedy and death.

33

HARD TO KILL

(Here is an experience related to me during my time in government service.)

I spent several years consulting with the United States Federal prison system (the largest most pervasive prison system on the planet.) These were the most fascinating years of my government service—because of the work I did helping officers and prisoners who needed my assistance so very much and also because there are unique stories in such places that cannot be found anywhere else on Earth.

The necessary preamble to understanding the gravity of a "prison inmate killing" is this:
It is extraordinarily difficult to kill prisoners.

The old saying is *"prisoners are as hard to kill as rats."* It's fairly a simple matter to hurt, maim, scar or even permanently injure prisoners but they have the devil's own luck in almost always managing, often miraculously, to stay alive—sometimes through horrific wounds that usually kill ordinary civilians just from fright, adrenalin rush and blood loss. The reason for this extraordinary survivability is quite clear. The conscious/spiritual energy, which animates prisoner bodies and minds, is always at a very high level relative to docile, free range civilians, who tend to sleep walk, at low energy levels, through much of their humdrum lives. Prisoners are always in survival mode. Unlike civilians on the outside, prisoners bodies and minds are in a constant state of readiness to rise to the challenge of defense, flight and survival.

I have seen prisoners receive: deep multiple chest stabbings, stabbings to the head—I've even seen their skulls hacked open, seen them lose kidneys and other internal organs and still get up and limp away. Most of these prisoners walk into the prison medical facilities under their own power while trailing pints of blood and then will even claim to medical personnel that *they have no injuries or they just suffered an accident.* Any other response would create an obligation on them to "rat" against the aggressors who harmed them and no one wants to be a "rat."

Prisoners almost always survive. If you have any doubt of the truth of this, simply peruse any available statistics from the U.S. Bureau of Prisons on serious inmate assaults, survey all the stabbings, slashing and how many "mortal" wounds occur during these assaults and then compare to the disproportionately miniscule number of actual prisoner deaths. The disparity is shocking. Prisoners harness an incredible amount of spiritual and conscious power that they put to no greater use than simple animal survival. All that being said, here is a story of a prisoner who *did not* survive and the Para-Investigator who tried to save him.

An executive in the United States Federal Bureau of Prisons shared with me the details of a notorious prison slaying that had occurred when he was a young Lieutenant Officer in the prison system. As a Lieutenant, he was on good terms with a bright young inmate named Edwin. Edwin only had one year left on his sentence for armed bank robbery. In prison life that is considered "almost out the door." Edwin saved his money from his prison job, kept out of trouble and provided information to prison authorities on inmates who were planning to cause trouble. His dream was someday to become an RN, a Registered Nurse.

Edwin then came into "friction" with another member of his own gang over an issue of disrespect. The other gang member had taken some of his personal photos of Edwin's girlfriend, used them to masturbate, and then told Edwin what he did *in front of other inmates*. The masturbator had meant the sexual act as a grotesque compliment to Edwin on how beautiful his girlfriend was in her lingerie pictures. Edwin took it as the worst possible affront.

The Lieutenant had found out about the conflict and spoke to Edwin about it. He had previously helped Edwin on several issues, including getting him to teach a class at the prison on the medical field for inmates. The Lieutenant got the masturbator to apologize to Edwin in front of the Shot-Caller (Leader of that section of the prison where both men lived). The men shook hands and the matter was put to rest. The Masturbator, who by all agreements had some mental issues, gave Edwin a picture of himself as a bizarre gesture of contrition.

"Here dude, do whatever you want with it so I can feel that we're even." Edwin took the picture and laughed that he would roll it as a joint for later. The Shot-Caller pronounced the issue resolved. The Lieutenant breathed easier.

They squashed the drama.

Edwin was one of the few inmates the Lieutenant knew would not throw his life away over fake issues of "respect." It was the end of the week and the Lieutenant had worked a Friday double-shift. He was exhausted but satisfied. At his apartment, he removed all his gear. In one of his pockets, he found he still had a confidential envelope from the prison Chaplin. He dreaded getting another envelope from the Chaplin. The Chaplin was a "yellow-jacket," a prison official who so nervous being around prisoners that he should be working anywhere except in a prison. He had received ten such envelopes from the Chaplin about suspicious behavior in just six months. They ranged from complaints about "obvious Islamic" inmates showing up for Christian services to prisoners who pretended to close their eyes during silent prayers but instead were "furtively staring at the Chaplin." He opened the envelope.

Lieutenant,
just wanted you to see this and pass it back to inmate Edwin. Strange that he left it behind but stranger was that it was in his hand during silent prayer time.

It was the picture Edwin had been given by Masturbator. Masturbator was in the yard standing alone against the handball court wall, smiling with his arms crossed. Edwin had taken a red pen, poked out the eyeballs in the picture, and drawn in thick, red, splashy crosses over the eyes of the masturbator. He did the same with even greater emphasis where the heart would have been. Something screeched inside the Lieutenant's chest, like a bird whose beak had been held closed but now burst free.

The Lieutenant threw his gear back on. He stuffed the picture in his shirt pocket as he ran. Driving back, he broke every speed limit and nearly crashed the gate. When he arrived back at the prison blocks, Edwin's cell was empty. He rushed over to the Masturbator's cell and found both men in there. On the floor of the cell was the cold, dead body of the Masturbator with nearly a hundred puncture wounds. A smiling Edwin stood over the body. The weapon Edwin had used was a modified and reinforced seven-inch long ice pick. The ice pick was still jutting from the back of the victim's head at the base of the brain where numerous persistent chops had severed the spinal cord from the base of the brain and released torrents of blood and fluids. He pulverized the liver, the back of the brain and the heart—especially the heart. The dialogue was as follows.

Recollected transcript:

Lieutenant: You were the last inmate I ever thought could throw his life away like this.
Edwin: I knew you would be disappointed Lieutenant but I gotta do what I gotta do. It's ok man. I'm ok with it. Cheer up Lieutenant. At least I did something good for the world.

(The Lieutenant called on his radio for lock-down of the prison, medical emergency response to the cell and he cuffed up the inmate.)

Lieutenant: Alright man, if you believe it was worth it then I guess it is. It looks like you were chipping away with that ice pick at about four points on the body. You really wanted to be sure there was no coming back from this.

Edwin: Yeah Lieutenant, I had to make sure it was done right so I targeted the most vital organs and I worked 'em to make sure it was *lights out forever.*

Lieutenant: So you don't care that he had a mom, that he was somebody's old man, he was a father to a couple of kids?

Edwin: (Laughing hard) You don't get it man! He was a piece of rotten meat— *nothing more.* That piece of crap was a *curse* on his mom, he was *shame* to his wife, and he was a *living, breathing plague* on his kids. They'll all find someone better than him by just opening their front door and spitting into a crowd. Anyone the spit lands on will be a hundred times better than this filth here. All I did was put a stop to this sub-human garbage breathing real people's air. (Edwin, hands cuffed behind his back, tossed his head sideways and spit on the corpse).

Lieutenant: So you don't feel that dude was even a human being like you.

Edwin: Not like me. Not even close. That guy is just trash people forgot to take out, so I had to do it. That's all I did here. I took out the trash.

(End of Recollected Transcript)

The Edwin that the Lieutenant had known previously, that was studying to be a nurse someday on the outside, that had a bright future on the outside, that was nearly out the door, that was mortified over past mistakes, that was anxious to rectify wrongs from the past, that was intent on making it up to his family; *was gone.* A calculating killer replaced him. The Lieutenant was sad for the young man and his newfound identity that would have to serve him well for the rest of his life inside. Edwin made his decision and would have to live with it forever.

§

No investigation can be complete without an inquiry into intuitive realities that shout to us whenever any investigative matter is scrutinized. The material based world and our sensory perceptions represent about .01 percent of the knowledge available to us as transcendent spiritual beings. Why do we deprive ourselves of access to 99.9 percent of what we can know about any particular subject? The only possible answer is *fear.* We, at some level, believe that our rational material based inquiry will somehow be invalidated by further inquiry into the metaphysical aspect of any problem. It's not true.

Para-vetting of evidence means intuitive examination of each physical piece of evidence or data. Whether we are talking about the remnant of an explosive device from the Unabomber or just a personal picture that was in the hands of an inmate prisoner, we must not reflexively toss these things in the mail for the laboratory without really looking at them first—not with physical eyes but with our mind's eye. Intuitive vetting of evidence is the intention to go beneath the surface facts and data and into hidden truth in a place that we must close our physical eyes to see.

34

DEBUNKER'S PARADOX

Debunking is a lie.

No one can prove a negative. This is one of the first universal principles taught in the study of logic and in first year study of any decent university or law school. Yet, that is essentially what debunkers purport to do. In truth and logic, anyone with intention can only prove positive propositions—that something *does* exist. Although, debunkers can prove that an active fraud is being perpetrated on an unsuspecting public in one single instance, they can never disprove *an entire class of phenomena*.

Debunkers have always tried to eliminate belief in an entire class of phenomena but instead succeed in chasing out the fraud artists and making it more likely those still remaining in the class are actually *genuine and supernatural*. That is the *Debunker's Paradox*: *That which debunkers are so eager to destroy: faith in supernatural realities—they only make stronger by their continual efforts to destroy that belief.*

So many self-proclaimed professional skeptics have spent many years exposing fake mediums—yet "amazingly" they have only made it more likely that those who remained in the "contacting the dead" business were the genuine ones. Also, debunking does not address the crucial center of every elusive mystery: what if that elusive mystery does not permanently exist in the physical world we know but just phases into our vibrational reality and phases back out to other plains of existence as it wills—paranormal UFO's, ghosts/spirits or channeling of elder warriors/spirits. How is it possible to debunk/disprove the existence with a purely physical examination, something that *mostly* exists on a different plane of reality?

The prohibition against debunking is the first principle that Para-Investigators must know before they alternate between criminal hunting and mystery revelation. Para-Investigators exist to find the truth whatever it might be—not to disprove anything or to show people what isn't true. No Para-Investigator executes his/her craft in order to debunk, criticize, ridicule or prove anyone wrong in the things they believe. No one has the ability to expurgate matters of faith and for every elusive mystery that has existed for longer than a decade; there are reasonable, sensible, sentient human beings with a very real faith in the existence of that mystery.

There have been innumerable members of the rationalist/scientific class who have "debunked" every elusive mystery from paranormal UFO's to ghost/spirits yet it is very apparent that *none of it has permanently taken.*

Paranormal topics, even thoroughly "debunked" ones, continue to expand in popularity among the most vibrant thinkers of our age. Cynics may prove a single or several incidents of that particular genre to be frauds but that has no correlation to the ten thousand other incidents of that same elusive mystery that continue to grow. Debunking elusive mysteries may be comforting to those hardcore rationalists bent on proving to each other that anything they can't feel, see, hear, touch or taste; can't possibly exist; but it does nothing to resolve the existence of the mystery. It is just cynics giving comfort to other cynics. Debunking elusive mysteries is an outdated practice in The Age of Mass Awakening. It stems from a paternalistic/ materialist worldview that is coming to an inevitable conclusion.

Scientists keep trying to find ways to preserve their purely material interpretation of the universe when their worldview has been exposed as mythos over the last century. Yet, Para-Investigation will be the synthesis of Advanced Quantum thought and Para-Investigative intuitive methods that will carry us into what is next. This will be an irresistible force for finding truth down to the root. Inquisitiveness, intelligence and the ability to connect to other human beings are the basic rational qualities that form the concrete foundation for any True Investigator. All investigators and even all human beings tend to have these abilities.

Para-Investigative Assessment (feeling and taking account of the problem from the inside out). This is approaching an investigation as a receiver of revelation from the great unknown rather than as merely a receptor of readily apparent details from the material world (a mere fact-finder).

Para-Investigative Connection and Empathy (being able to connect with on a spiritual level and then even become one with the subject of the investigation) is a process that will always succeed in bringing the Investigator closer to the truth because they *become a part of that truth.* When the Para-Investigator connects with and becomes the subject at the intuitive level, then they will know *what the subject knows.* In criminal cases, we are only trying to determine *who* did it. In paranormal mystery cases, we are always trying to determine if *it* exists at all and if this thing really does exist then: *what is it?*

The old axiom is true: *if you believe, no evidence is necessary and if you do not believe; no amount of evidence will ever suffice.* Humanity was created with a hardwired need for spirituality and supernatural belief systems. Because this need is part of our brain's hardware, it cannot be denied for long. This will express itself in spiritual terms or in any variety of ancient faiths or new mystical beliefs—but no matter what—it *will* be expressed in every single member of the human race. Even Atheists worship something. Sufficient investigation will always reveal it.

35

BLACK PARADE OF INNOCENCE

(In the late 1980's in New York state, I resided in Schenectady, New York; where the most gruesome trial of the century unfolded.)

The law school I attended was just a few miles away from Schenectady, New York, where a housewife and mother named Mary Beth Tinning was victimized by a mysterious death-plague that was visiting each of her children. Tinning often came running into one of the city's emergency rooms with one of her babies cradled in her arms. The medical staffs of Schenectady's hospitals knew Tinning well. From the year 1972 through 1985, all nine of Marybeth Tinning's children died suddenly and without reasonable explanation.

People reading the account for the first time of Mary Beth Tinning, the mother of these nine deceased children, often respond: *"this is obviously foul play."* The problem is that Tinning had massive, overwhelming and highly placed support throughout the medical community for her claims that these children's deaths were by "natural causes."

Here are the facts as they occurred according to neighbors and friends who were present. On a winter day in 1972, Tinning took Joseph Jr., age two, to the Hospital emergency room in Schenectady. He had some type of seizure. Doctors could not find anything wrong with him and so the child was sent home. Several hours later, Tinning returned with the dead toddler. The little boy's death was listed as "unknown."

Six weeks later, Marybeth was back at the same hospital with her daughter, Barbara, age four. There had been seizures. Tinning insisted on taking her home despite doctor recommendations for overnight observation. Several hours later, she returned with the little girl who was unconscious. The child later died in a hospital bed from unknown causes. Shortly, thereafter, a third young child died under the same circumstances. There were three dead children in about three months from the same family.

The working hospital that dealt with Tinning did everything they could to save the children but they were bewildered and frustrated. However, the medical community outside that hospital had a very different response. In a "eureka" moment of seeing their names splashed across medical headlines, several prominent physicians seized the opportunity to promote innovative theories for the deaths of the Tinning children. One such theory was a dramatic expansion of the parameters of Sudden Infant Death Syndrome (SIDS). The problem with this theory was that up to the time of their demise, each of the Tinning children had been quite healthy. Another group of physicians believed the only possible solution to this enigmatic mystery had to be a genetic disorder that passed from mother to all the children. Many physicians were certain that was it. They had hit upon the solution—the genetic disorder theory.

Tinning became pregnant with her fourth child, Timothy; a small baby weighing just five pounds. Just three weeks after birth, Timothy was brought back to the same hospital. He was dead. Marybeth told doctors she found him lifeless in his crib. The baby had been normal and active yet his death was listed officially as SIDS.

Two years later, in March 1975, Marybeth gave birth to her fifth child, Nathan. This beautiful baby was blonde and had blue eyes. In September, Marybeth showed up at St. Clare's Hospital with little Nathan, only five months old, in her arms. Again, he was dead. She said she was driving in her car with the baby in the front seat when she noticed that he had stopped breathing. The genetic disorder theory pulled ahead at this time since no possibility for SIDS could have existed in this last death.

In 1978, Marybeth and her husband, Joe, made arrangements to adopt a child. That same year, Marybeth became pregnant again. In August 1978, they received a baby boy, Michael, from the adoption agency. Two months later, in October, Marybeth Tinning gave birth to her sixth baby, a girl they named Mary Frances. In January 1979, the girl-baby developed some type of seizure, according to Marybeth. She rushed Mary Frances to a hospital emergency room, which was directly across the street from her apartment. A highly capable staff was able to revive her. They saved the baby's life, *but only for a time.* In February, Marybeth came running into the same hospital with Mary Frances cradled in her arms. The baby, just four months old, was dead. Tinning said she found the baby unconscious. The death was attributed to SIDS.

Tinning got pregnant again right away. She gave birth to her seventh baby, Jonathan. The Tinnings also cared for their adopted child, Michael, who was then 13 months old and in good health. In March 1980, Marybeth showed up at the same hospital with Jonathan unconscious. He was revived. This time, the child went to a major Hospital in Boston where he was thoroughly examined by the best pediatricians and experts available. Unfortunately, once the batteries of tests were exhausted the doctors could keep him no longer. *Jonathan was sent home with his mother.* A few days later, Marybeth was back at the hospital with a brain dead Jonathan. He died in March 1980.

Less than one year later in March 1981, Marybeth showed up at her pediatrician's office with Michael, then two and a half years old. He was wrapped in a blanket and unconscious. Marybeth told the doctor that she could not wake Michael. When the doctor examined the boy, he found that he was dead. An autopsy found traces of pneumonia but not enough to cause death. SIDS was ruled out since children three years old are not susceptible to SIDS. Also, since *Michael was adopted*, the long-promoted theory of genetic disorder was now eliminated. The two main theories of causation had been erased and still the black parade of innocent children marched on.

After so many deaths, some in local law-enforcement began daring to ask an unspeakable question: Could there be a monster targeting the Tinning children? Still, it was politically impermissible to ask such a question without proof. However, after the adopted child died, it was noticed that when she first realized that the child was sick that morning, Tinning could have walked across the street to the emergency room to obtain medical care. In fact, she had done that when the others had died. Instead, she let hours pass until the doctor's office opened for business. The business of murdering her own children had lapsed into routine for her. Tinning was starting to lack even the motivational energy for covering her tracks on the simplest things.

Local police investigators, who had long harbored suspicions, now had at least enough probable cause to begin preliminary inquiries into those around the Tinning family. Investigators were scrutinizing anyone who had access to the Tinning family on a regular basis. Anyone who had easy access to the children was a suspect in these possible murders. *Even at this point*, it was still inconceivable that this victimized, grieving, miserable mother, who had lost so much, could be involved with the monster targeting the Tinning children.

In August 1985, Tinning gave birth to her eighth child, Tami Lynne. Little Tami Lynne was lying on a changing table when Tinning called an ambulance. The child had no pulse and was not breathing. The ambulance team took the little girl Tami Lynne to the hospital. Tinning claimed the child was tangled in the blanket. At the emergency room, the baby was pronounced dead. All the previous hospital personnel support for Tinning's tales of plausible tragedy had been finally withdrawn. Later, after Tami Lynne's funeral, Marybeth had people over her house for a brunch. Witnesses reported she was smiling and conversing cheerfully.

This was the turning point.

Para-Investigators at the local police department were finally allowed to jump into the gap to put a halt to the black parade of Mary Beth Tinning. She was brought in for questioning. Long restrained officers at the Schenectady Police Department pounded away at Tinning's faltering deceptions. The interviews continued for hours. Determined investigators touched upon the deaths of all the children during the previous 14 years. After so many years of being unchallenged in her dark deeds, Mary Beth Tinning had fallen into the hands of True Investigators who *knew what she did* and would not stop until they uncovered it. They even reached out for a state police investigator, who was an old acquaintance of Tinning since childhood. He assisted local police with the interview. Every little bit helped. Although Tinning still protested her innocence, cracks were beginning to show in her defenses. Finally, at the culmination of more hours of persistent questioning, Mary Beth gave in. She admitted that she had killed three of the children.

"...just these three, Timothy, Nathan and Tami. I smothered them each with a pillow because I'm not a good mother."

Yet, amazingly the physicians and psychologists, who had been on the other side protecting Tinning *didn't give up on defending her.* At the murder trial, the medical scientific community took "one last stab" at continuing their previous coverage for Tinning. A pathologist claimed that the affliction that killed all nine children was an unknown new syndrome or disease. Another physician said the only way to figure out what this new syndrome really was would be to *release Mary Beth Tinning and to allow her to have more children as a medical experiment.* This would be laughable if it was written as fiction but it really happened.

Despite all this, Mary Beth Tinning was found guilty for the murder of just one of her children. It was for the murder in which the police had the most evidence. Tinning was sentenced to 20 years to life. Marybeth Tinning is housed at the Bedford Hills Prison for Women in New York. Tinning is up for parole every few years but it is unlikely she will ever see the outside of a prison again.

The mystery became a crime and the crime became justice thanks to Para-Investigators who never gave up faith in their own intuitive certainty—despite all the rational, scientific, psychiatric opposition right down to the very last moment of the sentencing.

Yet there was one parting gift from the serial-killer for the scientific/medical community that had enabled her crimes for so long. The scientific/psychiatric community salvaged one small scrap for themselves even while losing the Tinning trial—they were able to acquire Tinning as a poster child to promote a rare and mysterious psychological condition called "Munchausen Syndrome by Proxy (MSP)." The name is almost as complex as the tortured logic of the newly minted "psychological affliction." In this condition, the mother of helpless babies or very young children is uncontrollably driven to physically abuse her own children while feeding off the adulation and sympathy they receive from the community who are showering the mother/victim with love, sympathy and care. Tinning, to this day, is recorded in scientific and medical journals as a "victim" of MSP. Many pseudo-maternal evildoers who hurt and maim their own children continue to enjoy refuge in this "psychological condition" which insulates them from real criminal intention. *"They're not evil. They're just sick."*

The outdated scientific model cannot admit the existence of conscious, willful evil. That acceptance would force them to consider that there are causes for good and evil that they cannot process as psychological and medical conditions. Psychologists cannot counsel dark spirits away. Surgeons cannot excise a depraved and malignant heart. Brain surgeons cannot remove the perverse thoughts that solidify into evil deeds. Physicians cannot prescribe arrays of drug treatment for malevolence. To this very day, Munchausen Syndrome by Proxy is used to give aid and comfort to maternal abusers of children. Para-Investigation will be one more force moving our community away from the old model in which matters of the spirit must be treated as non-existent or are covered over with heinous mythology like Munchausen Syndrome by Proxy (MSP).

Whether we confront elusive mysteries or brilliant criminals hiding behind the assumed identity of a grieving mother while planning the next murder of a child, it takes True Investigators with a ferocious need to pierce the veil of the unknown to follow the truth no matter where it leads. Then, it takes even greater strength to continue to pursue the awful truths they find in the Superconscious Gulf despite opposition from rationalists who often unite behind false conclusions. Sometimes, the greatest opposition to relentless Truth-Seekers can even be the people in law-enforcement. The first generation of *open* Para-Investigators will be people with that unconditional openness and mental resilience, like the Investigators who (against enormous scientific and medical resistance) followed their quest to ultimate resolution of the Tinning serial murders.

PARA-INVESTIGATORS
AND NON-HUMANS

You can lead a horse to water but you can't make him drink;
You can lead a man to knowledge but you can't make him think.

36

GIANTS VERSUS THE POLICE

(Police tend to be highly trained observers so this mass police sighting is especially significant.)

The Southern Illinois incident was on January 5, 2000, and it involved more police officers in a single continuous sighting of Paranormal UFOs *than any other known instance in this nation's history.* This is highly significant is because police officers are "trained observers" who have learned over long periods of arduous training and experience to record factual observations in high stress environments. All the police officers involved on the record in this incident during radio transmissions kept their reporting very factual but they were very candid regarding what they saw and experienced—a soundless, enormous, intelligently-piloted Black Triangle.

Here is the geographic trajectory over Southern Illinois territories and jurisdictions followed by the soundless, enormous gliding object.

Highland Police Department,
Lebanon Police Department,
Shiloh Police Department,
Scott United States Air Force Base (The Base was closed at the time and any involvement or knowledge of this incident is denied by the U.S. Air Force),
Millstadt Police Department
The Regional 911 Center at Belleville (received the most calls routed to them concerning the appearance and travel of the object)
Dupo Police Department
East Saint Louis

If you juxtapose these towns/police jurisdictions onto a map of Southern Illinois, you will see the southwestern arc pattern of travel that the Giant Black Triangle followed. Shortly after the object entered the airspace over East Saint Louis, it disappeared. Here are just a few of the officers' publicly recorded first impressions concerning the giant black triangle floating soundlessly over their towns.

Officer 1 "Dispatcher, did they say if the truck-driver was DUI or anything?" (Referring to the witness possibly being under the influence of alcohol).

Officer 2 "Dispatch, I'll go over and see if it's an aircraft. It doesn't look like an airplane though. It definitely isn't the moon or a star."

Officer 3 "Dispatch, I see something but I don't know what the heck it is."

Officer 4 "Dispatch, this thing was about 500 feet above me and it was huge."

Here are some details the police observers agreed upon concerning the single gigantic triangular object involved in this mass sighting. It was definitely not an airplane or any known airship because it was missing navigation lights, stabilizers or any conventional air vehicle equipment. The majority of its lights were in its rear rather than towards its front to light the direction it was heading in. *It was enormous.* It was a floating triangular wedge with rounded corners that was at least two stories tall. Observed from the rear of the craft, there was an enormous white-glowing light-bar across the back where the propulsion jet engine would have been on an earthly vehicle. Alternatively, that light-bar strobed various rainbow colors and finally, it became all white light. Overall, the craft's lights were shifting and constantly changing in color and shape. It floated low over the ground, anywhere around 500 to 1,000 feet above ground level. It was as large as a football field from wingtip to wingtip—about 100 yards but it might have been larger than that. It could change course suddenly. It could slow down or speed up to incredible speeds. Yet a constant signature seemed to be that whenever people looked directly up into the base of the vehicle, it had several white lights spread out close to the three corners *and one red light directly in the center.*

Originally, five police officers from four separate departments stepped forward openly as witnesses who documented their own sightings in written reports or recorded conversations. That number unofficially later grew to at least eight police officers and more dozens of civilian witnesses on the ground who also documented their sightings of the same gigantic black triangle. This incident is very well documented and it qualifies on all counts as a genuine supernatural, non-terrestrial craft incident—Paranormal UFO.

The heavily touted rational/material theory that "this was a special military sponsored experimental craft being tested" has now expired. Although the Air Force base that created the Stealth Bomber and other experimental aircraft is near the area of this sighting, there is a ten-year window within which experimental aircraft are revealed through the military for widespread use. That expiration date passed years ago and no information has appeared on any vehicle such as this.

Indeed, only anti-gravity tech could explain such an immense vehicle being able to move without sound or conventional thrust. No national government may possess that kind of tech because it would make them too powerful and a threat even to the global system of control which all the nations serve.

Here is a typical comment from one of those same police officers made after the experience with the giant black triangle was over.

"Whenever I'm out on patrol in that area, I always wonder if I'll ever see it again or the different possibilities are in my head."

That is as much as these officers can speculate because they are still "on the job." The officers involved here are currently on duty and have openly identified themselves so they cannot really speculate on the paranormal aspect of this sighting but we know everything they observed was recorded in a methodical and precise manner. How do we know these officers were outstanding observers of detail under stress? Because what they saw, almost to the smallest detail, was also seen by numerous civilians on the ground who also reported these sighting to their respective police departments even as the police were deployed and chasing the phenomena from town to town. Yet even before this appearance of the giant black triangle in these small American towns in Illinois, the same phenomena had been previously viewed throughout the United States and all over the world.

From 1989 to 1991 in the nation of Belgium, thousands saw and reported the same vehicle, gigantic black triangles with the same pattern of lights as the one in Southern Illinois, on a regular basis in the night skies. In 1997, hundreds of Phoenix, Arizona residents saw and reported the same craft floating soundlessly over the city of Phoenix. There were so many witnesses, so many video recordings and so much belief that many concluded "the final triggering event" for open continuous contact with Alien Visitors had arrived. "The Phoenix Lights" incident became one of the most furious battles of establishment mainstream institutions against general awakening, involving cooperation among the corporate news media, the United States Air Force and even establishment politicians, all joining hands to ridicule, excoriate and deceive any Awakened Individuals who threatened to use this incident for mass awakening.

Additionally, there have been numerous more giant black triangle sightings in the United States since January 2000, when the Southern Illinois sightings occurred. All these sightings were of gigantic, black triangle/boomerang shaped, floating craft that traveled low and slow over populated areas as if *they wish to be seen.*

In all these sightings, these craft travel without sound or any sign of thrust or any conventional aircraft modalities. They can appear or disappear in an instant. The floating giants never show on radar and whenever people looked directly up into the base of the black triangular giant, it always has several white lights spread close to the corners *and one red light directly in the center.*

These officers, involved in the Southern Illinois incident, were extraordinarily accurate and they proved themselves True Investigators. Yet, they are no longer the same people they were before the "giant black triangle experience." They irrevocably changed as have numerous other officers and civilians throughout the nation and in many nations of the world who have experienced these giant triangles. Their minds have been forcibly opened to the unseen and mysterious reality—the Extra-Dimensional reality that exists just on the other side of the material veil; they can *never* be just conventional investigators again. They became Para-Investigators.

37

ELVES AND TROLLS

Often myths and legends matter more than rock-solid scientific data. This is because they reveal much more than the facts of our immediate physical universe. They expound on the deep psychological fears and hopes that all people have. They elaborate our deepest neurological responses and the causes behind those responses.

Para-Investigators will be open to anything. No matter how bizarre or far-fetched something might seem—an open mind, an open heart and a constant state of willingness to learn new aspects of reality are vital to every Para-Investigator. Human belief, no matter what it is, bleeds into human superconsciousness and that affects the physical matrix of reality. Pioneering students of the human psyche like Karl Jung and Joseph Campbell said that myths reveal more about the human experience and reality than do facts about people's lives, because myths reveal beliefs, not necessarily knowledge.

Para-Investigators will recognize this and once the physical world data is assimilated; they will insist on going further. They will be the first True Investigators to insist:

"Now, don't tell me anymore about the facts, tell me what you believe."

There are two races that live alongside human on the Earth and that appear quite similar to human beings physically but who, underneath the veneer of ordinary humanity, are as different as any creatures could be from homo-sapiens. Elves and Trolls are more similar to each other than to us. The common trait that makes them similar to each other is what makes them so different from humans. They derive a higher amount of spiritual energy and present consciousness from the Superconscious Gulf of the Cosmic Mind than ordinary humans do. They are like stronger funnels that pull more from the Source Matrix of Superconscious Power that swirls above us all.

Humans pull just enough spiritual power to animate what we are and what we need to do. Elves and Trolls pull more power from the Superconscious Gulf than they can possibly use for ordinary activities. They need outlets for their surplus spiritual power that must express itself outside their own physical bodies. Elves are the class of beings who are compelled to use that surplus energy to create. They build things—businesses, art, great ventures, inventions—things that serve the betterment and increase of humanity—things that benefit and empower humanity and will often persist beyond the creator's own lifetime. Trolls, in contrast, create mayhem, death and destruction, from the same overabundance of spiritual power and consciousness. Trolls are the malignant hunger for evil and human suffering, wrapped in human-appearing skin, which awaits the unwary under the bridge.

The man who taught me all this was a stone-cold serial killer.

38

"I AM NOT HUMAN"

(This is another of my experiences during my time as a consultant to the Federal Prison system. My position entailed the investigation, prosecution and deterrence of violence against officers and other inmates.)

Willy G. was in prison for life. He had a genius I.Q. and he enjoyed the game of taunting law-enforcement. As police from several states were closing in on him, Willy confessed to homicides that he knew involved Federal law. By submitting himself to Federal prison for homicides, Willy guaranteed that he would do his "easy time" before any states could ever get him. The Federal prison system would have Willy for two life-terms before he would ever answer for murders in the states. The reasons are technical and numerous but life in Federal prisons is much nicer and far preferable to State prisons. For inmates, it's like comparing the prospect of living in a one-bedroom, high-security apartment; to living in "Thunder-Dome" where you have to death-duel for your dinner every night. Neither option is good but given your druthers, you definitely want to get your chit in for the apartment.

We sat in a common interview room where Willy would grant me thirty minutes. Willy preambled that he was very happy to sit with me and that he requested that I forego use of the term *serial killer* because he considers it a silly, non-descriptive term. He prefers *Stone Cold Killer or just Stone Killer.* I agreed and he got ready to lay the *"real, real"* on me.

"So you have some unsolved homicides for me?" I began.
He smiled.
"My man, I can't tell you about something I've never done."
I was confused. "So you're saying you're innocent of killing those people you confessed for?"
"Naw, bro', I killed them—*but it wasn't murder.*" I shot him a quizzical look.
"How could that be?"
He leaned back in his chair as his shackles jingled.

"*Dig it. Under the system of laws that we all live under, murder means some form of criminal homicide. Even accidental, reckless manslaughter or criminally negligent homicide also qualifies as murder. A person commits criminal homicide if he intentionally, knowingly, recklessly or with criminal negligence causes the death of another person. Homicides that are not justifiable or excusable are considered crimes. But all these forms of homicide have one thing in common that is necessary for them to qualify as murder...*"

He waited, tapping the table.

"*O.K. Willy, what do they all have in common?*"

His chains jingled as his hands cut the air.

"*They must be the killing of a human being by another human being.*"
So what's the discrepancy? He leaned forward.

"*The problem is just this—I AM NOT HUMAN.*

Therefore, the people I have killed were a different species from me. Homicide is the killing...as you know—from the Latin Homo meaning "the same as" and cide meaning "to kill"...so linguistically it adds up the same way as the legal definition—it's the killing of someone who is human by another human."

I resisted allowing him to pull me into legal distractions.
"*Willy, if you aren't human, what are you?*"
Willy beamed.
"*I am a predator species of human beings...a hunter of humans...like the Trolls that wait underneath the bridges at night to trap humans who get drunk, lose their way and wander under the bridges at night. Even in fairytales Trolls look like humans but there's just something slightly off about them. Check my DNA chromosomes at the sub-molecular level and you'll see it has more traits in common with non-human DNA....like something the labs have never seen before. I promise you if you take my buccal sample and have a good lab examine it and compare it with a control group of normal human DNA buccals— you'll all be shocked. There will be unexplainable variations that cannot be present in True Humans. I know what I'm telling you is true and if you would listen to me; both you and the scientist who does the exam analysis would become world-famous. You guys would win the freakin' Nobel prize for discovering a new species.*"

He was selling hard and only stopped when he saw my hand up signaling him to stop.

"*Willy, I don't want the Nobel Prize. I just want you to look at this sheet of cold disappearances throughout your former geographical areas and tell me which ones you can help me with.*" Willy sneered at the sheet.

"*How do you think you are going to get me to confess to anything if you ain't even trying to hear what I'm about? You haven't even asked about the difference between Trolls like me and "mere killers."* Willy crossed his arms as best he could and snapped his head sideways looking at the wall.

"O.K. Willy, we are not *going to do sub-molecular examination of your buccal swabs but tell me why there is a difference between mere killers and Trolls like you?"* Willy brightened.

"Mere killers get most of their thrill from the terror of the victim and the whole physical aspect of the violence. They think everything is on the physical plane so they make it all about rape and torture. To them, everything is emotion and the physical—that's it. They wouldn't know about spiritual rewards or anything that happens in the non-physical world. Humans don't distinguish between just killers and Trolls. Do bunny rabbits care whether foxes or wolves tear them apart? But you have to care…you need to care about these differences."

I bit.

"Why? Why do I need to care about that Willy?"

He steepled together the fingers of both hands in a pose of pensive superiority.

"Because you are a hunter of the Trolls.

You can't tell me you haven't felt that let-down feeling when you think something is just a regular murder, some dirt bag, low functionary acting on the heat of passion or some physical need…booooring. But when you hit on something special, part of a pattern of killings, then the thrill hits you—that you are dealing with a Stone Killer—a Troll playing games with you, challenging you, daring you to try to find him. Trolls like me are working multi-level, sacred miracles of destruction and mayhem. We are the Demi-Urges of this universe. We do what we do for the quickening reward."

I wasn't following as well as I had hoped.

"What is a quickening reward?"

"The quickening is like charging a small soul tax for the killer as he releases the soul/ spirit of his victim out into the infinite field of consciousness. As the victim transitions over to the next plane of existence they pay out a small portion of their life force in gratitude or out of spiritual reflex (I don't know for sure why it happens). Whatever the reason, a tiny part of their life energy is paid back to the killer and enters his conscious field of spiritual energy. It's like….just imagine an orgasm that instead of happening in your genitals, happens in your heart and mind and for one moment it connects you to the life force of the entire universe, to the energy that moves the stars and planets around, that makes black holes swirl, that makes quasars explode and that connects to every living thing on our planet. It's better than any drug. That's why there's so many Stone Killers." He leaned forward.

"There's a lot more like me than people think. I know because I can feel them out there. That's part of my abilities that I took back from the field." He had me now.

"Where did you learn about this quickening?"

"It goes back to what the Greeks believed about paying the Ferryman who brings you across the river of death. Nothing is created or destroyed. Energy just finds a new home. You have to have the intention to receive the spiritual energy charge as their spirit goes to the next plane. I don't know why it happens. I only know it does."

"So, Willy are you saying that passion killers are not *eligible* to receive this spiritual payment reward?"

"Naw man, it's got nothing to do with eligibility. It's all about clarity and intention to receive what the universe offers. See, people who kill just one time out of jealousy or anger are people with clouded confused minds from the get-go. Their minds just bob up and down like a cork on the ocean taking whatever life offers them without any real direction or purpose of their own. They kill for stupid stuff...jealousy, money, rage. Stone-Killers have clear calculating minds. They know exactly what they are doing and they do it for eternal rewards."

I decided to throw Willy a curve.

"Willy, why would God allow a system like this quickening spiritual energy tax paid out to killers to exist when it will only encourage more killing of innocent victims?"

He didn't miss a beat.

"God didn't make this system to benefit killers. *He made it to benefit everybody.*

We all have the capacity and ability to share our spiritual life force energy. People just don't do it because they are living under the lie that everyone is separated and nothing is connected. In reality, everything and everybody is connected. Stone killers, because of our extreme actions just happen to have stumbled across an immediate way to share life force but it could happen with anybody that's next to the dying. If relatives would sit by a bedside of their dying grandfather with the intention to get a little something-something, spiritual energy wise—they would get it, the moment the relative passes over. Instead they are trained by other weak minds to sit by the bedside shivering with a giant cloud of community-taught fear blocking their only chance to feel above-human—like me."

I began taking notes and this greatly pleased Willy.

"Willy, I'm not going to have your DNA tested...so why are you still telling me all this?" He stared disbelieving that I could be so dense.

"Plan B, bro', you got to put all this stuff out so that all the stone killers wherever they are caught can be put down. They are a different species from human. There's no problem with the government using the death penalty because it's not really the death penalty at all. It's like putting a dog to sleep except humans would actually feel sad for a dog."

"Willy, isn't the serial killer's union going to be upset with you for letting out this little gem of information? Do you want to be put to death too?"

He smiled as if explaining to a small child.

"Well, true dat. I'll give you the real-real. Stone killers respect anyone who pursues death, even against the killers themselves so they wouldn't be upset with me. They would respect me even more than they do already. And, once the legal system gets wise and starts putting these guys down, it'll be just point forward in time only for new stone killers caught. I would be immune and I could help with a lot of the identifications."

I waved my hand for him to continue.

"And...."

"….and whenever they are put down I will get paid. I will get a piece of that spiritual energy as they pass over. There's no restriction for spiritual energy in time and space. That's why if an identical twin is hurt in Calcutta, India, his twin in New York City can feel it immediately with no gap in time—faster than the speed of light. I'd get the benefit of the quickening again without even directly killing anyone because I will have caused the death and I'll have the clear mind and the intention to receive the payment." Willy sat back.

"Willy, o.k. let's say I go along with everything you said. My next question is why me? There are psychologists here at the prison for you to talk to about this. Why not go to them with this?"

I knew about his history of refusing all contacts with the psychology.

"Those people don't know anything! You're an investigator so you know criminals in a way they never will. Most criminals and shrinks are dummies. They'll never know about that special spiritual charge that animates a select few to higher forms of life."

"Like you Willy?"

"Yeah, like me and like you too." Now I smiled.

"Willy, are you saying I'm a stone killer too?" He gulped his water.

"Naw man. You still don't understand what this is really all about? I didn't just pick you because you're an investigator. I'm an empath and an aura-reader—sensitive to other people's thoughts, emotions and energy fields. I can see people's spiritual energy fields around the crowns of their heads. There are two species that are not human—Trolls and Elves. Both are blessed with overflowing spiritual energy. Regular humans just have thin band of colored energy over the tops of their heads—about an inch. Trolls and Elves have several inches of jumping, flaring, explosive energy showing. Trolls use this overflow to destroy, but Elves use it to create stuff and help people. Here's the catch. Trolls can become Elves and Elves can become Trolls but neither can ever become just regular humans again." He paused to make sure I was absorbing every word.

"Neither type can turn off that faucet overflow. Both groups are like Major League baseball teams except they can't go back down to the minors. That's why it's so easy for successful businessmen, corporate officers and successful politicians to slip into the life of outlaw criminals and why so many guys who were criminals at a young age can turn it around and become successful, creative people later in life. What you don't ever see is any of these classes of Elves and Trolls become just regular people. It doesn't happen."

I felt like I was getting too far down the rabbit hole.

"Willy what's any of this got to do with me?" He was bewildered at my failure to understand.

"It's all about you. You're an Elf. I'm a Troll. Between the two of us, we could change the world. Our fields together automatically synergize. We can perform miracles together. We can send this message about my Theory of Alternate Species Development through the

entire world—not just the United States but the whole planet could use this to kill every single stone-cold killer in the world! I'll be exempt of course because of my good work and my thesis. There no limit to how far the power of my message—the truth about Elves and Trolls could go."

I took a deep breath like just before you jump into the deep end.

"O.K. Willy, I'll look at it."

It was nearly unreadable. Willy spoke *much better* than he wrote. Willy's "Theory of Alternate Species Development" was dense, scientific doublespeak, really better suited for a PhD deconfliction job than a cold reading by a non-academic. It appeared to have snatches of the right jargon but was overall incoherent. Willy was a hot mess in written form. I gave Willy back his manifesto (these things tend to be precious to prisoners) and shortly thereafter he was moved across the country to another prison. I never saw nor heard of him again but I will always remember the afternoon I spent with the killer who called me a kindred spirit (sort of) and asked me to help him plan the deaths of all the serial killers in the world.

A great deal of what Willy told me that day made sense to me based on long experience with both classes of what he called Trolls and Elves. As I mentally reviewed all the great executives, artists and great creative personalities I had known or investigated during two decades; I was confronted the granite truth of Willy assertions. Although I would qualify that, I believe criminal Trolls don't have to be serial killers or even murderers. They can mere just high-functioning criminals. Some of the former Trolls I had known—went straight and became successful executives and entrepreneurs (Elves). They switched from one supra-human team to the other supra-human team. A few that I had known just died during their Troll status; but NONE, not a single one of these two classes of people I have known over the years, ever fell into or reverted into or in any way entered the class of regular humans with ordinary lives. *They can't step down to the minors,* like Willy said. Their funnel draws too much power.

Para-Investigators will be imbued with the abilities that Willy displayed, not necessarily the ideas he espoused. They will be able to read auras and distinguish classes of people according to their spiritual energy matrixes. Para-Investigators, because of the nature of their constant exposure to paranormal topics and extra-sensitive individuals, will be plugged into the great matrix of all potentialities that unite all living things. By their vibrational abilities, they will traffic in thoughts and emotions that will resolve the most profound investigations and mysteries.

39

TROLL TO ELF

(During an inquiry into the death of a wealthy businessman in California, I uncovered the following story which jibed well with Willy's theories.)

Carl Z was a highly talented but troubled individual throughout his life. He grew up in Northern California in an affluent family. His father and brothers were surgeons and general physicians. However, as the youngest in the family, there was something different about him. He was never any good at school, grades or conventional academic tasks like the rest of his family. Carl was a restless spirit who could never sit still in the classroom and was anxious to actually get out and *do real things*. Carl's father felt his son had a chemical imbalance that made the internal chatter noise level of his son's brain operate at a higher volume than is safe for most people. His father medicated Carl with anti-depressants but Carl stopped taking them because he felt they "took away his personality."

Carl dropped out of college and worked a long series of menial labor, low-paying jobs. The only thing he really seemed to enjoy was working with general contractors with his hands, building, constructing and creating homes and buildings. During experimentation with various drugs he stumbled upon the use of heroin. Carl felt as if he finally found the calming balm for his restless heart and mind. For the first time in his life, the chatter in his brain lowered and the gates opened to the intense joy of life. Carl became an addict.

The bloom faded off that rose as he sank deeper into drug addiction. His family realized what he was using his money for and stopped providing it to him. It became more and more difficult for him to maintain the contractor jobs in the construction industry that he so enjoyed, due to his addiction. His lost his old friends and acquaintances.

Increasingly, his only friends were "drug buddies." Those friends got him involved in illegal activities to support all their habits: break-ins, robberies, muggings and even some assaults. Carl didn't *go down* for any felonies during this period and he said it was only because of God's Hand and his excellent acting skills that he escaped any serious criminal convictions. Yet, he felt the grim reality of being a full-time drug addict and part-time criminal. Several of his friends died from overdoses but Carl had one friend left from his happier days with his family.

Randall J was a successful businessman who had been close friends with Carl since the days when they attended high school together. They were together at college as well until, against Randall's advice, Carl dropped out and left California. Randall soldiered on without his closest friend. After college he took small companies owned by his father and magnified them into huge global ventures generating tremendous cash flow. Randall had a beautiful wife and three sons who all lived in a mansion in Northern California.

Randall's family sometimes wondered why he kept in touch with his old high school friend, Carl Z, since everyone in their circles had heard he had become a vagrant—a homeless bum. They were right. Carl had been living in shelters, spending time in alleyways or any place he could gather himself to strategize acquiring money for his next fix. Sometimes Randall Johnston would steer Carl toward construction projects for day-laborer work. Often, the menial workers at these construction projects would be shocked at the skill and expertise of this man who had the appearance of a vagrant off the street. They would often wonder what secret weakness kept Carl from being a Supervisor and climbing the ladder in contracting and construction, especially since this expert, general contractor/vagrant was *a personal friend* of the millionaire businessman Randall J?

Carl would always shrug off queries about himself or his friend Randall. He would repeatedly assert he just wanted to work as well as he possibly could for as long as he could. In truth, Randall J had a secret he shared with Carl since their teenage years growing up together in Northern California. *Randall J, the wealthy businessman, was also a part-time heroin addict.*

Randall moved smoothly between the reality of the "Troll" world and the "Elvin" world. Carl and Randall had appointments together about every two months, often in a hotel where Randall would allow Carl to stay afterward for a few days. This had been their arrangement for many years and they had enjoyed their shared addiction, but their addictions were consuming them as their appointments grew more frequent and more debilitating as time wore on. Now in their late thirties, they both sensed this phase of their lives was quickly closing. They tried to advise each other and finally they started uttering the phrases dreaded by all addicts—*getting clean, kicking the junk, and taking back control of their lives—REHAB.*

They entered rehab. Randall paid for a full course of therapy at a nice facility for Carl. It was nicer than being homeless. But they went to separate facilities as this is one of the minimum requirements of rehabilitation—complete separation from old drug friends. Carl completed rehabilitation and during that period read many books in an area he was interested in—buying and fixing up real estate for renting and resale. He had always worked in every phase of general contracting and home building since his teens. Carl had great skill and experience in this area and decided it was a way he could earn a decent living while quieting the chatter in his head. Carl had kicked heroin and he was striking out towards a new life. He acquired real estate and renovated it for resale. His self-owned business was doing very well.

Then the call came.

Randall called him from one of their old hotel rooms. He had relapsed and was crying, gibbering about not being able to *"get back this time."* Carl knew what that meant. He raced to the hotel room. Carl fell into a horrible déjà vu nightmare. It was broad daylight and he was in a four-star hotel room with every possible luxurious amenity the upper class could want but Carl's mind transported him back to those dingy, dark, bug-infested, Los Angeles drug dens at 3:00am when he had played out this same scene with other friends. He cradled his dying friend's head and Carl's mind swirled with images of: Randall's handsome family and the looks on their faces as they heard the news, all the business organizations that depended on Randall's talent, the community organizations that Randall had contributed to, the churches he had helped in doing missionary work, the journalists that had devoted so much ink to the positive impact his foundations had created; and Randall's blue blood, social register father and mother sickened and horrified with the news they somehow suspected might come someday.

Carl finished saying goodbye to his friend, sanitized the room of his own presence and of all traces of drugs and paraphernalia. Then, he anonymously notified the hotel front desk that he saw a guy clutching his chest and wincing who crawled up into Randall's room. The newspapers recounted the story of Randall's death from heart attack and the story of his life. Newspaper accounts omitted where his body was found and his family trumpeted a long history of heart problems. They rejected any autopsy. The coverage went on for quite a while in California with splashy tributes to Randall. All investigations were concluded as "death by natural causes."

Carl was pleased with the coverage and he awakened to the sacred present moment of his own life. Carl realized that he would always be a drug addict for the rest of his life and every single day that he does not fall back into drugs is a wonderful gift from God. Carl continued growing his business of acquiring small properties that required serious fixing up. He lost himself for years into the sheer joy of the manual labor involved in renovating his properties and turning them over. Today Carl owns several millions of dollars' worth of rental properties that began with a single trailer he had bought, renovated and sold with a small loan from his friend Randall twenty years earlier.

Carl resolves to honor the sacred memory of his friend Randall every single day. Carl overcomes the old urges with the approval and help of spiritual power that Carl receives partly from Randall himself. Carl is today the happiest most self-actualized person I have ever known. He stumbles at times but his new norm is thankfully, that of his Elf self—not the Troll that he once was.

40

SWALLOWED BY THE DARKNESS

(Teenagers can also be Para-Investigators. This is another of my own experiences as I went down the path that led to Para-Investigation.)

After my parents divorced, I was eighteen years old and my mother was raising me as a single parent. For a short period, my mother had a boyfriend who was one of the top executives at a hotel chain in New York City where she had worked. He was a widower and a wealthy, older man who carried himself with great poise. He was always a vision of buttoned down elegance in gray tweed. His name was Phil and he lived in a grim looking castle-like estate in upstate New York. As I pulled up with my mother to the luxurious looking stone mansion, I secretly hoped that my mother *would keep this one for a long time.*

It was then I received my very first Para-Investigative assignment: my mother asked me (if the opportunity arose) to help her in find out anything about what had occurred to her new boyfriend's wife—she disappeared mysteriously several years ago and no hint was ever found of her whereabouts. Phil's wife had been a well-known demonology/occult author who had written for many years on witchcraft, evil spirits and black magic sorcery. She had been an investigator of sorts—into realms where most souls dare not tread. She disappeared after writing her latest book and as the old saying goes was simply "never heard from again." Phil showed me the inside jacket of her last hard cover book in which her legacy publisher trumpeted that because of her relentless work to expose the dark powers *"she had been swallowed up by dark forces angered by her revelations."*

The inside even showed an illustration of how these evil entities may have unified their energies, created a vortex and swallowed her out of this physical world. It seemed in bad taste but Phil said he agreed to the portrayal "in order to warn others in the same field." I asked Phil what really happened to his wife. He stonily replied that she had told him that she needed to hurry and finish that last book because she had a feeling that "certain forces" were gathering to make sure that it was her last. He would say no real details or speculation on how she disappeared. The day we were visiting his home, Phil wearily confessed, was the anniversary of her disappearance. He related that years ago on this night, his wife had disappeared and he never heard from her again. I knew immediately he was lying. Not only did he hear from her but his withered gaze told me that, wherever she was, he heard from her constantly and that *what* he heard was *not good*.

He was a man in his fifties who appeared closer to his seventies. I later found out that he was a "reader" who would use ancient texts to read the spirits and the future, but it created a great stress on him every time he did a reading—a stress that would ultimately take many years off his life. Phil explained to us that the spirit world exists all around us at all times, that people who are blind to it are still subject to its effects. At the dinner table, Phil waxed mystical

"There is a saying that ignorance of the law is no excuse. You still go to jail even if you didn't know about the prohibition against what you did because when you originally decided to live in society, you agreed to live by its laws, whether you knew each one or not. Our physical bodies have agreed to dwell on the physical plane but our real selves: mind/soul and spirit; exist across the continuum spread from this physical world into a spiritual storm-field that is swirling all around us. We can be crushed by it or use its power depending on what we are willing to learn. At times, entities misuse the field to cross over into places they have no business being, to abuse their abilities and to abuse others who dwell in isolated places and know nothing about the field."

Phil then invited me to have my future read to which I reluctantly agreed. He opened a very large ancient looking text, unlike anything I had ever seen before. As he turned the leathery pages, ancient dust flew but it was not just dust. There were waves of particles that seemed to swell and ebb wherever he touched the ancient text. They were swirls that were *nearly there*. It seemed as if the book was thousands of years old. The writing was in an ancient language that resembled a Celtic dialect. I felt that I shouldn't look at it too closely. He asked me for several information reference points about myself including date of birth, place of birth and several other questions surrounding the circumstances of my earthly origination. Only my mother knew all the answers to these questions. He then seemed to do numerous cross-references with information about the positions of stars and planets and finally read to me my past at that moment and the future course of my life. Phil had told me things that had occurred up to that early time in my life that he could not possibly have known in any rational physical manner. Phil unveiled the impoverished circumstances of my early childhood in excruciating detail and elaborated that this upbringing had been planned for me in order to harden my character for later life. Phil said that I should forget about my difficult relationship with my father—that I should not continue to wear that relationship around my neck like a millstone because that burden was given for my growth so I should learn forgiveness. The negatives I had suffered from my father were over forever but the positives I had gotten from him were eternal. *I knew exactly what he meant by this painful truth.*

He elaborated about my dedication to my studies in school and that this would lead to a successful career in law and law-enforcement. He told me that there would be many instances in my life when men and institutions would notice my dedication and intelligence and this would open doors to unexpected opportunities. As he went into more detailed specifics about my past life, I saw why my mother would not have her own charts read by him. This was like being slowly stripped naked on stage in a full stadium at halftime.

I looked to my mother for some explanation. She had only known Phil for a couple of weeks and swore to me she had never mentioned anything about our personal lives. Her fearful gaze told me she was telling the truth. Years later, my mother would remind me how mathematically precise that reading had been but at the time it just seemed like a scary adventure. Phil told me about my life up to that point and then predicted several traumatic events through my young adulthood that at first seemed tragic but were later revealed as great blessings. He also went on to predict "that I would have a very successful career in law-enforcement and national security but that after that career was over, I would become far more successful as an older man."

Later, as Phil showed my mother photo albums of his family, he told me I was free to wander anywhere in the house. I quickly made my way upstairs in the expansive mansion, Phil added: "except don't go into my wife's bedroom." I asked him which one that was, as it appeared there were at least a dozen bedrooms up there. From downstairs, Phil responded.

"You'll know."

I raced giddily along several bedrooms all with similar New England décor and the musty smell of an ancient mansion. I popped in and out of those cavernous rooms. They were as interesting as giant mahogany furniture and mothballs could be to a teenager. Then, I confronted a door that felt different from the others. As I touched the old polished oak door, it seemed to give off the same misty tendrils that the ancient book had given off as Phil touched its pages. I could only see the bluish gray spirals out of my peripheral vision but they would disappear whenever I looked directly at them.

I stood in the doorway. The door swung open and I was peering inside to the gloom. Dark swirls throughout the room formed and dispersed as I tried to stare directly into them. Physically, this room looked the same as the others. It was essentially empty except for giant dusty furniture but I knew *this was it.*

This was her room.

Unlike the other bedrooms, something unearthly inhabited this space. I stepped inside as shivers ran through me. There was a swirl of dark energy throughout the bedroom that was not visible and yet I could almost see it.

This is what he meant. I would know.

That was when I realized that Phil knew more about me than what he read in his ancient book. He may have planned for me to carry out my Para-Investigative assignment for his own purposes. I felt I was being manipulated or *possibly tested*. I rifled through drawers, closets and dusty cabinets for any clues. There were just some woman's clothing and accoutrements that I ignored. I was looking for documents, letters, notes, address books—anything that might give a clue about her last known whereabouts. The final drawer I pulled was at the bottom of a giant dresser.

Books?

There were books that had apparently been removed from the elegant library downstairs and tossed into this large bottom drawer. There were about ten large ornately bound books.

The room had been sanitized of any documents but Phil could not bear to part with his wife's ancient tomes. I could see by the quality of the cover that it was of a material that was unfamiliar to me—black, metallic and secured by worn leather snaps. I ran my fingers across the letters on the front cover but something told me not to speak the words aloud.

I just pronounced them in my mind:

MALIFICARUM—DAEMONIUM

I put my fingers on the snap. A rush of moving images hit me. I saw a middle-aged brunette woman sitting with candles, downstairs in this house, with candles providing the only light, speaking in strange tongues. She appeared to be in a trance as she murmured incantations. Her eyes were turned up—just whites visible as she muttered. I saw a dark alien figure standing just off from her position. The creature was angry, hurling its body against invisible barriers that kept it contained—it demanded to be set free. The thing was cursing at her, but when she hit upon certain phrases, it became docile and obedient. I could almost see the mighty barrier that held the creature: it was nothing more than a line of white powder on the floor, traced into a large, multi-pointed, geometric shape. The powder line somehow manifested upward into shimmering walls of invisible energy. Although one creature seemed to speak for the rest, there were many voices chattering angrily from inside that transparent enclosure. A white cat, strode past one of the powder lines, and broke one of its perfect lines. The woman shrieked as her eyes opened. The creatures squeezed through the break created by the careless cat. She rose but it was too late. Several more essences whooshed out through the small crack in the shape and they kept coming at her—striking at her like rushing waves. They squeezed through the crack like rats. There were dozens, maybe hundreds, went shooting through the tiny break in the container. They surrounded the woman in a maelstrom of rage. Her hand outstretched from the swirling vortex before she disappeared—*swallowed by the darkness.*

I came back to my senses and closed the drawer. I backed out quickly and went downstairs. My mother saw I was pale but I protested that nothing was wrong. She was unsurprised when I told her about the wife's bedroom and what I had seen and perceived in there. My mother told me it wasn't just the bedroom. We were supposed to stay for the weekend but we made excuses and we left right after dinner. Phil's community was far in the rear view before my mother felt safe enough to speak aloud.

"That entire house was infected with evil. You didn't bring anything out of that home did you? If you have even a scrap of paper from that house, throw it away right now! The only reason Phil doesn't feel the evil there is because he's lived with it so long, plus they don't bother him because they need him to pull another woman to the house. Well, it won't be me."

I knew she was right about everything she said. I had always known about her psychic sensitivity. I considered it a wasted weekend but much later I realized how much had been accomplished that weekend. I had glimpsed paranormal phenomena in action for the first time and abilities at work (Phil's predictive abilities). I had successfully completed my very first Para-Investigative assignment. I learned about my own future and the experience spurred me to continue my studies into the paranormal and to eventually discover the truth of Para-Investigation.

41

DISQUIETING THE DEAD

(My most intimate study of the paranormal world was observing my own mother and her supernatural abilities)

My mother related several experiences to me that concerned spirits purporting to be the shades of the recently departed—like her mother. Whenever such spirits would appear to her, my mother would utilize a few persistent questions to expose the entities as frauds (in the sense that they *were* spirits but *not* of those they purported to be) and then she would send them away. She related to me that most "ghosts" of the dead are really "foreign entities" looking for a quick way to empower themselves with our conscious attention. They are desperate for this attention. They will do anything for it—impersonate anyone or anything she would advise me. Her conclusion on the rarity of true ghosts seemed right to me. Others believe there can *never* be true ghosts because the Bible says there can't be.

The Bible addresses the question of spirits of the dead directly.

1 Samuel 28:3-19—excerpted

"Now Samuel was dead, *and all Israel had lamented him, and buried him in Ramah, even in his own city. And Saul had put away those that had familiar spirits, and the wizards, out of the land.*
Then said Saul unto his servants, Seek me a woman that hath a familiar spirit, that I may go to her, and enquire of her. And his servants said to him, Behold, [there is] a woman that hath a familiar spirit at Endor.

….And the king said unto her, Be not afraid: for what sawest thou? And the woman said unto Saul, I saw gods ascending out of the earth. And he said unto her, What form [is] he of? And she said, An old man cometh up; and he is covered with a mantle. **And Saul perceived that it was Samuel,** *and he stooped with his face to the ground, and bowed himself.* **And Samuel said to**

Saul, Why hast thou disquieted me, to bring me up?

And Saul answered, I am sore distressed; for the Philistines make war against me, and God is departed from me, and answereth me no more, neither by prophets, nor by dreams: therefore I have called thee, that thou mayest make known unto me what I shall do. Then said Samuel, Wherefore then dost thou ask of me, seeing the LORD is departed from thee, and is become thine enemy? And the LORD hath done to him, as he spake by me: for the LORD hath rent the kingdom out of thine hand, and given it to thy neighbour, [even] to David:

Because thou obeyedst not the voice of the LORD, nor executedst his fierce wrath upon Amalek, therefore hath the LORD done this thing unto thee this day. Moreover the LORD will also deliver Israel with thee into the hand of the Philistines: and tomorrow shalt thou and thy sons be with me: the LORD also shall deliver the host of Israel into the hand of the Philistines."

(Emphasis added by author)

This section begins by making it clear that the great Prophet of Israel, Samuel, who raised up King Saul and later raised up King David; *is dead*. Then it depicts a desperate King Saul resorting to outlawed necromancy. The biblical text clearly advises that Samuel's spirit is brought up and not only that, the spirit very emphatically identifies itself as being Samuel by saying something that *only the real prophet Samuel* would have known or dared to say to the King of Israel. Samuel's spirit (ghost) predicted that a great battle was coming the next day and it would end in a terrible defeat for Israel, and in the deaths of Saul and his sons. The King responded as one who knew the spirit of Samuel was genuine. Saul was inconsolable in his grief and certainty that the prophecy would come to pass—*and it did.*

I've heard Christian pastors twist and turn logic, reason and language; in their attempts to posit that this ghost was not really the spirit of the great Prophet Samuel—supposedly because God set up a system, according to the Bible, whereby the dead cannot return to this plane and even trying to bring them back is prohibited by God. Their words always rang hollow to me and only propelled me to further study. This study corroborated that those pastors and scholars who dared to address this passage were contorting the biblical text to fit their own suppositions.

It is true that God has set up the basic rule that the dead may no longer contact the living. Jesus once told a parable of a man in Hell requesting to go to his living brothers to prove to them that they must repent so they don't end up like him. Jesus' reply was that God's rules allow no such visits:

"Betwixt the living and those in Heaven a great gulf is set up which neither may cross"

Throughout the universe and in nature it is evident that the Creator sets up rules (for laws of physics or biology for example) but then it pleases the Great Designer to create exceptions for His own laws. The solid form of every liquid in existence is denser and heavier than its liquid state—except for water. Why was this exception created? Because that way ice would float so that life on Earth could exist. Why can bees fly when under the laws of physics—the bees' mass/weight to wing-size ratio—such a thing is not possible? An exception to the laws of physics allows us to experience sweet honey. If you still don't believe the Creator-Source carefully sets up systems of rules and then breaks them—*go look at information on the creature known as a "platypus."*

In the same way, God allowed Samuel's spirit to cross the great uncrossable chasm because it pleased Him and served His glory. The Creator-Source allows exceptions to His own rules when it serves His glory (and sometimes because it's funny—platypus).

42

UNFOLDERS AND COSMIC INTROSPECTION

A few locations around the world are confluence points for spiritual/mystical energy —morphogenic energy sites. Out of these concentrated geysers of supernatural energy, manifest phenomena of miracles and magic. Such geographic locations are permanent vortexes of superconscious power that can be tapped into by those with the ability to connect to the great Superconscious Field. These sites affect both spirits and the living. In these places, even those who cannot connect directly, still sense and feel the ancient power and even a little dread—they just don't why.

Egypt, at the Pyramids of Giza is one such place. There is no reasonable material world explanation how technology several thousands of years ahead of its time suddenly appeared at this place to make the Great Pyramids of Giza. Another such place is the Teotihuacán ("teh-oh-tee-wa-khan") ancient sacred site, located 30 miles northeast of Mexico City, Mexico. The ruins of Teotihuacán are an ancient place of magic and necromantic blood rituals where again, the Meso-American peoples had access to astronomy technology that was thousands of years ahead of its time with no explanation for how they acquired it. Many of these "wonders of the world" sit with quiet, suppressed energy awaiting reactivation by some unknown future event. Others have vortexes of present energy for everyday purposes.

I posit that in the latter category of currently active confluence points are the ancient Indian burial lands of Tucson, Arizona—a sacred place at a confluence point in the healing energy field of the planet. This historic, ancient town has an incredible healing energy that permeates all the land and its mountains, lakes, and its lush desert. Its phenomenal healing energy is the reason why this ancient town is a global center for Mind-Body medicine and rehabilitation centers. Whether their bodies have been ravaged by alcohol, drugs or like the majority of people on our planet—infected by out-of-control neurosis purposefully created by the stress of everyday living—they all go to Tucson for healing. They have their minds quieted and their bodies healed. Tucson, Arizona, is renowned all over the world for its Mind-Body transformation centers.

If you know anyone in the movie or television business who are on the Hollywood "A-list," they have either experienced or heard of these centers.

Partly for this reason, the University of Arizona at Tucson has become a global center for studies in mind-body consciousness and various paranormal topics. This university recently did a study into the "Accuracy of Mediums Channeling Dead People." Quantum scientists there recently claimed that they were able to produce proof of life after death. They call these "survival of consciousness" studies. This university is doing pioneering work with scientists from the fields of psychology, medicine, neurology, psychiatry and surgery; and are constantly in the forefront of paranormal and consciousness studies. World famous mediums and psychics go to this University to prove their abilities and participate in non-biased experiments (as much as such things are possible). These investigators, visioneering scientists and psychics are adding voluminous data to our storehouse of understanding about paranormal topics. In short, they are acting as Para-Investigators.

It will be visionary universities such as this that will train, educate and equip the first generations of *formally recognized* Para-Investigators. They will teach True Investigation, not criminology, as if crime was a separate area of human endeavor divorced from other parts of human existence. They will instead teach True Investigation as an opportunity to dive into the Superconscious Gulf that connects all things.

There will no longer be separate academic studies of crimes and mysteries. Instead, there will only be studies of consciousness that *happen to be involved* in the world of crimes and mysteries. Then, formally recognized Para-Investigators will be augmented by investigators already in place with special Paranormal Abilities who no longer have to hide their abilities like fugitives. Solution rates for crimes and mysteries will jump geometrically.

However, since statistics are the realm of old world scientists, they will twist figures and numbers around to attribute the increase in crime solving to other things—anything besides non-material things. As the influence and success of Para-Investigation grows, the emergence of the new paradigm for successful investigation will become apparent and undeniable. Fortunately, it will not be long before the visioneering scientists at the University of Arizona, the rising Para-Investigative class, and all those who share their belief in this new paradigm; will become the majority in a new technological-shamanistic culture. The stultified scientists frozen in the old model of the purely physical universe will mercifully lapse into an irrelevant minority. Presently, there are many universities both in the United States and throughout the world that are hard at work in developing academic programs in the Advancing Sciences such as mind-body consciousness and paranormal studies. Hospitals are increasing their participation in holistic naturopath medicine that treats the human spirit and uses its natural energy rather than using harmful pharmaceutical drugs to suppress and destroy the body's natural responses.

The Centers for Well-being and Mind-Consciousness all over the world must join one another and share databases and personnel; towards the day when *they* will become the dominant "new shamanistic science" and cultural-medical system of the world. These networks will create a genuine world of holistic health and well-being among populations that were previously being slowly poisoned by pharmaceutical conglomerates and their armies of well paid pill-distributors disguised as medical doctors. The Western world will finally emerge from the dark age of scientific materialism.

Para-Investigators will be a new class of beings with abilities that will prove a great blessing for all those who are Seekers of Truth. They will be students of the human spirit and investigators of human consciousness with powers to see through people, to see what they truly are and what their true purpose is. Often, a Para-Investigator assigned only to uncover whether a person is guilty of murder will confront the intuition that the suspect is not guilty but the person who actually did the murder is someone never even considered a suspect by conventional investigators. This is usually unwelcome news in the world of conventional investigation. Other times, Para-Investigators, when confronted with elusive mysteries, will conclude that the subject of the mystery does exist but is unavailable for physical scientific inspection on our material plane of existence. These are investigative conclusions that are difficult to understand and are very unwelcome in the conventional world. There will be a difficult adjustment period during the shift to a new paradigm of investigative reality. It is for this reason that only the most resilient personalities will have the mettle to become Para-Investigators—*unfolders of the abyss.*

Here are further areas that will be taught by this new class of Para-Investigators, both in the supernatural and the metaphysical. Concerning incidents of malevolent spiritual encounters that people ascribe to ghostly activity, many are just evil spirits seeking to attach themselves to or to simply do damage to human beings. These spiritual entities are from other dimensions of existence and, at times, might assume the guises of loved one, family members or familiar earthly departed; all in order to do damage from a more intimate place. Many such spirits dress themselves up as our relatives, former friends and ancestors in order to make us believe they are a part of our realities. This appearance gets them much farther in becoming a part of our perceptions and therefore they seize our conscious energy and it empowers them. It feeds them.

If your next query is then *what are* these supposed evil spirits—the answer is that "they are *other than human*." They are from another plane of existence and come to our physical plane to wreak mischief and sometimes worse upon those who invite them into our existence. They existed since before man was on the earth and lived within strict guidelines/rules as to when they can inject themselves into human planes. Yet, you probably already know, "rules are made to be broken."

There are several required accommodations for such entities to attach themselves to the lives of humans.

1. An Invitation—Invitation can be in several forms but it must always be a conscious act of will by some human to invite spiritual entities into our plane of existence, for example, playing with Ouija boards, mystic incantations or use of charms and enchanted objects.

2. Physical place—a receptive field for these purposes is a place that has high levels of mystic/spiritual energy and so is conducive to the transmutation and dwelling of spiritual entities. Any place can serve this purpose because it's the energy that matters.

3. A Willing Host Connector—a physical entity from our plane of existence must serve as an anchor for spiritual entities to dwell here, at least initially for the first period of ingress/dwelling. The physical host may then try to dislodge the entity or even die. Even when the original anchor is gone, the malevolent spirits are still able to dwell and try to find other willing receptors to power their existence on this plane. (*For Para-Investigators investigating possessions, attachments, oppressions by spiritual predators: the host/victim, at least for a moment, was involved in the convergence of all three of these elements--no matter what you are being told **or not told.** Sufficient investigation will always reveal it.*)

When all three of these conditions converge, something transitions into our physical plane and can remain here in contravention to the rules of ordinary existence for an extended period. Again, there can be genuine ghosts but genuine episodes of haunting by the spirits of former humans who physically departed from this plane, are exceedingly rare.

Yet, no one can be a Para-Investigator if they do not first know themselves. No one can even be a fully realized human being unless they conduct the one investigation that everyone must do. The great truth revealed through the Advancing Sciences is that we are not physical creatures that happen to have a spiritual base underneath; but instead *we are spiritual creatures* temporarily overlaid with a physical body. But the comprehension of that truism is only the beginning of understanding who we really are. Beyond discovering our spiritual potential, there are many chambers with unique treasures in each of us, and we must discover, in each case, what they are.

Unfortunately, the majority of humanity leaves this imperative search undone until they die and their earthly lives prove to be a fleeting exercise in wasted potential. Upon death, other forces take over the decisions associated with spiritual unfoldment and the individual spirit may lose control of that process.

One way or another every human being will develop a course of spiritual unfoldment; be it a small step in spiritual evolvement or a complete process of spiritual transcendence over the temporary material world. We will each learn to look inward and upward at the same time. All must embark on the most important investigation there can be—an investigation inward into the most profound parts of themselves.

Those who will be Para-Investigators must unfold their inner potential by awakening a fuller, deeper more profound consciousness.

They must awaken.

They must let go—of all constant streams of desires and thoughts.

They must unplug from the Mind Dampener: the great mass of cable and major media broadcasting programming that pumps materialist refuse across the globe.

They must dare to shut off the many sources of the Dampener and regenerate peace, harmony and presence for the mind.

Cosmic Introspection is just one nomenclature for this process. It means looking within oneself yet simultaneously looking upward into the Great Abyss that connects us all into the cosmic mind of Creator-Source. Our consciousness expresses itself in our minds as a localized phenomenon effecting biological responses and physical reality but the source of the consciousness *is not localized*. The true source of human consciousness is so far away as to be unimaginable. The source is what Jung called the Cosmic Mind. It's what Emerson called the Oversoul. It's what Deepak Chopra calls *"the Non-local Field of Consciousness in the Infinite Field of Limitless Possibilities."*

Our physical bodies are like suits of clothing animated through an infinitely long cord from that limitless field. Like electric appliances that do not function unless they are plugged into an electrical outlet; we require a constant connection to that field of Infinite Intelligence. In eastern traditions there are many different names for this invisible cord. Some say the connection is through our solar plexus, which is the perfect center of our bodies. Others believe the connection is through the top of our brains (the crown chakra) which is the hardware system filtering usage of the spiritual power (consciousness). Wherever the invisible cord is plugged, it is the transmission through that cord that animates these physical bodies into the constant miracle known as *human souls* which can see, feel, comprehend, imagine, and create; beyond the physical animal level of the material world. It is here that creative imagination creates and no one in the universe has this ability except for fully ensouled human beings.

We are the only physical beings on the planet that can imagine being something far beyond what we presently are. A lion cannot imagine anything beyond being and acting as a lion. Humans imagine themselves far beyond what they are and that is because they *can* ultimately become and do anything they imagine. We recreate reality through consciousness into new and varied forms. This is precisely why if we imagine ourselves as Para-Investigators, with all the attendant powers and abilities this position implies; we will achieve exactly that.

One of the greatest truths about you has to do with your brain. Your brain is a receiver of consciousness, *not a producer*. If primitives from a pre-iron age civilization confronted a plasma television for the first time, they would be alarmed at the magic of the dynamic, full-color images they see. They would naturally assume that the images are real beings generated by the machine—the television itself. In reality, the television only acts as a receiver picking up television station signals from the nearest technological civilization. It reproduces. It does not create anything original—real or image based. If we believe the scientifically fabricated (based on nothing really) falsity that our consciousness is produced by our brain, then we are acting just like those primitives, thumping the sides of the television to see if the small people hidden inside start thumping back. Understanding the truth about our source of consciousness will ignite the beginning of a powerful awakening and will lead us into the second step in this process.

We must also let go.

Our minds are in terrible turbulence. We are in a constant stream of desires for material things and our brains are constantly running multiple streams of chatter and mental static based on the wants and needs of the false self—the ego. Whether the desire is to be a Para-Investigator or to live in a big mansion, we must let go of those desires and streams of thinking in order to clear our consciousness. Goethe said: *"There are none so enslaved as those who falsely believe themselves free."* Truer words were never spoken. How can we break free of a prison that we do not see? Once we quiet the desires, chatter and needs of the ego/mind, the incredible power of our consciousness will easily sense the truth no matter what it is. Let go of desires. Let go of constant thinking/worry. Quiet your mental turbulence. Once we feel the truth of the Mind Dampener's existence and of its malevolent purpose, we will achieve the pivot point in our lives that will change everything.

Whether we are Unfolders of the Abyss or just seeking truth of the world that surrounds us, Cosmic Introspection will lead us toward the ultimate truth of what we were created to be. As we awaken, let go and regenerate peace and harmony, our consciousness will ignite a greater reality than the facade we are presented with in the deceptive mediums of this material world.

43

MIND DAMPENER HYDRA

Cosmic Introspection which is so vital for human development and for the development of our paranormal abilities, is up against a terrible obstacle—the Mind-Dampener.

In Greek mythology, the gods assigned Hercules ten "impossible" tasks or labors. There was only one rule in the accomplishment of these labors—Hercules could not seek nor accept help from another person or being. He had to stand alone or the labor would not be counted. Hercules clashed with the most undefeatable foe he had ever faced. It was the gigantic, nine-headed, Hydra lizard-dragon. According to the legends, Hercules confronted the great beast whose breath and blood were poison to ordinary humans. In some versions, he used a club, in others a sword or a razor sharp scythe to destroy some of the Advancing Heads as they attempted to devour him. Yet, in all versions, it was the same result. Each time he destroyed one of the heads—two more grew back in its place.

Hercules had no solution and he had to do the one thing he was forbidden to do. *He had to ask for help.* Hercules appealed to his nephew Loalus for ideas. His ally came up with a bold plan. As Hercules destroyed each head, his nephew Loalus, used a powerful firebrand, a hastily composed jet of Greek fire, to burn and cauterize each destroyed neck stump. This was to prevent new Hydra heads from growing back. It worked.

After a long day and night of slashing and burning, the headless monster finally died. Cooperation and imagination succeeded where superhuman brute force had failed. No matter how undefeatable an obstacle or a monster may seem, there is always a way we can work together to destroy it.

Like the great Hydra Dragon, the global media complex has been elevated into the status of undefeatable foe of` humanity. The EPIC (The Elite Powers In Control) utilizes this Hydra to subjugate through fear and to devour resisters who dare to stand against it. The Mind Dampener blurs our vision, interferes with our intuitive hearing and dampens our mental and spiritual abilities. This Mind Dampener is: the great seething mass of cable, satellite, radio, and major media broadcasting channels that continually pump electronically beamed refuse across the planet infecting humanity with electronic malaise. They infect the world with a relentless torrent of irresistible materialism, consumerism and a mad frenzy to be entertained every moment of our lives. These Western values keep us as far away as possible from a meaningful exploration of our own consciousness so that we are condemned to continue as a populace of wage slaves and rampaging materialist mall-dwellers rather than discover who we truly are. Most importantly, it disrupts our access to our own consciousness twenty-four/seven.

The human mind was designed as a precision tool, like a cutting instrument—laser beam or an electron microscope. Unfortunately, from almost the time we are born, terrible forces work in concert to dull and dampen the abilities and sharpness of this fearfully and wonderfully made instrument. The "Hydra's breath" is a scalding stream of cerebral noise and mental pollution ludicrously disguised as mainstream entertainment, information or even as "mainstream news."

Any possibilities of meaning reflection, contemplation or meditation upon the things that really matter; becomes almost impossible. The negativity-filled mind is similar to a computer hardware system that is so infected, like a computer virus infected software system that the horrible infections eventually compromise the hardware system as well.

The first individual Hydra head of the great chatter machine is the establishment Global News Media complex that pervades the entire globe and directs the thinking of so many people by distraction, using 2 percent of the news throughout the world in order to distract the global populace from the 98 percent of events and happenings that truly matter. If you listen to mainstream news, read or even look at any mainstream newspapers or mainstream publications, pay any attention to mainstream news media in any of its vile forms—*you are eating baby-food.*

It is very difficult to wean ourselves off this vile stuff. Independent thought always requires action so it is much harder than passively accepting predigested, spoon-fed, baby food. Proactively working in the cyber-network to find information that actually matters to us as independent, thinking individuals; *requires real effort.* But more than anything, it requires an extraordinarily high value placed upon independent thought and truth.

But if you are willing to put forward that effort and if you place that kind of value on independent, critical thinking; *then* there are things that you must do immediately. Seek out specialized/alternative news sources that do not censor themselves because of the EPIC mandate to control what the general populace may view or have access to. These news sources should be cyber-sources, peer-to-peer sources, and live broadcasts from friends/neighbors/members of *your* community. This will be almost up-to-the-minute news; not news that is 48 hours or even a week old from the moment it gets to you.   Reject filtered, censored, predigested, mainstream information crafted for infantile minds.   It is for slaves and prisoners.

The 2nd individual Hydra-Head is the Cosmic killer of initiative and independent thought known as "series television and cable programming."   This second brand of insidious noise is the modern incarnation of the British Imperial Army Drum Corps beating out a steady tune as they roll over every corner of the globe.   Rather than military domination, the Elite Powers In Control, EPIC, are achieving mental domination.   Cable programs are the 24/7 pounding of the great mass of humanity into giving up their God-given ability to think in exchange for privilege of becoming non-critical thinking, non-creative, risk-averse grist for the global corporate labor mills of the planet.   Cable programming acculturates our children's minds into accepting that humankind's conflicts and problems can be resolved each week in 30 minute to 60-minute increments of drama, comedy, mystery or witty banter in any genre.   It is incredibly damaging to our mind's ability to function on higher planes.   After too much exposure to this sort of disguised attack, you can kiss your abstract thought capabilities goodbye.

The third individual Hydra Head of the Dampener is commercial advertising, propaganda and marketing advertisements.   In the 1950s, during the height of the Cold War against the enormously powerful Soviet Union, the United States government took a great deal of advice and management from a descendant of Sigmund Freud.   His name was Edward Bernays and he became the father of an industry called "public relations."   He became fabulously wealthy by creating the marketing and propaganda industry based upon the realities that people/consumers/the masses react in a more visceral manner when you use advertising and propaganda that taps into their unconscious fears, doubts, worries and even hatreds—the reptilian part of the human brain.   The U.S. government used this advice to manage the "Red Menace" campaign and to increase their control over events and the nation.   This lesson was also learned by the Global advertising/marketing industry and they have used it ever since to motivate the minds of the controlled populace through the deepest negativity rather than positive messages.

This third Hydra Head eases us into believing that it is normal and not harmful for our minds to be in a constant state of siege from multiple, constant streams of advertisements and commercials that propose poisonous messages: *that we probably exhibit symptoms of horrible diseases, need prescription drugs they are selling, have dirty kitchen floors, are at risk for every terrible malady known to man and suffer innumerable desperate conditions that require whatever product or service they are pushing at the moment.*

Commercials and propaganda are pieces of media that often have 60 seconds up to a few minutes to make you believe you are: incomplete, miserable, in sorrow, uncool, unpopular, unhappy, not as good as you could be, desperately unhappy and not as good as your neighbor.   These are bullets of intense negativity that most people don't believe do much damage to their psyche—until they go methodically through the process of Cosmic Introspection and calculate the massive psychic damage they are undoing.

We are being poisoned by ear. Although we believe innocuous background noise doesn't affect us, our minds are both more vulnerable and much more powerful than we can imagine. Like the Shakespearean King assassinated by poison poured in through his ear, our brains are being murdered by toxic noise pouring in slowly. It drips in bit by bit. The power of our subconscious mind picks up, absorbs explicit negative programming, and even picks up semi-hidden messages in the background. Negative messages, pain-based advertising, envy-based programming, raw materialistic messages and music videos; this all is absorbed and synthesized into our psyche and becomes a part of our own internal programming. This small section of the Mind Dampener disperses its bile all over us, consistently over years and decades, in multi-faceted forms. It sets up negative parameters and neural pathways in our brains that are difficult to repair.

The global elites who perpetuate the vast powerful networks of the Dampener as overlord of our lives, know that the *last thing* they need is a society of "common" people accessing their great potentialities—becoming artists, magnates, successful business owners—competitors to the status quo and independent thinkers and creators of new systems that challenge the EPIC world order. These are the things that would destroy the corporate/government dominated culture they have carefully installed over many centuries.

In Latin, a well-known phrase is "Ordo Abchao"—"order out of chaos." I use it to refer to the government finding (or quietly creating) a societal problem, then exacerbating it into chaos while pretending to try to resolve it. Exhaust the people mentally and emotionally—and they will accept any solution—then the Great Solution appears: increased government power, centralization, and control in the hands of global bureaucrats. They can't do this if the Great Dampener loses power. If we had a true investigative journalistic class that began asking real questions, if the population of our countries were to unplug, shut it off and rebuild their peace and the power of their spirit and minds, if cosmic introspection broke out on a massive scale; then this fraud would come to a close.

Here is what EPIC *does want*: a great seething mass of loyal obedient wage slaves for their corporations, companies, global conglomerates, government administrations and a Western World full of voracious consumers for their products and services. We learn from commercials and cable programming that we must live as purely sensual/physical beings and strive only for the material comforts that life can provide. We follow the conditioning by obediently staying trapped in cycles of credit card debt, consumer debt, and various personal debts that keep people unable to climb out of this tar pit. The loyalty (to this depraved system) exhibited by mind-slaves is further demonstrated by their acceptance of fear language manifested in tender concepts like "job security" and "corporate retention rates."

These worker bees couldn't tell you the accomplishments of people like Mahatma Gandhi or Deepak Chopra but can recite chapter and verse of the latest travails of the number one music pop star. That's because the "bread and circuses" at the coliseum of the Roman empire have now been replaced with thousands of satellite cable programming channels on television, Internet, radio and various other media.

This Hydra does not had three heads but hundreds even thousands of reptilian heads snapping at our souls eager to consume any threat to its continued subjugation of the general populaces' freedom and independence. I am here as Loalus to give you the long overdue key to destroying the power of the great modern Hydra—the Mind Dampener of humanity before it's too late. The final defeat of the Global media complex can be accomplished; but its overthrow must begin by reducing its power and influence, by recognizing it for what it truly is and by beginning to take away its nutrition—our money, our patronage and our consciousness. Then the Hydra Dragon will weaken and it will become vulnerable for the cutting and cauterizing of those evil heads.

We need a popular movement that commences with massive unplugging. It will be composed of the most daring among us showing how to unplug from the global noise machine. Turning off those televisions, shutting down cable television, shutting off satellite radio, refusing to buy the old "news print media" (that for some bizarre reason still exists); are the greatest acts of freedom loving independence and resistance to EPIC dominance any individual can accomplish. The new resisters of tyranny will not stand on street corners making speeches or run with mobs throwing rocks at government buildings. They will take their index fingers, call their cable providers, satellite providers, subscription providers and they will shut off the noise machines that keep them from getting in touch with powers far greater than anything broadcast cable can muster—and this must be done quickly because *time is running out.*

No one can be a Para-Investigator unless they are deconditioned from culturally imposed Mind Dampening first. Once the prospective Para-Investigator or any recovering mind has completed the process of Cosmic Introspection—letting go, unplugging, shutting off and regenerating peace and presence for the mind; they will become sensitized to and revolted by negativity. They will be unable to tolerate: commercials on radio and television, mainstream media news, cable series television or the innumerable forms of noxious mental pollution.

The few times recovering minds and Para-Investigators must listen to those mediums for business or social reasons, the mute button on the remote will become a vital part of that process. The best part is still coming. After de-conditioning, *comes the Awakening.*

44

THE CULTURALLY CONDITIONED MIND

Those who are awake and aware, face the most overwhelming force for slavery and conformity that has ever existed—the Culturally Conditioned Minds of the populace. This is the average mental state of the great mass of people trained and controlled by mainstream institutions and programming.

There's no real "mind-control" anymore. Tragically, there's very little need for it—at least not on a mass scale of any sort. Actually controlling the thoughts and actions of individuals was a labor-intensive process that required sometimes years of specifically targeted work, all to achieve the promise of some robotic "Manchurian-candidate" like outcome in the future. The return on investment was speculative at best. Now we have the much more pervasive and mass scale success of *Mind-Conditioning*.

Cultural training and mental conditioning is so rampant in every mainstream population that they reflexively respond to unapproved new ideas with condemnation, judgment and without investigation. This type of mind conditioning does not control outcome but instead guarantees inaction, lethargy, indolence on a massive scale so the architects of societal fate will have little to no interference in their plans for humanity. When the cultural guardians and interpreter institutions: school systems, mainstream news media, popular culture and materialist sciences; are able to dictate the limits what you believe is possible; then you have entered the prison built for your mind, stepped in and slammed the cell door on yourself. Your jailers have their surrogates in the media, in banking, in education, in cultural institutions, in all popular mainstream media; jingling the keys to your prison every time they succeed in making any of their mentally conditioned sheep utter phrases of allegiance to their jailers:

...Show me proof of what you're saying—not just blanket statements!
(subtext: *once you show proof you've fallen into my trap because my thought masters have taught me to deconstruct evidence as a weapon against any dangerous innovative thinkers*)

…who else is reporting this?
(subtext: *until I hear it on the corporate-government media, I'll never believe it*)

…where are you getting that information?
(subtext: *unless you are getting that information from a culturally approved source, I've been trained to disregard it.*)

Why would the government lie?
(subtext: *I'll keep believing what the government feeds me right up until the moment me and my family are pushed into ovens and the heat is turned all the way up.*)

That person is "conspiracy theorist/nut…"
(subtext: *according to my mental conditioning, the application of this label to this person gives me approval not to think about, analyze or even consider what this person is saying*)

He's anti-government.
(subtext: *Again, according to my mental conditioning, the application of this label to this person gives me cultural approval not to think about, analyze or even consider what this person is saying*)

He's just a truther, she's a birther, he's a hearer….
(subtext: *Again, according to my mental conditioning, the application of any of these labels to this person gives me cultural approval not to think about, analyze or even consider what this person is saying*)

Throw off this sheepish thinking. Free your mind.

Currently throughout the earth, approximately only about three to four percent of the earth's population is "awake." The rest are imprisoned and in slavery under the various global systems. In the Western World, the figure is worse at about 2 to 3 percent. Due to higher levels of materialism and organized religion, the Western nations have much fewer people who are engaged in the Awakening Process through increased spirituality or purely higher awareness. "Awake" simply means (like Para-Investigators)—able to discern truth from lies and deception. It means able to perceive the Mind-Dampening systems that EPIC uses to sap the will of any population to escape global control and manipulation. "Awake" also means impervious to the many energy-sucking constructs that impose absolute control over the imprisoned populace.

There have been some modest gains in recent years in weakening the great reptilian Hydra. Mainstream media has declined in power and influence with the rise of the Internet. The concurrent freedom it has brought to the cyber-masses has greatly alarmed the EPIC, but global powers are working 24-7 even now to bring the world and the Internet into global taxation, control and domination. Additionally, technological forces are working to reinvigorate the global Hydra and reassert its power over our minds to a level undreamed of in the previous age. We are in a race towards ultimate unfoldment before the vise of global tyranny closes on our planet forever. Para-Investigators will be a crucial tool to help humanity win that race.

PARA-INVESTIGATIVE AWAKENINGS

Reshape your language and you reshape your destiny.

45

PARA-INVESTIGATIVE TOOLS

We have come to the first "great reveal" of this work. Something is coming very soon that makes awakening a much more urgent imperative than ever before. Cosmic Introspection, self-awareness, understanding of the self or any journey of self-discovery and turning inward to face yourself; is about to go from difficult *to nearly impossible* for those unfortunates still trapped in the great mainstream of global society.

There are several places on the earth, technological research centers, where several of the next generations of technology are being developed at a breakneck pace. These are purely scientific technological research facilities dominated and run by non-governmental global institutions. These are not to be confused with the numerous underground governmental and military underground installations built to serve future globalist purposes.

There are five traits these technological research centers have in common:

1. They each have installations and structures that are underground and out of site to general civilian populations. There are numerous other reasons as well for this placement beyond plain practicality.

2. While they sometimes pretend to be sponsored by the nations that host them, they are actually sponsored by networks of global organizations, known and unknown "NGOs" (Non-Governmental Organizations) that receive virtually no national supervision of their operations and they are almost completely free of oversight from the various nations that supposedly host them.

3. They each have leading scientists and pioneers in the "hard sciences" working around the clock at these installations; along with some of their best students and assistants. As a matter of fact, if you have known one of these upper echelon minds in the hard sciences and he and his family have disappeared for a couple of years;

its highly likely that they went voluntarily to live at one of these installations for a Temporary Duty Assignment in high salaried positions. However, sometimes they never come back.

Most dangerous of all, there are cells of these scientists who are seldom seen even by the main body of workers in the installation. These cells are working with encapsulated "black technology." The word "black" in this context is said to refer to the sources of funding. (*But the term resembles "black magic" doesn't it?*) This is "next level technology" whose original sources are not allowed to be fully known even by those working with it. Additionally those who are working with it are allowed to know *just enough* to operate a small piece of the whole. The great alternative thinker, Dr. Richard Dolan explains in his book: "A.D. After Disclosure: When the Government Finally Reveals the Truth About Alien Contact" that these insulated mini-societies are actually "breakaway civilizations." These are human-hybrid cultures that operate independently from mainstream human civilization with abilities and technology that is unfathomable to ordinary humans.

4. These installations typically release information about benign, easy to understand projects they are working on for public consumption. This is a cover. They keep the "real projects" classified at levels above Top Secret. The establishment media in any case does not report on these installations. What little is reported about these places is again on the benign, humanitarian work that is funneled out through corporate publicity agents (the global news networks). The only truth about what goes on at these installations only comes out through alternative and highly specialized news sources. Only the relatively tiny Awakened Community has any idea what actually goes on at these bases.

5. Some of what is developed at these installations will remain hidden from popular consciousness forever—unused in mainstream society. Some of the tech is already being used covertly but will never be openly revealed. Some of it will be released in the near future and used throughout mainstream society to great fanfare.

Much of the current technology in the mainstream world will be rendered obsolete by CSIT: **Complete Sensory Immersion Technology** (*Not True Name*)—the first generation of true virtual reality devices for widespread use—cost effective to build, cheap to buy, easy and convenient to use; and staggering in the realism levels that will be achieved. The hardware will be the tiniest plug which will fit easily inside the ear or in some other unseen bodily venue. The software will be based on quantum liquid breakaway tech. The applications for CSIT will be endless and wildly popular throughout the globe. It could replace some or all portions of the current hardware media systems of the Dampener Overlord—television, radio, etc. The old overlord would be finally be overthrown by a new greater overlord that seizes human minds on a level undreamt of by the previous one—but each overlord will still be under to same ultimate master—the EPIC.

That old Hydra—global corporate media—may not be necessary anymore as the global hardwired Colossus it is today. CSIT will take its place with higher efficiency and far greater connectedness. "Meet the new boss, same as the old boss—*but much worse.*"

The potential manipulation, dampening and control of the human mind will be staggering. This will be a system enacted on the body by tech as small as a pea stuck in the human ear and it will place the wearer into a vivid, waking dream of his or her choice. That dream will be as real to all the senses as a concrete wall. This dreamscape will be more real and vivid than our physical reality and will function under preprogrammed parameters—at least for a time. The dreamscape will be rife with trap doors under the control of others and what emerges from those trap doors will be as benign as ten second commercials at first, but later that will change.

If we have not increased the number of people who are self-aware and self-unfolding by the time this CSIT technology pervades throughout our society; it will be much harder to increase our numbers once this insidious system takes root throughout humanity. Technology must not be allowed to destroy our abilities to reach the Great gulf of peace wherein resides all creative imagination and self-actualization. There are alternatives to this grim imminent scenario.

A person does not need to be an intuitive Para-Investigator to know that CSIT will take us much deeper into the chatter and noise that surrounds our minds in the modern world. It may actually insulate us completely from any ability to self-unfold. Once we and our children are addicted to CSIT, it will be exponentially more difficult to convince people of the need to look inward. It will become a Herculean task to get people to consider the importance of reaching serious levels of the self in meditation, spiritual pursuits, natural vivid dreams, sensory deprivation exercises or any of the ways to go into the Ekashic Field.

When CSIT technology becomes available, it will be hailed as the greatest miracle human entertainment has ever seen. Unawakened mainstream consumers will demand it at any price, not realizing the vulnerable position they will be placing themselves in. CSIT will function through direct connection to the brain—not hardwire connection but through technology that wirelessly accesses the brains' neural pathways. Despite this incredibly dangerous requirement to participate in CSIT, only those already Awakened will have the resolve to resist its lure. Many who accept it will find themselves in the new opium dens of the Information Age.

CSIT will be asking for direct linkage to the human brain. However, they will actually be acquiring a direct linkage *to the human soul.* That will be the hidden agenda of CSIT—to find the broadcasting bandwidth *of human consciousness.* Then they will exploit it for purposes so nefarious that most will brush the warnings aside under the old, reliable mind control trigger words: "conspiracy talk."

CSIT will ultimately be used to further enslave humanity. No matter how attractive the Mind Dampener makes CSIT appear, free human beings must reject it as technological violence against the spirit of humanity. Most will not listen to The Awakened. The Western World has been so ingrained with consumerism and materialism that nothing can stem their mad rush for shiny new baubles. Yet, we must try to save as many as we can right now. Once CSIT spreads, it may be too late.

Here is the beginning of what we must do right now to diminish the Dampener Overlord before it becomes more empowered over our minds than it already is.

Refuse all information from the major media establishment that report on two percent of the news in order to distract us from the other 98 percent that actually matters.

We must turn off television.
Shut off the news.
Shut off cable television.
Shut off satellite radio.
Shut off satellite television.

Shut them all off and cancel them and then go to the next section in this chapter subtitled
"Para-Investigative Tools" and repeatedly read and learn each of these tools. Use them over and over to discover another world of experience and power that is available to anyone and to all who dare TO SHUT IT OFF.

SHUT OFF THE JAILERS OF YOUR MIND.

SHUT THEM OFF FOR YOUR CHILDREN...FOR YOUR WORLD AND FOR YOURSELF

SHUT IT ALL OFF and dare to create a new better future based on YOU.

If you were brave enough, daring enough and bold enough to take this giant leap to cutting down the chatter entering your brain by 90 percent then you may be ready for the next great leap. You should be spending several weeks and then months free from the established-media-mind-conditioning devices of the Western world. You should have replaced the loathsome mainstream chatter with fresh alternative news sources and cyber media that is specialized for you as an individual and for the *highest aspirations* that you have as a human being.

You should redirect any reaching for media into the active pursuit of specialized knowledge, both spiritual and material, that uplift and excite the highest values in you. Carefully, slowly build new sources of information from alternative media in the same way you would lay the foundation and pipes for a new home you've always wanted.

The house is your mind and the pipes will carry data like clear, fresh, non-fluoridated water to your home. With these new pipes and new water, no longer will you and your family be numbed into a narcotic stupor and into accepting anything EPIC decides is best. Once your alternative sources are set up and nourishing and uplifting you, you will no longer be tempted to relapse back into the old world of cultural conditioning that victimizes the global population.

Once you have cut the noxious toxins going INTO your brain, we must next cut down the chatter coming OUT of your brain. There is a great deal of noise and chatter entering your brain from the useless noise of society's Dampener but there is another great portion of noise also regenerated by your brain (again due to mental conditioning) going outward toward the universe. It is the memories of yesterday's noise and every day before that—regenerating past noise and negativity, thoughts of future problems, worries and concerns thereby creating new noise in the future. Unplug that also.

Several Para-Investigative tools used for resolution of mysteries and crimes are the same tools for regeneration of a recovering harmonious mind. These are vital agents for reconditioning the suppressed, dormant mind/consciousness. The central Para-Investigative tools for regeneration of a harmonious mind are: transcendental meditation, lucid dreaming and waking contemplations.

Transcendental meditation in the past has been directed, by those who approach it as a mystic process. It is nothing of the sort. It is a humanistic, proven method for achieving higher mental planes. Also, it has universally been taught as an end unto itself—as a process for achieving relaxation and an improvement in general disposition, attitude and demeanor but it can be far more. It is true that it should be mastered first as a method for relaxation and improving general attitude but after ten to twenty sessions, once that has been done, it should be used for even higher purposes.

Here is the process explained so that even any typical Westerner like me can understand and follow.

Equipment needed for successful transcendental meditations:

one sitting pillow
one reliable alarm clock that can be set for 20 to 25 minutes
one set of earplugs
one blindfold that completely covers the physical eyes
one set of people in your household/family/loved ones who will respect that you require 20 to 30 minutes of complete undisturbed silence

Process

Establishing a space—Find a place, corner, small space with no phones, no communication devices or noise making devices within earshot so you can attain 20 to 30 minutes of total silence

Set alarm for 20 to 30 minutes, set earplugs and blindfold in place, settle into the correct spot comfortably on your sitting pillow. Stretch your muscles, relax your body, and begin to empty your mind of all concerns, worries, negativity — let the darkness flow out of your mind. Breathe in light and exhale darkness. 20 to 30 deep cleansing breaths.
Visualize it and it will happen.

Completing the circuit—cross your legs, straighten your spine and lace your fingers/hand together across the middle of your lap so your body forms a three-point triangle.

Relaxation and position—Relax your entire body as much as possible while still maintaining posture and the three-point triangle. Begin deep breathing.

Quieting the chatter—*Clear your mind of all thoughts.* Concentrate on nothing except the sound of your own breathing. When thoughts pop up involuntarily, just imagine them as scenes on floating, balloon-like television screens and gently push them away. Continue this process, just listen to your own breathing and push away all thoughts until your mind remains cleared and all chatter is gone.

Successful conclusion—Final Result

Etheric state achieved—your breath will diminish slightly and energy will begin to descend from the Superconscious Gulf. You will feel energy you never have before and the world you return to will be slightly changed.

Follow this process for 15 to 20 successful sessions to establish your ability to achieve the most difficult step—quieting the chatter. This is, by far, the hardest to achieve due to the incredible volume and intensity of mental noise that fills our modern lives. This is the step where most people tend to give up. It may seem impossible but it is not. We can completely shut down the chatter in our minds. If you persevere in 15 to 20 successful sessions, you will have established regular contact with the Superconsciousness Gulf wherein the Great Cosmic Mind resides and awaits to commune with you.

Aside from making it possible for you to tap into the abilities needed to be a Para-Investigator, there will be numerous personal benefits as well. Negativity directed at you will have lost its edge whether it is anger, envy, jealously, hostility, indifference, insulting behavior any type; it will not affect you nearly to the degree that it did before. There will be a layer of serenity of protecting your spirit (the real you) at all times. The ego-self that is based on vanity, arrogance and fear will be withdrawn further inside to farther reaches in a place where it cannot control you. The superior spiritual portion of your soul will have grown to give you better covering. This spiritual part is the luminous part of each person that has no: pride, ego, self-serving motive, desire for selfish gain or self-serving motives of any kind. It exudes humility; desire to serve and *it can only act out of love.*

Every law-enforcement institution should establish a space for individual and group meditation. This would not be an area for rest but for work; where law-enforcement officers would come to unfold the abyss containing all the answers about their investigations. These tools are not occult stunts but simply focus exercises for increasing the external power of the mind when infusing ideas and thought with conscious power and drawing strength and guidance from the Cosmic Mind.

Another Para-Investigative Tool is lucid dreaming. In our continuing efforts to pierce the veil of the Superconscious Gulf, we must use the power of the subconscious mind to guide us to the Oversoul. It is vital to enlist the profound power of the subconscious mind in pushing toward goals and the achievements we wish to attain. Even if that goal is just self-knowledge, all of our Para-investigative tools will assist toward that simple goal.

Lucid dreams are extraordinarily vivid dreams that have a purpose or lesson to teach us that can aid us in our waking life. They are also dreams in which we realize that we are both the dreamer and the dream. We can control our actions and outcomes in the dream to differing extents. Lucid dreams will often provide the answer to a question that has dogged us for a very long period or at least will point the way to wherein the answer lies. We cannot, with full certainty, induce lucid dreams at will but we can make it very likely by following a simple procedure and using the greatest power available to each us—the power of our intention and faith.

At bedtime, we should follow this procedure:

1. Quiet the hardware operating system of the mind so that only "the query" is in your mind. Silence all other chatter. Acquire a comfortable position and make all accommodations so your body will know by muscle memory that it is time for sleep. Make certain you have a pad of paper and writing utensil set nearby.

2. As you begin to relax in preparation for sleep, upload a request from your conscious mind and just "point it" toward your subconscious. Request and intend that you will have dreams that will answer your query or lead you to an answer on a conflict you are attempting to resolve.

3. Your query or request should be answered in dream and if you do not recall the dream (sometimes our mind does not allow us to remember important dreams) the imprint of the response/solution/answer will be left on your awakening mind—like a spiritual post it note stuck on your forehead. It should be vivid in your mind as

soon as you awaken so you must write it down immediately. These illuminations can begin to disappear soon after we awaken.

Waking contemplation exercises are excellent for strengthening the mental muscles in short bursts for opening channels of focused concentration through visualization exercises. These are easier ways for someone to start who might have problems with more extended meditations to begin with.

1. Take a long hot bath or shower in dark silence. Water with silence is a powerful combination. This must to be done without other occupants in the home for complete silence. We should shut off phone ringers and all technical communication devices. The only light, if any is necessary, should be from small night-lights or candles. Before beginning, there should be the preconceived intention to focus on *gratitude and goal attainment* during this period. Prepare any particular query or request for upload to the Superconsciousness. Stop all thoughts temporarily—cease all mental chatter, thought pollution and ego-based efforts to think into the past or the future. Bring the full awareness of your spiritual presence into that continuing moment throughout this process. Do not allow the chattering mind to try to propel you into future thoughts or past thoughts. Stay focused in the present. As a part of this focus practice, allow the spirit to expand throughout the reality of the present moment in order to truly feel and sense the fullness of all stimuli present in the situation you have set up. Each time your brain resists the present moment, you must use the power of your intention and spirit to bring yourself back into the present moment. Great revelations will occur to your mind and spirit as the water soothes your physical being.

2. If the shower/bath contemplation is not yet practical, an even simpler exercise for sharpening the ability to enter the present moment and sharpen intuitive abilities can be increased with just a silent abode, darkness and a candle. With a focus on gratitude and goal attainment and a complete attainment of the present moment, we must slip out of time and drop completely into the now. This is done by stopping the efforts of your brain to constantly take you into the past and the future. The brain is always trying to get you out of the present moment because if you attain complete presence in the present moment, you begin to feel who you really are—a spirit managed by a Cosmic Consciousness from a nonlocal field. The brain as a hardware system is completely invested in tricking you into believing that you are just an ego wrapped in a flesh bound identity. The brain/ego struggles to keep chattering out thoughts about your past (worry, doubt, fears, concerns) and about your future (again worry, doubts, fears and concerns) so that you will always miss the real truth of what you are—an eternal spiritual power emanating from the Gulf of Superconsciousness. When you quiet your brain from chattering about the past and the future, you will slip "out of time" and into a place you may not have visited for a long time—the actual present.

Slipping into the present moment may affect different people in different ways but the only common denominator is that you will feel different. I usually begin by setting up my lit candle in a dark room and I sit on a pillow in front of a table holding the candle. Then I take a deep breath and still any chatter in my mind. Complete halt. No thinking about past or future. There is only the sacred present moment. My breath deepens and slows. Time slows down and disappears. Everything appears to be in extreme slow motion.

Honor the present sacred moment...

If a ceiling fan is spinning, it suddenly is moving very slowly, impossibly so. My five senses increase exponentially and my spirit expands outside my physical body sometimes to fill the entire room or several rooms. Yet I can hear a loud whooshing sound from the slowed down ceiling fan. Any tiny sounds in the room like the ticking of an old-fashioned clock become deafening booms impacting in my ears like steel mallets smashing rocks. I see my own body motionless from the ceiling and I see everything else in the room in relationship to my body. But my vantage point is not just from the ceiling. Somehow, I can see from everywhere in the room and into each other room. In the actual present, I can be everywhere in my immediate area. I don't know how it is possible but it does happen when I slip out of the artificial march of time created by the chattering deceptive brain and into the eternal present moment that is generated by The Mind.

Then, stare into the lit candle and check that you are still feeling gratitude and thankfulness to the Creator-Source for the joy the present moment brings you. Focus on the resolution of your crime or elusive mystery as you stare into the candle. Things will be revealed. Not only the solution to your crime or mystery, but also the true purpose of your existence and the plans upon plans the universe has designed you for will bloom like flowers of Divine Beauty.

These are the Para-Investigative Tools that can lead you through Cosmic Introspection and once you have completed this journey, you will see it is not just the abyss that has unfolded, but Yourself. You need to follow the direction of this chapter over the course of several months to complete the entire regimen for a recovering mind. Once you have completed several weeks of faithfully following this course of self-treatment, you will be a Para-Investigator or even better—*a fully self-aware human being.* You will now exist outside of the sphere of influence of those who would enslave your mind. You will now see the cultural conditioning everywhere you look but you will be unaffected by it. Instead, you will pity those still caught up in the massive global delusion that had you firmly ensnared until recently. You can call it deprogramming, taking the red pill, enlightenment or awakening. The results will be the same. You will be a different person and you may find yourself on a slightly alien landscape unable to comprehend how you wasted so much of your life on so many meaningless things.

You will be unable to listen to negative chatter anymore—it will assault your senses like nails across a chalkboard. Whether it is pain-based commercial advertising, music videos promoting materialistic hedonism or even toxic people spewing acidic bile disguised as conversation, entertainment or news—you will find it intolerable. You will need to flee such things. That will be how you really know.

You are awakening.

46

PARANORMAL PROGRAMMING BY EPIC

The most unsettling effect of becoming an Awakened Being is an unceremonious ejection from the composed institutional reality designed to keep the population sedated, bedazzled but most of all…distracted. This world has trained the population to be manipulated from cradle to grave. In a society that is largely based on the Elite Powers In Charge (EPIC) using their institutions to contain and manipulate the minds of the population, the truly Awakened Mind (recently liberated from the old constructs) emerges onto an alien landscape. Now, things they barely noticed in their previous incarnation are burning their senses like holy water burns a vampire.

Things we took for granted before as mere background now cause us unbearable anguish. Things as simple as crass commercialism, party politics, mainstream religion, the media networks, the big game, the bowl, the championship, the latest hit songs and the thousands of radio, TV, satellite and cable programs across the globe many of which were previously important are now simply intolerable. Friends and family will often say; *"why can't you just be like you were before—normal?"*

The awakened Truth Seeker will hunger for serious consistent treatment of spiritual and paranormal topics. The seeker should resort to the less lucrative (and therefore less controlled) mediums: books, radio and internet.

EPIC "green lights" voluminous programming to deal with the unending demand for paranormal programs; yet they carefully control the linguistics and instill pervasive shallowness into such programs. Look at a small sample of such programs that have been started and then mostly cancelled during the last few years:

The Antiques Ghost Show 2003, Living TV (UK)
Ancient Aliens, History Channel (USA) 2009 - ?
America's Haunted Castles 2005, Travel Channel

Beyond 2005 (Canada)
Creepy Canada 2002 – 2006 (Canada)
Celebrity Ghost Stories 2009 - ? Biography Channel
Crossing Over with John Edward 1999 – 2004
Dead Famous 2004 – 2006
Derek Acorah's Ghost Towns 2005 Living TV (UK), Travel Channel
Destination Truth 2007 - ? Syfy Channel
Encounters: The Hidden Truth 1991 Fox Network
Extreme Paranormal 2009 A&E Network
Exploring the Unknown 1999 Saban Entertainment, Fox Kids
Fenómeno 2000 RTP2, Mínima Ideia (Portugal)
Fortean TV 1997 – 1998 Channel 4
Ghost Adventures 2008 - ? Travel Channel
Ghost Hunters 2004 - ? Syfy
Ghost Hunters Academy 2009 Syfy
Ghost Hunters International 2007 - ? Syfy
Ghost Lab 2009 Discovery Channel
Ghost Stories (TV series) 1997 - 1998 FOX Family
Ghost Stories (2009 TV series) 2009 - ? Travel Channel
Ghost Story (TV series) 2006 (UK)
Ghost Trackers 2006 YTV
Ghost Whisperer 2005 – 2010 CBS
Ghosthunters 1996 Discovery Channel Europe

The majority of these shows created to "satisfy" the relentless public demand for serious treatment of paranormal topics are *ghost hunter type* shows which are little more than bad theater with former celebrities or underemployed people running in circles and acting terrified while assistant producers rummage around in "haunted attics" clanking chains and dropping objects. Such shows often portray the paranormal as an area of ridicule fit only as titillation for the lowest strata of human society.

Another level of the paranormal shows listed above are thinly disguised "debunker shows" which are meant to tickle people's curiosity and draw believers in with a promise of "balanced" examination of paranormal themes. Then, these shows scientifically grab them by the collar, but then by the end of the show, they disprove the paranormal subject and throw the watcher/believer back into the box with five holes. They are usually staffed with rationalists, non-believers and scientific types; anxious to debunk the topic and indirectly ridicule those gullible enough to tune in.

Very rarely, shows on this very lucrative medium (television, cable, satellite TV) make it through to a television market with a staff of true believers and enormous popularity; yet EPIC still carefully controls the dialogue by controlling the language. A successful show on paranormal topics is degraded from the beginning by being forced to use the language previously invented by materialists as pejorative—language that drags along an enormous burden of stigma from a previous age.

Conspiracy Theory
Fact or Fiction
Myths and Legends

There is also nomenclature that reinforces the idea that you will never be sure paranormal truths are real:

Unknown Mysteries
Unexplained (but really unexplainable) Mysteries
Strange But True?

Probably the worst appellation, most loaded with negative connotations is the old acronym "UFO." A 1950s U.S. Air Force pilot invented this term. Yet despite use of the old loaded language; shows like "UFO Hunters" and numerous other UFO programs (not listed above due to space considerations), have been consistently popular and yet are always cancelled from cable television whenever they are becoming "too popular."

Rarely (very rarely) there may even be one or two paranormal shows in a decade managed and populated by true believers, enormously successful in the ratings and actually accorded respect even by critics; yet regardless of all this success, *even these will always* be cancelled within about three years (again with little or no explanation). In the last decade, even with interest in the paranormal exploding to higher levels than ever before in modern history, I'm certain no genuinely paranormal television show *will ever* break the five year barrier. After five years, such programming might begin to cause Mass Awakening. If you can show me the exception, I would be delighted to demonstrate why and how that show stays within a preset formula designed to strictly limit what viewers may think and discuss on the paranormal subject area.

We, the Awakened believers must continue to develop and utilize alternative methods (outside the control of mainstream corporate media) to spread the word and support the growth of the paranormal Awakened Community. As we can see above, depending upon the media minions of EPIC in the constant effort to awaken others is *not* a workable business model for long-term success. Even if we must stand on street corners, on our own time, without remuneration, to grow the community of The Awakened, we must do so gladly.

47

RECOGNIZING CRIME

There's no conspiracy.

There's no longer any need for one. Since the global corporate news media complex works in complete obedience to the EPIC masters—secrecy for EPIC machinations is unnecessary and obsolete. Also, because the global media has worked tirelessly for the last fifty years to create the convincing illusion of "freedom" in the Western World; conspiracy is also outdated except as a poisonous label used to excoriate anyone with ideas outside the mainstream paradigm. EPIC institutions and minions commit their deeds out in the open every single day. There is *no* reportage. There are no recriminations or calling out of EPIC and their lackey institutions; except among that three to five percent of the population that is already Awakened but *they are only speaking to each other.*

EPIC has conditioned most of humanity to immediately reject (without analysis or consideration) any ideas outside the culturally conditioned paradigm that the materialist, global media has created; so that even as we develop an alternative media interconnected among the Awakened Community the question remains; who else will listen?

The system of the national governments continuing to implement endless cycles of generated Crisis-Chaos-Control will only grow more deadly to the populations they purport to protect. Government finds a problem and then with help from the obedient mainstream media and their own bureaucratic machinations—increase and amplify the problem so that it will perceived as a genuine crisis. Then, Government reliably makes the former problem spiral seemingly out of control until the alarms ring that extreme measures must be taken to prevent the fall of society and all the values we hold dear. Then, the true endgame of this cycle is inevitably reached and National and Global Institutional Control is increased over the people who are, by then, clamoring to have more of their liberties taken away in favor of security. This methodology is not just centuries old—it has been used for thousands of years and it still works all too well.

We need a shift.

The major urgency for a cadre of independent, lucid True Investigators unaffected by the fossilized paradigm of materialism, is that presently there are *no* remaining guardians of the people's well-being and survival. The governments of the nations of the world are becoming more and more brazen in their use of the model that is so terribly familiar to watchers and seekers of truth. Governments attack liberty (while pretending to attack a crisis) and the corporate controlled media is delighted to publicly discredit and character-assassinate anyone who dares to point out such truths as "Conspiracy-Nuts" or whatever might be the latest pithy extremist label.

In this process, the national Government leaders who answer to higher authorities can often believe they are acting in the best interests of their people but they do so against logic and reason. They exacerbate a problem into a potential holocaust and become part of the global CRIME system—CRIMEs against humanity and against freedom. Some high minion national leaders are fully aware of the process, if they are part of the Bloodlines of EPIC but the EPIC Overlords keep most in the dark. *They just follow orders.*

CRISIS—false, manufactured human problem created or exacerbated by the national and global governments

RESPONSE—apparent reluctant action by the government with cover provided from the global mainstream media and

INCREASED—magnified/amplified

MISERY—a degraded/animalistic/enslaved state of humankind...

ENTHRONED—permanent reduction in quality of life especially when disguised as temporary, fleeting or as interim measures—liberty-reductions with eternal bureaucracies to enforce these reductions forever

We need a shift.

When a crisis is created or exacerbated by Government, Mainstream Media plays a vital role by trumpeting and amplifying the horrors that loom over society. Usually it must be of a nature that creates great fear in the general population. Fear leads people to cry out for any solution—even *extreme* solutions that will inevitably result in a loss of life, comfort and loss of freedom.

Usually the response is a dramatic acting job by the same Government who created the crisis in which the Government "reluctantly" offers their subjects a series of oppressive options to address the people's "security." The Mainstream Media again plays a vital role by beating the drums in print, broadcast television and in every available venue for the absolute dire need to give up liberty, freedom and independence in order to remedy this impending catastrophe. The national government must appear to offer this reluctantly because they have no interest in further increasing their domination over the people they already dominate with oppressive taxation and immoral over-regulation. This model of governmental behavior has been reliable for so many years (about the last sixty years since the Mainstream Media gave up any pretense of being investigators or seekers of truth); because it invites the culturally conditioned minds to beg and plead with the national governments to take away their liberty. The taxes are increased. The new war launched against drugs, terrorism or poverty invariably turns out to be a war *against us.*

Increased misery enthroned always refers to the imposition by government bureaucrats of measures that increase the power and control of government bureaucrats for the benefit of government bureaucrats who have only disdain for liberty of the people they rule over. The new oppression is enthroned because despite talk of: abolishment, election recall, redress of grievances, repeal, exemptions, waivers or any other such doublespeak; once new governmental abuse is established—it's there forever. If you doubt the permanence of that condition, go back in the historical record and check politician promises right after any governmental agency is caught in massive abuses and illegal actions. There are extensive records of speeches promising abolishment or downsizing of that agency but nothing ever results. Instead of serving the people, such bureaucrats are in a constant state of CRIME against their people's liberty, independence and sovereignty—and worse of all, *the people begged for these abuses.*

This is CRIME against humanity, against our right to life, against our right to be free and against our right to live outside the globalist system of slavery and obedience to an EPIC Order that cares nothing for our families or our nations. Yet these crimes are committed everyday by "national" institutions and organizations whose true loyalty is not to their people, their oaths or their country but to their Order—their EPIC Order.

We definitely need a shift.

From the moment of JFK's assassination to the mass shooting incidents against civilians around the world by *"individual gunmen acting alone"* to the innumerable mysterious genocidal events that occur in "coincidental convenience" for the EPIC agenda; we now live in a world controlled by agendas that have nothing to do with any nation's "strategic national interests." National leaders do not dare attack the private, centralized, global banking system that governs their currencies and economies. Entire Western nations vote hysterically to disarm their civilian population and nations obediently agree to go to war over events that ultimately are found never to have happened.

The natural progression has been that EPIC has become more brazen every year in the "operations" they have run to push forward their agenda. They know that no matter how much we improve our methods, our independent media, our technology, our passion and our message; we the Awakened Community are still *just talking to each other*—the tiny minority—but that is changing even now because *we all need a shift in the current paradigm.*

We are growing beyond the tiny four to five percent of every population. It's a tough slog but it is happening. Someday we will reach that magic six percent that it takes to change the world—to effect the Mass Awakening and it will happen sooner than anyone thinks. EPIC is overplaying their hand and the Para-Investigators only need be in place when the Age of Mass Awakening ignites and changes everything.

The Para-Investigators will be a cadre of unrelenting finders of truth who will be unfazed by the crisis distractions regularly provided by globalists and their guard dogs. They will be just one group of the Awakened (there will be many). They will always dig deeper, uncover what no one thought could be revealed and due to their intuitive abilities; *they cannot be lied to or deceived.*

The doors to many interrelated mysteries will be opened very soon as revelation erupts in one area after another—not just in the area of genuine paranormal UFO's but in numerous other areas. Once we attain full revelation that paranormal UFO's exist and that Alien Visitors are awaiting the breaking of a tripwire—open recognition and mass conscious invitation to fully enter our extremely narrow spectrum of reality. Once that line is crossed, it can never be uncrossed. If we do not have cadres that are set up as "voices in the watchtowers of truth telling," then we will be on the precipice of extinction.

The Para-Investigators will be the Quantum Age Shamans of humanity...the Advance Guard of a higher paradigm of Earthly consciousness. They will be only one among many diverse groups dedicated to the proposition that *all men are created spiritual* but then are conditioned to be pitifully physical...*like birds that forgot how to fly.*

As the wise man counseled...*we will be the shift we want to see.*

48

TOTAL AWAKENING TO MASS AWAKENING

The Para-Investigators will be leading the way into the Age of Mass Awakening. Total Awakening is a decision, method and attitude while Mass Awakening is the final goal of that crucial decision. The tribes leading us into the throes of Awakening will declare "Total Awakening"—the continuance of the Awakening Process at all costs. It will be similar to the historical concept of "Total War." In human history of its most desperate struggles, war was declared in a fuller sense than ever conceived before, in which women and children, the elderly, animals, resources, every blade of grass in a town are directly committed into a war effort against an approaching army. Women and children are given weapons to fight to the death, or if none were available, they would create makeshift weapons out of farming tools and kitchen utensils. The horrors that would subsume the defenders if they were taken alive were described to them in graphic and odious detail. The elderly were assigned to leave displayed food in abandoned homes with wide-open front doors and set horrible traps for any enemy troops lured by that poisonous feast. Livestock were purposefully infected with rabies to create another brand of welcome for the troops—vicious and uneatable. Total War left no gaps. When used in its purest form, it could not be overcome because it was fundamentally pyrrhic in nature.

It left nothing to be victorious over.

No matter how superior a military force might be it could not win when there was nothing to be gained. Total war has not often been used in history because it required two rarely found set of circumstances:

1. It required a defending populace that fully understood they were in the most desperate circumstances of imminent destruction with no hope of conventional victory.

2. It required a people whose dedication to their ideals was absolute and unshakable. This had to be a people who above everything else valued *freedom and victory above life itself.*

In the rare circumstances when it has been used, it has *always* been triumphant and will always be so because ultimately no one can defeat those who are willing to give everything for freedom. Yet the most important quality of Total War is not the fact that it always succeeds, it is that it begins with the mindset *which has already won.* The defending individual must adopt the worldview that victory, liberty and freedom are more important than this temporary, physical life. That mindset spreads and that community converts from a herd of sheep to den of wolves awaiting their attackers.

The Age of Mass Awakening will be similar to Total War. Once embarked upon, Mass Awakening will be complete commitment and total devotion of resources toward the goal. Humanity will have no choice but to go forward into the paradigm shift *or* into complete slavery. In Mass Awakening, we will use everything we have to awaken others. There will be total dedication of resources, ideas, love, emotion, determination to the active awakening of all those willing to awaken. Once Mass Awakening is underway, there will be less and less of any value left in the mainstream of any value for EPIC to claim a victory over. There will be a massive unforeseen withdrawal of resources, participation and cooperation with institutions of slavery and imprisonment. Eventually, with great sacrifice, the old EPIC institutions of mainstream imprisonment will finally be left empty, irrelevant and abandoned.

The Para-Investigators will show the way into a new era of Mass Awakening against the wishes of the globalist systems of control and manipulation. EPIC has run their CRIME system for eons and they are very confident in its efficiency. In addition to the CRIME system, EPIC has another system tightening their control every generation. EPIC also uses a system of "date setting for societal shift" which always ends in no shift at all and devolves into more secure imprisonment than ever before. Yet, this time our new "date for a grand global shift" is developing in ways that have never been seen before. *Things are different this time.* One of those things is the Para-Investigators.

49

THE COMING POLE SHIFT

In a planetary pole-shift, earthquakes could move every land mass on the planet—fires and floods could occur that devastate entire continents. Some say this impending planetary catastrophe is the reason national governments have been so busy quietly building so many underground facilities and even small cities beneath the earth. Many observers have asserted that, although these facilities are ostensibly only for military and science research bases that are immune to the needs of surface dwellers; yet these structures are sometimes referred to as arcs that will carry global bureaucrats into the future of humanity.

I would not rule out this possibility, but neither does it concern me. Even if those who issue marching orders to government leaders are planning these arcs for themselves, their families and their bankster cronies (because they fully plan to expel from safety those military and government drones who so fiercely protect these facilities for their masters); they are still doing nothing more than creating very deep and expensive gravesites for themselves.

There is a great pole-shift coming for the Earth but it is not of the type that some believe. It will be, in a way, more radical than the shift of the Earth's physical poles. It will be a shift in the Earth's mental/spiritual poles that presently hold the people of this planet in their disempowered position. The great seemingly indestructible scientific rationalist dome under which we all labor, suffer and to which we render constant homage; will be overthrown and subjugated. That pole will swing over to the bottom of the earth rather than the top where it will occupy a lower place forevermore. In its place, the Spiritual/Intuitive/Metaphysical Overmind of man, which connects us all to the Mind of Creator-Source, will assume its proper position of preeminence of all the systems of humankind. It will be our new North Pole reigning over the top of the world. It will be the first filter of all human systems of thought and action. The poles will be shifted henceforth and forevermore.

Some even in the Awakened Community (refugees from the scientific/materialist paradigm) have long labored to perpetuate the belief that we are approaching a time when the spiritual/metaphysical will finally achieve parity and legitimacy co-equal with the hard sciences and rationality. This is wrong. They beg for crumbs that will never be given and should not be asked for. This mistaken belief is the reason why so many "enlightened" individuals who are part of the Mass Awakening still trumpet their "scientific" credentials, their Ph.ds, their M.D.'s and their previous scientific professional backgrounds. These people assert that spirituality and science will sit side by side, like co-captains of a sports team who graciously share equal credit for victories and hug each other—a lot. They believe these two will, in this harmonious relationship of equals, address all the problems of man with new success undreamt of during common hours. Again, they are wrong.

This false hope only serves to discredit whatever metaphysical truth they labor to put forward. Here are some sayings that dilute the message of so many metaphysical compromisers:

"...having been trained as a scientist/physician/engineer I am quite familiar with the other side of this argument from the point of the view of the hard sciences...."

"...my background in the hard sciences allows me to see both the scientific angle on this paranormal issue and also beyond what scientific fact allows as possible."

"...these experiments under the old scientific model support the new meta-physical theories that may actually show us a new truth..."

These apologies go on ad nauseum in the world of alternative thinking and quantum-consciousness studies. By trying to have a foot in both worlds (the obsolete scientific world and the quantum, emerging, paranormal world), these people will ultimately earn contempt, not accolades, from both sides.

Whenever pioneering thinkers have tried to justify Para-Investigative truths by sidling up next to the fossilized scientific materialist model, they succeed only in appearing ridiculous to fully Awakened Minds. Materialist science of the previous age must be subjugated to new spiritual/metaphysical truth, not bargained with for an equal partnership. The poles must reverse. Only then, will we enter by the narrow gate that leads to salvation.

50

OPENING OF THE AGE

(Following is a prediction I wrote on December 21, 2011)

There are two major skill sets in being a Para-Investigator: one is the real world skills of any true-life investigator. The other skill set is the intuitive ability of the Para-Investigator to find and connect clues to each other and to great hidden truths inside the black maelstrom of universal mind. What makes the Para-Investigators so uncanny is not this ability to connect facts and clues that people can see—it is the ability to find and connect clues that others can't imagine exist.

By way of partial/full disclosure, I have uncovered great truths, as a Para-Investigator, only when I have ruminated upon a matter for weeks or even months at a time. However, I have known Para-Investigators, some of whom are mentioned in this work, who decipher, connect and resolve hidden mysteries within hours and sometimes even *within minutes* of learning the conundrum. They are not just Para-Investigators. *They are Para-Seers.*

Para-Seers are the final evolved form of the Para-Investigator; investigators who have fully developed the ability to go directly into metaphysical intuitive mechanisms and Superconscious Abilities in order to resolve crimes and mysteries. Para-Seers then allow the use of conventional modalities as physical corroboration of truths they have already uncovered supernaturally. There aren't many of them but when you find one, they make Para-investigation look effortless.

One of the things that Para-Investigators and Para-Seers know is the future—just by connecting previously hidden clues to hidden truth. They are *not* prophets but they *can* tell the future. One of the worst obstacles to those who know the future is "date-setting." This is when individuals declare a certain upcoming day, time or event as "The Date That Will Change Everything."

At Sunrise on December 21, 2012, for the first time in nearly 26,000 years, the Sun rose to conjunct the intersection of the Milky Way and the plane of the ecliptic plane. According to the Mayans, who were assisted in some way by unknown entities with incredibly advanced technology in their knowledge of astronomy, this date marked the end of one world and the beginning of another. It was predicted that perhaps those whose minds and spirits cannot enter the new paradigm that will take over our reality *may enter a different reality* or simply enter oblivion. On that morning, our Sun was to be aligned with the black hole that is the center of the Milky Way via its equator. The Galactic Center is a giant Black Hole. This new alignment, we were told would have a strong effect on the gravitational field of our planet. Consequently, many EPIC institutions created and spread tremendous fear throughout the planet surrounding that date.

History is *not* cyclical, as many have been taught. *It is climactic.* The cycles do exist within the great rising crescendo of human existence but to focus on cycles is a distraction from our greatest truth. The history of humankind is like the base of a giant pyramid all rising up into a climactic cymbal crash at the top of the pyramid. The consciousness of man will soon be openly challenged at the nexus of the future to graduate into freedom or slavery. *There will be no third way.*

At such moments, we will always see the importance of intuitive investigators like the Para-Investigators who will have a magnified ability to discern truth from deception. Utilizing Para-Investigative techniques, *I determined what would happen on December 21, 2012.* These words are being written and memorialized on December 21, 2011.

Do not read any further unless you can handle the truth—*and I mean down to the bone.*

Are you ready? Are you sure?

Here is what is going to happen on December 21, 2012:

nothing.

absolutely nothing.

I did warn you. This truth will not be welcome in paranormal circles and even outside those circles. It doesn't sell books or DVD's or seminars and it doesn't promote paranormal conferences or create giddy excitement that translates into market share and television ratings; but it is the truth—as they say on the streets "that's the *real-real.*"

Date-Setters are always wrong and their dates only serve to take you out of your true power—the power of right now—this very moment that you should focus on as you reach deep inside yourself to discover and utilize your genius to free your brothers and sisters. Unfortunately, many people have reason to love date setting and they *will continue* setting them for as long as people keep falling for them.

Again, in the physical world we live in, nothing will happen of any real consequence but in the spiritual, metaphysical, in the unseen black abyss of multi-universal Overmind (which connects every Awakened and Awakening human mind)—something tremendous will be happening because it's happening already—*it's happening right now.* A new age will begin—*The Age of Mass Awakening.*

Our consciousness as a human race will rise up to new unknown heights. People in numbers never before seen on the planet will poke their heads out of *the box with five holes,* if only just for a moment, to see what wonders might exist outside the ubiquitous prison for their minds. Millions, *perhaps billions* will: take a break from shopping for trash they don't need, pause from channel surfing for news about celebrities who have only contempt for them, stop serving and reinforcing a non-human cultural system; if only for a moment. They will: take a moment from their narcotic stupor in front of the plasma screen. They will: stop following their teams, their political parties and "the big game." They will take a moment out from: the daily grind, from keeping up with the Joneses, from staying on top of politics, the stock market and organized mainstream religion. Then, they will step into a crackling morphogenic field that will initiate their permanent transition from this materialist facade.

We may become two trans-human races at that moment—one branch will be "transcendent beings of higher vibratory reality" and the other will descend into abject terror—"Homo-Luminous and Homo-Indomnitus"—beings of light and beings of savagery side by side. Nothing will happen and yet *everything will happen* just as it is happening right this moment because you are reading this book.

§

"The date that would change everything" is a slogan used numerous times throughout the centuries. Even during my father's childhood, several dates were the "appointed dates for societal transformation." After two world wars, a failed attempt with the League of Nations and decades of global anticipation; finally the major nations imposed the ratification of the United Nations Charter. October 25th, 1945, was advertised as the official *end of all wars and military conflict throughout the globe.* This date: 10/25/1945 was the awaited paradigm shift that would change everything we had known especially during the 1900s—wars, conflicts, conflagrations, constant societal violence would convert into a new golden era of peace, harmony and gentle co-existence. The date finally came and the new United Nations enjoyed great fanfare and celebration.

Nothing happened. Nothing changed.

Since the enormous global bureaucracy of the United Nations hatched, there have been more wars and armed conflicts than ever.

Nearly a quarter century later, as we approached July 20th, 1969; planetary consciousness again rose in anticipation of a shift in the human paradigm as humankind prepared to put a man on the moon. The awaited date 7/20/1969 finally came and astronaut Neil "Armstrong pronounced: *"that's one small step for man and one giant leap for mankind."* In that moment, humankind believed that nothing would ever be the same again—that we were just moments away from sentient humanoid robots and anti-gravity cars. Advanced technology would resolve all the problems of humanity—disease, hunger and scarcity of any kind.

Nothing much changed at all.

Today, instead of using technology to teleport us around the earth and to do instantaneous replication of food to end world hunger; NASA spends much of its time furiously scrubbing data files and erasing evidence of structures and former humanoid occupation on the Moon, Mars and other places in our solar system. Like so many national authorities, the only discoveries NASA can tolerate are the ones that they have knowledge of and control over. If they can't explain it, then *you won't be allowed to see it.*

Yet another next date that would change everything was January 1st, 2000—Y2K. This was a little different from the previous dates because it was a pure negative—a predicted technological apocalypse. Supposedly, there was a universal glitch in all the computers, which would render all computers, and mechanisms that function through computer chips inoperable. Planes, trains, and automobiles would crash. Homes, installations, buildings would spontaneously burst into raging infernos and all the cities would go up in flames. Again, universal consciousness of every human on earth, on this day, would rise and people would pause from their material lives to peer outside the box with five holes. At the opposite end, the EPIC engineered the perpetuation of books, programming, movies and all manner of products that promoted this same date. EPIC also encouraged people to believe this date would change their lives forever.

Again, nothing happened.

The familiar pattern had completed itself again. The Awakened latched onto a date that would bring a great paradigm shift to humanity. EPIC commanded their corporate control structures to push products and programming to push the same date for paradigm shift. This begs the question: why would EPIC whose interests are in keeping the great herds of workers and cogs asleep, go along with and even encourage the promotion of a specific date that could shift the paradigm that keeps their prisoners securely working on their corporate farms? It's because EPIC knows date setting *always* fails.

I am reciting this history of global date setting because EPIC and their minions will use it again and again in the future as we prepare for the coming Blood Moons. Getting the global population focused on a date in the future is a very low cost but highly efficient method to keep the global population subjugated by keeping their attention away from things that could actually free them from EPIC subjugation. This is why there will always be another date-setting campaign and another. The only question is how long the people will keep falling for the same deception.

The EPIC have multi-generational memory. The origins of the ancient bloodlines that make up the Elite Powers In Control stretch back into the misty dawn of man's pre-history—they were the rulers of the Sumerians, Babylonia and they were the Pharaohs of Egypt. They have been the advisors to Kings, Presidents and Prime Ministers throughout the ages of man. The EPIC has learned over many generations of witnessing the natural cycle of man's awakening and slumber, that it is far easier to use the Slumber/Awakening cycle instead of fighting it. So they encourage and promote the anticipated dates of awakening. After the date fails (*because it always does*) all those who were in the process of awakening and were peering out of the box with five holes—fall back into materialist despair and give up all hope of anything valuable existing outside the box. Then the lid of the oblong box is affixed even tighter than before and another generation throughout the globe will be again firmly sealed inside their oblong boxes. A con artist once said "old tricks are the best tricks."

The EPIC are so confident in their ability to manipulate the globe that they are playing the game on a grander scale than ever before through their consolidated power over global mainstream media. Again, as in times past, those who are already awakened have promoted this date, December 21, 2012; with products, books, endless conferences—in order to seize the opportunity to awaken others. They act out a genuine desire to awaken and help others and they succeeded to a certain extent as they do during every such cycle.

Again, the Elite Powers In Charge (EPIC) have given green lights to innumerable projects (movie studios, publishing houses, cable programming) that promote the same date. EPIC again knows the date will fail to produce anything of substance so their victory will be complete except it will be greater than ever before. On December 22nd, 2012, after nothing happens, yet another generation will sheepishly go back into the boxes with five holes, never to begin awakening again.

Except, this time *something's different*.

I believe that EPIC has overplayed their hand. Already, the Awakened are rising above the normal 2 to 3 percent of every population. As we know from the history of every great rebellion in history, slight differences can make *all the difference*. The EPIC may have finally outsmarted themselves because *now* there is a realization going on among those already awakened. For the first time in man's history, they are beginning to realize how they are being used in this game the EPIC plays every generation. Perhaps this realization is because of the interconnectedness of the Internet or maybe because of an expanded access to the universal consciousness. While they will continue to use the momentum provided by the EPIC's promotion of the 12/21/2012 date, the Awakened Community are beginning to understand that by shifting focus gradually from the *date* of Awakening *to the idea of Awakening;* they can salvage much of the cache built up for usage during 2013 and even into 2015. They can possibly prevent the great mass of humanity from simply falling back into their slumber and imprisonment within the box promptly on the dawning of 2014 and far, far beyond.

51

THE FINAL REVEAL

Here is the final big reveal of this work that has already been disclosed in the title of this book. Mass Awakening *will not be any date or even any year*—it will be an Age. During an age, it is the individuals that are the trigger for revolution and permanent change—not a date. We will be the shift we wish to see.

Dates empower systems but Ages empower individuals.

During a transitional age, the universe has changed its conditions but still awaits bold individual leaders to carry forward and break through the old mental barriers to effect the revolution which is so desperately needed. Ages can only open the gates but people must boldly step through those gates as sovereign determined purveyors of paradigm shift. That age began in 2013/2014 and will be unlike any previous Age of Man. The Awakened will finally use EPIC's power against EPIC's own interests and Para-Investigators will play a vital part in this Age of Mass Awakening.

We, The Awakened throughout the planet must come together and prepare for the greatest rescue operation in history—and the most unexpected. EPIC will be shocked and dismayed as they helplessly watch the world's first organized rescue—not for people's bodies but *for their minds*. Operation Awakening Rescue commenced in 2013 and 2014. Once that first year, 2013, is upon us without major seismic change, millions who are awakening will begin to sink back into the despair of the box with five holes. Instead of following the script the "global masters" have carefully laid out; we will lay the groundwork for their train of despair to *jump the tracks*. All that fearful momentum will be harnessed toward a Mass Awakening process that will last for an Age instead of a date. All who dared to believe the world was changing will be held by the wrist and urged *"don't go back in to your box—stay out here with us and see what you can achieve."*

Every great rebellion and revolution that swept away old orders—reached their tipping point when they achieved the active participation of less than *six percent* of the populations of the nations involved. The "Mass" in "Mass Awakening" means reaching just six percent of each population of the nations, states, towns and cities. If just six percent of each population takes action against EPIC's old systems of control—*they will collapse* and freedom will break out.

The freight train that EPIC had planned to go off the cliff on 12/22/2012 will instead be switched to a different track where it will collide into EPIC's most treasured institutions of control—major political parties, mainstream media, cable television, dependence on the energy grids, government controlled public schools and fear of governmental coercion. EPIC institutions will be abandoned and deflated. Alternative systems will be created by the Awakened and built up to service the refugees.

Only six percent is required to ignite permanent change and it will happen so long as all the disparate Awakened Community groups hang together through 2014 and beyond. Otherwise, we shall assuredly hang separately.

The hour grows short.

For the first time in humankind's history, EPIC's awakening boom and bust cycle will be interrupted and for the first time, it will be used for humanity's benefit instead of to increase the current slavery and prison system. The EPIC have miscalculated in a way they haven't done in over twenty eons. National Governments, corporations and all the old gatekeepers of the old society will be apoplectic as 2014 unfolds and the Para-Investigators join with other segments of Awakened Society to expand the ranks of the awakened geometrically rather than arithmetically.

This will be the only time in man's history that the recognized ranks of the awake and aware will join with many other tribes that were considered outcasts by respectable society; to awaken many more. EPIC will be frozen in disbelief as one of their most dependable scripts, for the first time in eons—fails. EPIC will again put their corporate media to work globally to discredit the awakened who dare to disrupt their plans. Corporate media will for the first time begin to feel how truly diminished their power is when confronted with an awake/aware populace. Rather than be cast out, The Awakened will be sought out as potential saviors because they will have the ingredients that make the difference in such transitional times, between life and death—belief and passion. For the first time in man's history, mainstream populations will feel themselves detached from the institutions of mainstream society.

Para-Investigators will become only the tip of the spear of The Awakened who will guide us into Total Awakening and then Mass Awakening. Para-Investigators will join themselves to other emerging awakened tribes: Angel-Speakers, Paranormal Believers, the Clear-Hearers, Christ-Based Transcendents, the Western Absolutists and many others will become a single force merged towards a single purpose: to effect a Total Awakening that cannot be stopped. Every group that joins toward this effort will bring unique special skills to the effort. The Para-Investigators will be only the beginning of Operation Total Awakening for these reasons:

- No one (no national government or any other puppets of EPIC) can successfully lie to Para-Investigators, no matter how official the lie or how loudly trumpeted it will be by the global corporate media. This is the very purpose for which Para-Investigators exist.

- The Para-Investigators cannot be *thrown off the scent* of genuine Paranormal phenomenon by hundreds or even thousands of false reports and distractions created by the minions of EPIC in order to drown out the few genuine events they are so desperate to hide.

- The Para-Investigators are aware that the Age that opened in 2013 and beyond may very well be the final chance that mankind will have to affect the beginning of a Total Awakening and escape from all the mental and spiritual imprisonment systems that EPIC has held us in for so long. Again, the Mass Awakening will not occur on any date—*it will occur during an Age*. This is why the Para-Investigators will go to any lengths and make any sacrifice to ensure that as many minds make the jump to freedom as possible.

- It will be the Para-Investigators who will prepare The Awakened to stand firm in apartness while the EPIC unleashes mainstream institutional attacks against them.

Yet, the truly awakened all know Total Awakening is happening today—right now, this second. We must do everything we can to help others to escape from the comfortable boxes they are laying in. We must do it now because you don't have to be a Para-Investigator to know—*this may be our final chance*.

52

THE NINE WAVES

It's already happening. We sit astride the shifting from the previous Age of mankind and will unite and synergize humanity into the turning of the globe toward the Age of Mass Awakening. This work began with an anecdote about Indigo children. Anyone who has worked in the Paranormal Community during the last decade has noticed an explosion in interest and participation to levels undreamed of in the past. Previously, paranormal believers, experiencers and participants kept themselves behind locked doors with the curtains drawn as they met in secret rooms away from prying eyes. Their numbers were miniscule and their attitudes were paranoid.

Today, participation in paranormal believer groups is bursting into the open. Their numbers are burgeoning and they come from every age group, social status and area of the globe. They are overt and even proud in their apartness from mainstream society. Instead of an easily manageable remnant of Awakened/Empowered non-cooperators with mainstream control systems, the EPIC will be confronted with the beginnings of global, spiritual revolution. An active, thriving and growing minority of supernaturally empowered individuals cannot be controlled, assimilated or deterred. We are currently seeing the birth of *an "Indigo Generation."*

The Indigo Generation are people who have re-invented themselves as Starseeds, Lightbearers, Lightworkers, Path Cutters, Energy Transmuters, Clear-Hearers, Angel-Speakers, Plant-Whisperers, Transcendors, PLASMA Seekers, Out-Reachers and Way-Showers.

No longer are they duped into labeling themselves with the exhausted mainstream language and concepts: "UFO's, conspiracy theorists, psychics, mediums and channelers." Awakening people using these obsolete ancient terms are like escaping prisoners making a run for the walls with cowbells clanging around their necks. No one suggests the Awakened Community will ever be in majority numbers. On this plane of existence that is not required. Ancient indigenous peoples, as a rule, maintained a core of Transcendent/Awakened, shamanic guardians who kept alive the tribe's connection with the Universal Overmind. This core collected and maintained for their tribes all the eternal and temporal advantages of genuine connection to the Earth and the universe. In numbers, these High Heart Conscious beings only amounted to probably just several out of every few thousand people. Despite all the global efforts of EPIC's guard dogs, we are approaching similar numbers today.

Many respected/Awakened scholars have interpreted the Mayan prophecies. One major portion of those prophecies concerns "The Nine Waves of Ascension" toward a shift in Universal Consciousness. They are explained and diagrammed by Carl Johan Calleman in his book: "Solving the Greatest Mystery of Our Time : The Mayan Calendar." One of his major contentions is that the Mayan Calendar is not just about the flow of time but it is also about the flow of human consciousness. Terrence McKenna does similar analysis of the Nine Waves in his book: "Timewave Zero." Many cultures around the world also refer to the eternal importance of the Nine Waves.

These Nine Waves are harbingers of an increasing growth of humanity's awareness toward a final crescendo of shift and they have many parallels in other prophecies and studies of ancient texts. The prophecies and process of the Nine Waves is supposed to end in a Unity Consciousness for humanity. Other scholars call it the "birthing of a Golden Age." This will be unity, not under the boot of EPIC prison guards, but under a new form of Supra-Human, individual, Super-Consciousness that will keep us free, independent and sovereign. Some say that these Nine Waves will occur during a period of time that may last several decades as the planet sorts out the lower consciousness descending souls from those who ascend into the next evolutionary cycle of transcendent consciousness. The universe will effect a cosmic reshuffling of human souls in a new stratification for a New Age.

Prophecies can have several fulfillments in different manifestations and they can all be true. In the Bible, it predicts that an Anti-Christ would come who will fit certain personal traits and will cause genocide throughout the planet. It is consistent with that prophecy to find that the most evil of the Roman Emperors during the 1st century, Emperor Domitian, was the literal fulfillment of that prophecy. Yet, there will be another realization of that prophecy in one who is yet to come. Prophecies can have several fulfillments along different points in the timeline and even in different forms altogether.

I believe the Nine Waves are people.

These are nine individuals who fit the traits of the Nine Waves—they will effect radical change in human consciousness at a planetary level by exploding the old paradigms and institutions. They will be at the core of "tidal waves" of change that they create by altering the reality filters that humans use to navigate the universe. They will overturn industries, economies, institutions, systems of control and they will break down the walls of global prisons. They will burst open institutions, sometimes from within. The Nine Waves will be protected and supported by the rising Indigo Generation. Numerous diverse groups in the Age of Mass Awakening will rally to them as well. The Nine Waves will become tsunamis for radical transformation of global society.

Former physicians/scientists will overturn the medical/scientific establishment. A former teacher may lead us to overturn the government public education system that does so much harm to children's minds. A former banker may create the Tsunami of change that will erase the private, global, centralized banking system that still hold the nations and their economies in subjugation. Some of the Nine Waves have already appeared. Others are yet to come. You don't need me to name them because the Nine Waves are identified by their accomplishments, not by anyone's words. You'll know exactly who they are when you see their ongoing battle against malicious mainstream institutions resulting in glorious victories for humanity and liberty. You will see our most malevolent EPIC structures reeling and ready to fall. Then you'll know.

That's them. That's one of the Nine Waves.

Wherever they might arise, the Para-Investigators will be there to identify them, support them and encourage them. It is the Para-Investigators who will also be there when EPIC tries to gain control of the situation by employing their ancient tricks of merely triangulating themselves into that new paradigm. As they have done so many times in the past, EPIC will set up actors to pose as one of the Nine Waves. They will speak the right words and issue platitudes but their actions will not match the fervors of their words. Then they will set up false conflicts against the Wave by their own mainstream institutions. They will own/create/manipulate both sides of the new conflict and encourage people to pick a side and inject themselves into the new dialectic. This has been a reliable and proven formula for EPIC for thousands of years. *The only Agents of Change who can be trusted are the ones we see truly reviled, ridiculed, despised and persecuted by mainstream institutions.* Then we know they are "the genuine article."

Be on the lookout for counterfeits because they will be plentiful. Whenever you see mainstream institutions open the gates wide for any purported "agent of paradigm shift" beware the ravenous wolf in sheep's clothing. Periods of global transitions are highly dangerous times. EPIC knows this and so must the Awakened Community. Use Para-Investigators. This is precisely what they were bred for and what they are best at—gleaning truth from situations where enormous resources are brought to bear for the sole purpose of hiding the truth and active deceit. True Para-Investigators can be lied to but they can't really be deceived.

The highest truth of the Nine Waves is that there aren't just nine of them—there can be Nine Hundred or Nine Thousand traveling across the planet and effecting radical transformation everywhere they go—and because you are reading this work you are probably one of them.

Each of us can become a Wave for shifting. Each of us can become the explosive that detonates the rotting old institutions whose only purpose is control. Each of us can be the very Wave of change we are looking for. The Age of Mass Awakening isn't triggered by a date in time or a date range. The Nine Waves don't come into being because of a period of time. Both Ages and time periods don't mean anything without individual action. *They are just changes in our environmental conditions* that will be far more favorable to the Cosmic Shifts that must be sparked by individuals—by us.

We must go to any lengths, scale any heights for revolutionary global change. All Awakened Tribes must unite in this effort. Para-Investigators will act an impenetrable shield for the tribes as this unity consciousness goes forth. They will shield against the malicious deceptions of EPIC—against artifice, false flag operations, misinformation operations, disinformation operations, dissension sowing operations, newly minted false dialectics and the global deception of the CRIME system. Our legacy to future generations should be liberty and the elevating of human consciousness into a brighter Age of Mankind. Even now EPIC is locking down the nations in a tightly controlled fascist global society. Systems of surveillance, defense, and militarized control are being unfolded across the planet that will slide our world gently into many years of governmental tyranny and prison. Let us create for our future generations a higher, better future than the prison-planet EPIC has designed for humanity. Let us go forward into the Age of Mass Awakening with a certainty that unity shall be our strongest weapon and freedom our greatest destiny.

INVITATION

If you have stories of law-enforcement or civilian truth-seekers using their paranormal abilities to help humanity, reach out to us to share them. (Do not compromise any ongoing prosecutions or appeals in any court system.) Please visit TamaBooksPublishing@gmail.com. God Bless you and may your investigations always unfold the abyss.

John DeSouza

THE AGE OF MASS
AWAKENING—TAMA LEXICON

Unless we break away from the old code words, control verbiage and false labels of the mainstream; we can never show the way of freedom to others. False labels are in place to limit discussion and imagination, not to encourage it. Ludicrous descriptors are invitations to ridicule anyone who opens a paranormal topic for discussion. Breaking from this "control language" is the purpose of the New TAMA Lexicon. Again, attempting to escape the old paradigms of the mainstream while still using their mainstream labels and language is like escaping prisoners running for the walls at night with cowbells clanging around their necks.

Para-Investigation—a systematic inquiry or investigation which utilizes rational scientific methods initially but primarily relies upon intuitive paranormal mechanisms from Superconscious Abilities to resolve crimes and mysteries.

Para-Investigators—conventional investigators such as ghost-hunters, police officers, detectives, private investigators, field investigators and even civilian truth-seekers who uncover and connect: clues and evidence utilizing rational investigative methods initially and then utilize intuitive paranormal mechanisms order to reach investigative conclusions.

Para-Seers—the final evolved form of the Para-Investigator, investigators who have fully developed the ability to go directly into metaphysical intuitive mechanisms and Superconscious Mind in order to resolve crimes and mysteries. Para-Seers then allow the use of conventional modalities as corroboration of truths they have already uncovered supernaturally.

Box With Five Holes—The version of reality which teaches that humans are nothing more than flesh covered containers in a purely physical reality—that they will live the span of their lives in a box with five holes. The five holes represent their five physical senses, which they are taught, are the only methods by which they can perceive the universe.

TDE's—Although misnamed as "Near-Death Experiences" by materialist scientists, these are True Death-Experiences (TDEs) which have proven beyond any shadow of doubt that our brains are not producers of consciousness but rather are merely receivers of it in the same manner that a radio receives the signal that fires it to life from somewhere else.

The Persistent Consciousness Corollary—If the basis of all reality is actually human consciousness—not time, space and matter; then this truth shifts the priorities of all things. Things come into existence and remain in existence because we give them our energy in the form of attention, belief and our consciousness. This is a switching of the chicken and the egg. We do not give them our energy because they exist. They exist because someone, somewhere has given them energy in the form of consciousness. So the Corollary states: therefore, if any spiritual or paranormal subject has persisted in human consciousness for decades, centuries or eons, that is the best evidence that it is real, that it truly exists and that its existence is incontrovertible. Otherwise, that subject would have just disappeared from human memory shortly after it was suggested. That is especially so in light of debunkery, secular cynicism and culturally conditioned responses. The moment we understand this truth, the fruitless search for scientific minutiae becomes irrelevant. We know it exists because we believe it exists. The LochNess monster is real because it has persisted in human consciousness for eons regardless of what technical scientific equipment does or doesn't reveal on that topic.

First Investigator's Query—a group of six "first responder" questions for those investigating any crime or elusive mystery: who? what? when? where? how? why?

The Ephemeral Postulate—the doctrine stating that paranormal truth can only be understood in proportion to the realization that genuine paranormal phenomena is never fully perceivable by our five senses in our physical universe, except partially or temporarily.

The Quantum Paranormality Theorem—the doctrine stating that individuals who encounter supernatural situations are not stumbling across these events. The perceivers of the paranormal phenomena are themselves passing through a quantum flux field (or being made by supernatural forces to pass through this field) so that they are translated temporarily into a parallel field of non-corporeal existence.

The Six Percent Resolution—the doctrine stating that in paranormal areas, approximately 94 percent of reported incidents are those in which there are natural, physical or even fraudulent explanations ultimately provided or proven. This resolution still leaves an average of six percent of reported paranormal phenomena that are genuinely paranormal or supernatural in origin.

Para Vetting—this is the methodical examination of items of evidence utilizing supernatural modalities and abilities as the primary method of testing authenticity and origin.

Rationalist Cover—these are the spoken word formulas that are permissible for professional investigators to use in order to avoid admissions that they used paranormal abilities to solve crimes and mysteries: e.g. *"in light of my previous knowledge and experience as a criminal investigator in this neighborhood I knew it was likely that the suspect had a revolver with only six shots as these types of cheap, old-fashioned guns are in favor in this area."* Yet this doesn't explain how the officer (who did not arrive until after the original shooting) could be **so certain** that the criminal was out of bullets that he was willing to allow him to put the barrel to his face and pull the trigger before he disarmed and arrested the man. Had he not used the acceptable rationalist cover, he could lose the arrest/prosecution in a court of law.

Para-Investigative Assessment—This is the method of feeling what the situation really is—not from this physical world but from the unseen abyss wherein resides the Cosmic mind that connects us all. This is examination and inventorying of the subject and evidence in the investigation on levels that have nothing to do with the physical world.

Para-Investigative Connection—This is the method of cessation of our participation in the falsity that we are separate from fellow creatures in this universe. We then enter into connection with the most heinous liar, criminal, even non-human entities. This is just a moment between assessment and empathy.

Para-Investigative Empathy—This is when the investigator merges spiritually with the subject. The Para-Investigator *becomes the subject* and works through all their mental processes. This skill, if it is engaged in for too long a period it can leave an indelible mark on the investigator's mind and can render them permanently sympathetic to the subject they are investigating.

The Para-Investigative Prohibition—the only disallowance in Para-Investigation stating that debunking people's beliefs, whether paranormal or spiritual, is never a legitimate goal of Para-Investigation.

The Extra-Dimensionals—non-terrestrial, intelligent life forms who are visiting our dimension of time and space as transitory beings *from outside* our plane of physical time and space—e.g.: from outside our material existence and who return to outside this physical existence.

PLASMAS—the replacement for the term UFO is the acronym PLASMAS:

Paranormal—having supernatural qualities such that no explanation or qualification can be provided for this particular event or thing in the physical/material iteration of time and space.

Living—a living creature, sentient, intelligent but also programmable like a computer

Aura-Reading—able to read the auras and emotions of living creatures, especially humans

Soul-Printing—able to record, collect and store a blueprint of a soul for later reference

Mobile—able to move through physical or non-physical media and even able to dematerialize

Aerial—most likely to be in the air because it wishes to be seen by as many humans as possible

Scanners—these are unoccupied scanners constantly roving to carry out their programming—to collect soul-prints of as many "interested" humans as possible.

Direct Voice Channeling—the brand of channeling during which the channeler gives away their own spiritual sovereignty by allowing another entity to directly enter and control their soul, spirit and persona.

Clear-Hearing—This well-documented ability is the perception of a Voice of Authority that has its origin from a non-local field of Superconsciousness.

Morphogenic Energy Sites—geographic locations that are permanent vortexes of Superconscious Energy that can be tapped into by those who are sensitive and open to the great field of unlimited potential.

Unfolders of The Abyss—another name for Para-Investigators

The Mind Dampener—the great seething mass of cable, satellite, radio, and major media broadcasting channels that fills our existence no matter which way we turn. It is the generator of the chatter, noise, interference and negativity; that disrupts our access to our own consciousness. It is the machine that creates the pollution which seeps into our subconscious minds and keeps us occupied with purposeless, non-sensical, non-critical buzzing.

Cosmic Introspection—looking within oneself yet simultaneously looking outwards into the Superconscious Gulf that connects us all into the Cosmic Mind of God; in order to unfold the meaning of our own Soul Identity.

Culturally Conditioned Mind—the average mainstream mind—conditioned, trained and subjugated by all the mechanisms of Mainstream Culture designed to create docile, non-critical-thinking prisoners who only accept as truth whatever the Mainstream Cultural authorities tell them.

EPIC—The Elite Powers In Charge of the world that come from the ancient bloodline families that have ruled humanity since the very first world empire came to power. These same bloodlines have persisted at the tops of the pyramids of humanity through every successive world empire right up until today. They are not in charge of us as free and sovereign individuals directly but they are directly in charge *of the global institutions*, which tell national political leaders what they must do from day to day. We detach from them when we detach from their institutions.

CRIME—An acronym for the typical methods employed by the national governments to reduce liberty of their subjects while pretending to rescue them from crisis:

Crisis—Problem or chaos created or exacerbated by government

Response—government presents to their subjects a series of oppressive options for the people's own "security"

Increased—Magnification and amplification on a national, sometimes on a global scale

Misery—Loss of liberty, sovereignty and freedom.

Enthroned—the imposition by Government bureaucrats of the measures that increase the power and control of Government bureaucrats and which will persist forever, long after the temporary crisis that "caused it" is over.

The Age of Mass Awakening——this is the Age of Man, which will begin the year after the Mayan calendar date setting has produced nothing—from the year 2013 and 2014 forward, during which millions, will awaken from the current reality paradigm/ prison.

BIBLIOGRAPHY–
ADDITIONAL RECOMMENDED READING

BIBLE QUOTATIONS

Any scriptural quotations in this work are derived exclusively from the King James Version (KJV) Bible, originally published 1601, Public Domain rights apply.

THE TRUTH ABOUT EVIDENCE

US Federal Bureau of Investigation (FBI) Handbook by USA International Business Publications

This is a non-classified, non-sensitive handbook of basic investigative procedures in keeping with standards recognized by the United States Federal Bureau of Investigation (FBI).

Myths to Live By Joseph Campbell

This book is an excellent examination of the driving forces that often make myths far more important to the development of a society than "solid facts" and about the ways in which myths actually tell more truth than facts.

True-Death Experiences (TDE's):

Evidence of the Afterlife: The Science of Near-Death Experiences by Jeffrey Long and Paul Perry

Consciousness Beyond Life: The Science of the Near-Death Experience by Pim van Lommel

Beyond The Veil/NDE Near Death Experiences by Lee Nelson And Richard Nelson

Science and the Near-Death Experience: How Consciousness Survives Death by Chris Carter

Saved by the Light: The True Story of a Man Who Died Twice and the Profound Revelations He Received by Dannion Brinkley and Paul Perry

Life After Life: The Investigation of a Phenomenon—Survival of Bodily Death by Raymond Moody and Elisabeth Kubler-Ross

Amazingly, this is an area of the paranormal in which numerous M.D.s, physicians and even scientists have dared to write books. If you are more scientifically inclined, read the first four books above. If, hopefully, you are already a paranormal believer, indulge yourself with the last two books. Regardless of your personal proclivities, all the books are astounding in the clarity of stating their case: *you are far more than the body and brain you temporarily occupy.*

Cattle Mutilations:

Hunt for the Skinwalker: Science Confronts the Unexplained at a Remote Ranch in Utah by Colm A. Kelleher And George Knapp

Strange Secrets: Real Government Files on the Unknown by Nick Redfern and Andy Roberts

Enter the Valley: UFOs, Religious Miracles, Cattle Mutilations, and Other Unexplained Phenomena in the San Luis Valley by Christopher O'Brien

These works capture the exasperation of people confronted with a very real threat to livelihoods and safety by forces they cannot understand. They further depict that all the normal defenders of safety in mainstream society absolutely refuse to consider honest investigations of this situation.

The Threat: The Secret Alien Agenda What The Aliens Really Want And How They Plan To Get It by David M. Jacobs

Though more focused on abductions than mutilations, this seminal work elucidates the arrogance of Extra-Dimensional alien beings whose technology is so far ahead of our own that they have only contempt for human beings and all other terrestrial creatures (like cattle, horses, sheep and others).

The National Commission On The Terrorist Attacks Upon The United States "The 911 Commission Final Report" by United States Of America
Some of the best fiction I've ever read.

What Every BODY is Saying: An Ex-FBI Agent's Guide to Speed-Reading People by Joe Navarro
Machines cannot tell you if anyone is being deceptive and polygraphers can't either. That's just common sense. Joe Navarro can tell all these things and much, much more. I've sat in classes taught by this man and I can tell you first hand, if you want to understand how to interpret deception even people's thoughts and intentions—then don't rely on machines, rely on yourself and on Joe Navarro's books to teach you how.

THE PARA-INVESTIGATORS IN ACTION

Industrial Society And its Future (The Unabomber Manifesto) by Theodore Kaczynski
about as good as the average peer-approved doctoral thesis

Minority Report by Phillip K. Dick
Minority Report is hallucinogenic and nightmarish vision of future law-enforcement in a dystopian society (I still don't know what *dystopian* really means but I plan to look it up).

From Cradle to Grave by Joyce Egginton
This book is the final heart-breaking documentation of the heinous crimes of Mary Beth Tinning and the medical establishment's succor and dissemblance that allowed her to go on committing her murders of young children for so very long.

PARA-INVESTIGATORS AND NON-HUMANS

UFOs: Generals, Pilots and Government Officials Go On the Record by Leslie Kean
This work is the final authoritative and ultimate documentation of the fact that people with the most credibility and also the most to lose by telling the truth, are now coming forth and telling the rest of us what we already know—that Extra-terrestrial beings have been visiting us for a very long time and that the national governments are lying to us about it. Despite the best efforts of the national governments to deny and obfuscate this truth, the floodgates are now open and there won't be any closing them again.

***DECLASSIFIED H.P. ROBERTSON PANEL PROCEEDINGS AND
REPORT OF SCIENTIFIC ADVISORY PANEL ON UNIDENTIFIED
FLYING OBJECTS CONVENED BY OFFICE OF SCIENTIFIC
INTELLIGENCE, CIA, January 14 - 18, 1953***
Facts reported in this typical Government Commission are true but the conclusions
are disinformational fakery.

PARA-INVESTIGATIVE AWAKENINGS

Human Race, Get Off Your Knees by David Icke
Don't read if you are unawakened or cling to the current version of reality promoted
by the mainstream. And if you come across this book, *don't even think* about
cracking it open unless you can take the truth—*and I mean down to the bone.*

***The 2012 Story: The Myths, Fallacies, and Truth Behind the Most
Intriguing Date in History by John Major Jenkins***
This work is the definitive final word on the meaning behind the date 12/21/2012
expertly laid out by a master researcher.

ACKNOWLEDGEMENTS

Many thanks go out to my assistant/editor Goldie Serrano who has advised and counseled the fruition of this project and to the fearless iconoclasts at TAMA Publishing. Great respect and admiration goes to the greatest Book Designer in the industry, Scarlett Rugers, because she makes everything and everyone look so very good. Eternal gratitude also goes out to all those brave souls referred to in this work that gave testimony, interviews and encouragement that many would be helped by what this work had to say.

AUTHOR BIOGRAPHY

John DeSouza has researched and collected experiences on paranormal and spiritual topics for two decades. Previously, he was an investigating official of the U.S. government who maintained a Top Secret security clearance during many years at one of the major "three letter agencies." He labored in the fields of the (GWOT) Global War on Terrorism and the (WAD) War on Drugs. Subsequently, the author has represented national companies as legal General Counsel. Currently, John DeSouza manages a national sports recreation company and serves as the Author and Chief Editor of The Age of Mass Awakening (TAMA) books.

The truth of Para-Investigation revealed itself to the author through his own paranormal experiences and those of innumerable others across many professional fields. The author lives in the great Southwestern United States and devotes himself to his companies and to The Age of Mass Awakening (TAMA) series. He can be reached at johntamabooks@gmail.com. All business queries should go to Goldie Serrano, (520) 544-3863, goldietamabooks@gmail.com.

CPSIA information can be obtained
at www.ICGtesting.com
Printed in the USA
BVHW041912031019
560165BV00008B/316/P